Praise for *The Forgiveness*

D1045362

"*The Forgiveness Solution* is a wonderful, passionate, healing book that is easy to read, practical, integrative, and powerful. Readers will not only learn how to forgive themselves and others but will also be on the way to developing a forgiving personality and reconnecting with the inner goodness and light within themselves and each other."
—GERALD G. JAMPOLSKY, M.D., author of
Forgiveness: The Greatest Healer of All, Love Is Letting Go of Fear,
and co-author of *A Mini Course for Life*

"The most practical book I've ever read on forgiveness. From beginning to end, it focuses on giving you a direct experience of forgiveness and helps you to incorporate this way of being into every facet of your life. If you do the exercises in this book, I know your life will be changed forever." —DAVIDPAUL DOYLE, co-author of *The Voice for Love: Accessing Your Inner Voice to Fulfill Your Life's Purpose*

"There is no doubt that the #1 solution to so many of our personal, political, and social problems today is forgiveness. In this book Dr. Friedman offers a wealth of forgiveness techniques and processes that skillfully blends science, spirituality, and clinical practice into a seamless garment of love, peace, strength, and resilience."
—COLIN TIPPING, author of *Radical Forgiveness*

"If you were to have one book on the all-important subject of forgiveness, this is the one. In an easy-to-read style, *The Forgiveness Solution* deftly compiles research with exercises, case studies with concise insights. It's a clear handbook on how to forgive, written for the layperson and professional alike. To have a great life, you need to know how to forgive. This book really maps out what you need in a fascinating and comprehensive way." —DR. PHILLIP MOUNTROSE, co-author of *The Heart & Soul of EFT and Beyond* and co-director of the Awakenings Institute

"A comprehensive and powerful book that teaches hurt people to recover their center and let go of painful wounds and grievances. The book is well written and carefully researched." —FRED LUSKIN, Director of Stanford Forgiveness Projects and author of *Forgive for Good*

"*The Forgiveness Solution* is a treasure trove of inspiring quotations, powerful examples from Friedman's clinical practice, and numerous effective and healing exercises that bring the material alive. Whatever your orientation, you will find doors to walk through and abundant resources to continue your journey toward greater peace, happiness, love, and joy." —MARTHA CRAMPTON, Ph.D., founder and former director of the Canadian Institute of Psychosynthesis in Montreal

"There are many solutions to personal, social, and interpersonal problems, but *The Forgiveness Solution* is one of the best. With empathy, care, wisdom, and intuition, Dr Friedman gives you a detailed, step-by-step, and focused approach to healing, wholeness, peace, and happiness. Drawing on scientific research, spiritual teachings, and years of clinical experience, he teaches you how to forgive yourself and others." —DR. LOREN TOUSSAINT, associate professor at Luther College

"Forgiveness is quite possibly one of the most misunderstood words in the dictionary. We've all been told we 'should' forgive, but why is it so important and so difficult to do? Dr. Friedman's book answers these questions. Not only does he point to the benefits of forgiveness for your own health and inner peace, he gives you numerous ways to actually forgive and release the pain, hurt, guilt, and anger. World peace begins with inner peace; you owe it to yourself and the planet to read this book." —MARY T. SISE, LCSW, former president of the Association of Comprehensive Energy Psychology and co-author of *The Energy of Belief: Psychology's Power Tools to Focus Intention and Release Blocking Beliefs*

"*The Forgiveness Solution* is an in-depth course on cognitive, emotional, spiritual, and energetic healing. With its many inspiring stories and practical exercises, this treasure chest will empower you to overcome negativity and live life to the fullest. All students of energy healing and spirituality will benefit from assimilating this amazing contribution to the field that draws upon scientific research, clinical experience, spiritual wisdom, and cutting-edge methods. Keeping this resource handy will help anyone navigate the toughest of times." —FRED P. GALLO, Ph.D., author of *Energy Psychology* and *Energy Tapping for Trauma*

"*The Forgiveness Solution* makes two bold claims—that unforgiveness underlies virtually all psychological problems and that the solution to that underlying problem (and also other problems) is to forgive. Philip H. Friedman, equipped by years of practical psychotherapy experience, offers you a practical, powerful, and personal book that will help you forgive. Doable exercises are engaging, useful, and therapy-tested. While many psychologists integrate scientific findings into their practice, I know of no therapist who does as often as Friedman. His integration of research and practice has resulted in a book that will help you, teach you, and heal you. It is the best blend of science and clinical practice."
—EVERETT L. WORTHINGTON, Jr., Ph.D.,
professor of psychology at Virginia Commonwealth University and
author of *Forgiving and Reconciling: Bridges to Wholeness and Hope*

"*The Forgiveness Solution* is a comprehensive, in-depth look into every aspect of the power of forgiveness. Drawn from a wide variety of perspectives, it has more exercises, techniques, and energetic processes than any book about forgiveness on the shelves today. Dr. Philip Friedman shows us how one simple act can transform our personal lives and the world around us. If you're experiencing challenges of any sort and don't know what to do, forgiveness is your next step and this book will guide you true. *The Forgiveness Solution* is a winner!"
—TONY BURROUGHS, author of
The Code: 10 Intentions for a Better World

"If you want more peace, satisfaction, and joy in your life, then *The Forgiveness Solution* can be your solution. This book will not only change your life, it will change the world you live in. You can't afford the luxury of being unforgiving." —STEVAN THAYER, Director, the Center of
Being and author of *Interview with an Angel*

"Dr. Friedman's years of study and practical application of his deep knowledge, along with his obvious grace in dealing with this most sensitive and significant psychological problem, will inform and inspire you to new freedom from unforgiveness. Unforgiveness runs deep in all of us; it is ingrained in our childhood and highly reinforced in our society. *The Forgiveness Solution* will help you enormously, both personally and with your clients who suffer silently with this debilitating problem

of how to become free through forgiveness. This book is a treasure and is well suited for laypersons as well as for professional practitioners."
—LARRY P. NIMS, Ph.D., author of the
BE SET FREE FAST™ book and DVD set

"Wow, what a rich and comprehensive resource *The Forgiveness Solution* is. Though the theme is 'forgiveness,' Dr. Friedman offers us a rich resource to guide us to a positive, fulfilling, and satisfying life. Not only does he present us with a compendium of ways to perceive, assess, and take action to heal ourselves, but he even provides the questions and answers we might ask him to have the confidence to apply these methods. This is a book we could all use."
—BARRY G. GINSBERG, Ph.D., Director of the Center of Relationship Enhancement and author of *Relationship Enhancement Family Therapy* and *50 Wonderful Ways to Be a Single-Parent Family*

"Dr. Phil Friedman's *The Forgiveness Solution* draws upon extensive knowledge of contemporary forgiveness research and then charts new territory by fusing that research with a deeply spiritual orientation. It offers a veritable gold mine of practical exercises drawn from years of guiding therapeutic clients into the experience of forgiveness. Friedman's profound commitment to helping his clients and his readers along the road to true forgiveness shines through on every page. If you are serious about walking on that road yourself, read this book—and use it."   —ROBERT PERRY, founder of the Circle of Atonement and author of *Path of Light* and *Signs: A New Approach to Coincidence, Synchronicity, Guidance, Life Purpose, and God's Plan*

"I opened this book and could not stop reading it! If you want to give up guilt, suffering, or painful distance from loved ones who have disappointed or hurt you, definitely get yourself a copy of *The Forgiveness Solution*. This is the most practical book you can buy on forgiveness. It can help you restore your own peace and happiness and make a rapid 180° turn in healing the most important relationships in your life!"
—DIANA KIRSCHNER, PH.D., author of *Love in 90 Days: The Essential Guide to Finding Your Own True Love*

THE
FORGIVENESS
SOLUTION

The Whole-Body Rx for Finding
True Happiness, Abundant Love,
and Inner Peace

Philip H. Friedman, Ph.D.

Conari Press

Clifton Park - Halfmoon Public Library
475 Moe Road
Clifton Park, New York 12065

First published in 2009 by
Red Wheel/Weiser, LLC
With offices at:
500 Third Street, Suite 230
San Francisco, CA 94107
www.redwheelweiser.com

Copyright © 2009 by Philip Friedman
All rights reserved. No part of this publication may be reproduced or transmitted in
any form or by any means, electronic or mechanical, including photocopying, record-
ing, or by any information storage and retrieval system, without permission in writing
from Red Wheel/Weiser, LLC. Reviewers may quote brief passages.

ISBN: 978-1-57324-462-6
Library of Congress Cataloging-in-Publication Data is available upon request.

Cover design by Maija Tollefson
Text design by Maxine Ressler
Typeset in Adobe Garamond Pro and Avenir
Photographs by Raymond W. Holman, Jr.

Printed in the United States of America
VG
10 9 8 7 6 5 4 3 2 1
The paper used in this publication meets the minimum requirements of the Ameri-
can National Standard for Information Sciences—Permanence of Paper for Printed
Library Materials Z39.48-1992 (R1997).

4536

Dedicated to my wife Teresa Molinaro-Friedman, my son Mathew A. Friedman, and to the late Martha Crampton, a close friend and colleague.

Contents

Introduction

MANY BOOKS TALK ABOUT forgiveness. I'm sure you picked this one up expecting something a little different. I think you'll be very pleased. Unlike the other books available, this book, which I've set up as a kind of workbook without the blank writing space, leads you through a process of examination and healing so that you can forgive at the deepest levels of your being. The power of this forgiveness work is that it can release you from the grip of old—sometimes very old—unhealed wounds once and for all.

You probably come to this book with one or more people in mind to forgive. In fact, we all have many people in our lives to forgive, including ourselves, and this book will help you identify who those people are and *how you can forgive them* for good.

In fact, it is the thesis of this book that *underneath all other emotional and psychological problems, there is one core problem—unforgiveness—and one core solution, which is forgiveness.* As you read, you will learn about this idea in much more depth. You will also have the opportunity to work with the many tools of forgiveness that I have found most helpful to my clients in my many years of practicing psychotherapy. You will find practical ways to incorporate these tools and techniques into your life as you work to resolve whatever is blocking you from living the fullest possible life. My goal is to make forgiveness practically automatic—not something you have to think about but more a matter of how you function in the world. Because if there is one thing we know, it is that the more forgiving you are, the more at peace, the more joyful, the more satisfied and fulfilled by life you will be.

What Is Forgiveness?

In the research literature, forgiveness is often defined as having benevolent feelings toward someone or some situation that you previously perceived harmed you. It is also defined as giving up anger, resentment, or indignation against another person or circumstance for a perceived offense, difference, or mistake. In other words, it focuses on *releasing an unpleasant emotion that is based on a perception.* It is also defined as giving up the desire for punishment or restitution. In this case, forgiveness focuses on a desire and an action. I use both a broader and a deeper definition. After forty years of work in the field of personal and spiritual growth and psychotherapy, I see forgiveness as the process of:

1. Releasing the negative emotions of anger, resentment, bitterness, indignation, hurt, irritation, and guilt not only toward others and circumstances but also toward oneself, God, and groups of people.
2. Giving up the beliefs that generate these emotions, such as the grievances and judgments behind them.
3. Shifting your perceptions toward the person or circumstance that triggered the unpleasant or negative feeling so that you learn to see things differently.
4. *Choosing* and *deciding* to forgive.
5. Developing positive or benevolent feelings and attitudes toward the person or circumstance that was previously perceived as hurtful, including oneself. These include feelings of compassion, kindness, warmth, and love.
6. Developing an authentic sense of peace and contentment when thinking about the person or situation you previously perceived as hurting or harming you.
7. Giving up the desire for retribution, punishment, or harm to that person or people.
8. Discovering that the events or circumstances that were perceived as harmful or hurtful were learning experiences that existed for the personal and spiritual growth of all the parties.

Don't be daunted by the long list! My point is that the process of forgiveness is a profound one. It isn't something one-dimensional, with a simple beginning and end. It is a thorough examination and repositioning of oneself that leads to lasting feelings of peace, love, and joy and a sense of inner balance and calm.

The chapters in this book will address each of these aspects of forgiveness through a series of powerful exercises and processes that include journaling, affirmations, imagery processes, relaxation/meditation, and some work with energy and spiritual healing. Sometimes these processes and techniques will trigger quantum and sudden positive shifts in you; sometimes the changes will be more gradual. There is no right or wrong way for any of this to happen. However it happens for you is the right way.

Who Will Benefit from This Book?

If you are experiencing depression, anxiety, guilt, shame, stress, and anger or are just generally not at the level of well-being you desire, this book will help. It will also help anyone who wants to shift to a higher level of awareness or consciousness in their life.

Why? Because I have found time and again that underneath an enormous range of psychological problems are issues of unforgiveness, either consciously or unconsciously experienced. For any of a great number of reasons, many of us walk around with grievances, judgments, and *shoulds* that have the intent to harm, injure, criticize, hurt, or weaken us or someone else in some way. These attacking thoughts, however "justified" they may seem, are separating us from our true or core Self, that place within us that knows deep peace, happiness, joy, love, strength, creativity, resourcefulness, and wisdom.

Doing the practices I prescribe here will help you find your way back to that core Self. As you discover what and who you need to forgive and do the work of forgiving in all its facets, you will find yourself happier, more peaceful, joyful, loving, and fulfilled. Your relationships and feelings about yourself are almost guaranteed to improve as well.

How to Use This Workbook

I strongly recommend that you work the chapters in order. They are sequenced as I teach them to my clients and the exercises build on one another. But if it seems to work better for you, feel free to skip around.

Books like this one don't just work on a mental level. There is a certain energy and vibration at work here, too. The stories are designed to be uplifting and the book overall is designed to have a high positive energy to it. That positive energy alone might be beneficial to you.

I recommend reading one or two chapters a week and doing the exercises they suggest. You'll want to use a journal or notebook, or your computer, to record your responses to the different exercises. If you prefer a faster or slower pace, that's just fine. Please don't get too hung up on whether you're doing it right or wrong. Any way it works for you is the best way.

The most important "tool" of all for doing this work is a good attitude and a "little willingness," a desire to learn a new perspective and a desire to develop some new skills. Also, I think you will find it helpful to drop your goals for now and simply enter this adventure as if you were conducting an experiment, with the intention of finding out what will happen as you go. If you discover that very strong feelings surface during this forgiveness process and that you feel overwhelmed by them, it would be wise to put the book down for a little while or contact a good therapist, support group, or facilitator to further help you with the forgiveness process. For most people, however, that won't be necessary.

One caution: if you are working on forgiving someone who you feel is hurting you a great deal, it is okay to remove yourself from that person's presence and/or to assert yourself appropriately even while you are learning how to forgive him or her. In other words, please don't feel guilty if you deem it necessary to limit contact with that person while you become stronger using the forgiveness solution process. In fact, it might be necessary for your safety.

Because my own path has been varied and instructive, in *The Forgiveness Solution* I pull from a wide range of therapy methods and ideas, including Western and Eastern techniques and concepts. I draw from cognitive behavior therapy (CBT), psychospiritual therapy, attitudinal healing, energy therapy, and others. Some ideas will be new to you, and it's perfectly understandable if you are skeptical about them at first. I encourage you to bear with me and try my suggestions. I think you will discover just how powerful these different approaches and perspectives can be.

Reading the book once will give you much to work with. Read it three times, however, and do the practices and exercises regularly, and you will get maximum value from it. Then you will begin to develop a mastery of forgiveness that will greatly benefit you, and others, for the rest of your life.

I know everyone is pressed for time and that sometimes it's hard to stay motivated to do exercises learned from a book. Most of us end up picking and choosing. *If you do nothing else,* please practice the Psychological Uplifter regularly. It will help you create a positive frame of mind, which greatly facilitates forgiveness.

Do You Work Better Alone or with Someone Else?

Most of you will be able to do the exercises in this book by yourself. They can, however, be done with a partner or even in a small group. Once you have developed some level of mastery of the techniques and attitudes, in fact, you might want to share them with your family and friends. The most important thing, though, is to first do the work on yourself and your relationships. As you will see, one of the ideas that runs through my work is that all minds are joined, and when you are healed, you are never healed alone. Once you use the forgiveness solution on yourself, in many cases it will have a positive ripple effect on others, and that will make your forgiveness experience even more powerful. Then you can go on to use it in a group setting.

If you do decide to do it with a group, it will probably take about twelve sessions. Some of the chapters take more time to read than others, and some chapters have more exercises than others.

What Are Some of the Major Benefits of Forgiving?

Researchers and psychologists have been looking at the benefits of forgiveness for some time. We have discovered much about the negative impact of *un*forgiving on the body, the mind, and the emotions and how important it is to forgive, not just for peace of mind but for our physical and social well-being as well. Excellent research shows us that various forgiveness strategies can have powerful positive effects with people who have experienced the death of another and/or perceive themselves as victims of incest, abuse, affairs, lying, violence, post-traumatic stress disorders, postabortion grief, abandonment, mistreatment, assault, or marital problems.[1]

Forgiveness and Health

Everett Worthington and his colleagues have summarized much of the literature on forgiveness and health.[2] They pointed out that chronic unforgiving responses can contribute to poor health, especially in the areas of cardiovascular reactivity and blood pressure. In general, those people who were unforgiving have higher blood pressure than those who were forgiving. In addition, researchers have found some preliminary evidence that certain areas of the brain tend to be activated when people are making forgiveness judgments, especially certain areas of the frontal lobes, while other areas of the brain, such as the amygdala and limbic system, tend to be activated when fear, anger, and other distressing feelings are the predominant emotions. Research has also shown that forgiving people engage in more healthy behaviors, have a better physical health status, have better social support, are less likely to drink alcohol and smoke cigarettes, have less depression, anxiety, and stress, and fewer interpersonal problems.[3]

Learning to forgive can also be very beneficial to families dealing with health problems. Studies have shown that people who are forgiving decrease their risk of heart attack and experience less anger and physical pain than their unforgiving counterparts. So one of the many benefits of forgiving is that it may improve your health.

Forgiveness in Marriage

According to Frank Fincham, J. Hall, and S.R.H. Beach, forgiveness is essential in understanding marital satisfaction and relationship dynamics.[4] In general, couples who are able to forgive experience greater marital satisfaction and longevity, better communication, and enhanced intimacy and empathy. Forgiveness in marriage also decreases hurts, disappointments, anger, revenge, and destructive arguments. Forgiveness is especially important, of course, when dealing with infidelity (more on this in chapter 12). So another benefit of forgiving is that you may discover that not only do you experience greater peace of mind and happiness from forgiving but also a significant improvement in your intimate relationships.

Forgiveness can also be very important after a divorce.[5] Just because the other person no longer lives or interacts with you doesn't mean the emotional underpinnings aren't there. Learning to forgive an ex-spouse is not only good for the children, it's good for your own mental, physical, and future relationship health.

Over the Long Term

My own clinical research has shown that within four or five sessions of focusing on forgiveness, people are less distressed, more grateful about life in general, and have much higher levels of overall happiness.[6] They also experience a greater openness to life, reporting much higher levels of meaning and purpose and far fewer negative feelings and beliefs, particularly depression, anger, and anxiety. They obsess less about their problems and just generally take things less personally. (See the following graphs.)

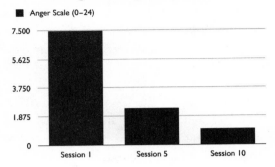

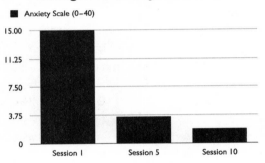

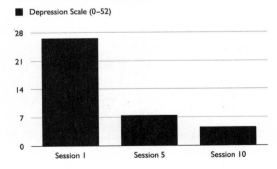

Changes in Forgiveness Over Time

■ Heartland Forgiveness Scale (0–126)

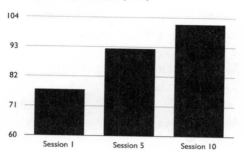

Changes in Unforgiveness Toward One Person

■ TRIMS Unforgiveness Scale (0–60)

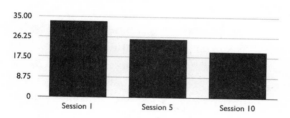

Changes in Well-Being Over Time

■ Friedman Well-Being Scale (0–100)

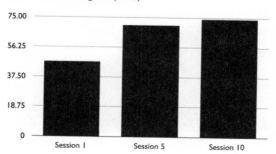

In summary, if you have a "little willingness" and practice the exercises in this book diligently over a period of weeks and months, you will almost certainly feel better and better and develop a more even, positive outlook on life. If for some reason you have difficulty working through this book, then it would be wise to seek help from a therapist, coach, facilitator, or support group experienced in forgiveness-oriented work.

"But What If I Have Blocks or Resistances?"

It is natural to have blocks, barriers, or resistance to forgiving, especially at first. After all, when we hold on to intense negative feelings for a long time, we can come to believe that they protect us, and, however unconstructive it can seem, we can be loath to give them up. In fact, removing these blocks and doubts is part of the process of forgiving. With time and practice, you will find yourself liberated from the burden of these feelings and finally be able to reach your goals for love, joy, peace and happiness.

The fact that you even picked up this book tells me that you are ready to learn how to forgive. Congratulations on starting this process! Make forgiveness a part of your life, and its benefits will be far-reaching for you and the people you care the most about.

Now, let's begin.

CHAPTER 1

Where Are You Now? Some Basic Self-Assessments

"What could you want [that] forgiveness cannot give? Do you want peace? Forgiveness offers it. Do you want happiness (consider that forgiveness offers it), a quiet mind (could forgiveness offer that too), a certainty of purpose, and a sense of worth and beauty that transcends the world? Do you want care (being cared after), safety, and the warmth of sure protection always? Do you want a quietness that cannot be disturbed, a gentleness that never can be hurt, a deep abiding comfort, and a rest so perfect it can never be upset? All this forgiveness offers you and more."

—ROBERT PERRY, *Return to the Heart of God*

"The end result of all 'unfair' pain and suffering is burning hurt and resentments. You have carried these resentments for years.... To heal from them, you must forgive the individuals involved. Until you are willing and able to forgive fully, you weigh down your soul with these prisoners."

—CAROLINE MYSS, *Entering the Castle*

This and every chapter begins with a story. You will notice that I often provide no commentary for these stories. They are here to set the mood and offer hope. Let them just wash over you.

In his book *The Code: Use the Laws of Manifestation to Achieve Your Highest Good*, Tony Burroughs has Alan tell his forgiveness story:

> When I first decided to serve others, I didn't realize that it also included forgiving them. I thought I would help them out by cleaning or running errands or doing whatever they wanted, but what I came to understand was that I could help them in other ways as well.
>
> The instance that brought all this home to me was when I made an intention to help my aging mother. In 1998, I gave up my own apartment, moved in with my mom, and began to prepare her food, bathe her, and do all of the things necessary to make her last days as comfortable as possible. Up until then, I really hadn't made much of an effort to get close to her. She lived three states away, and we really didn't get along all that well anyway. In truth, there were long periods of time when we never spoke at all because I was still carrying a lot of anger toward her for things she'd done to me as a child. Mainly, I never understood how she could just stand by and let my father abuse me like he did.
>
> But in the last few weeks of her life, as she lay in her deathbed with me sitting in the chair beside her, we began to talk about some of the things that we might not have otherwise spoken about. One particular evening after we finished eating and our barriers were lower than usual, I asked her why she let my dad beat me without ever coming to my rescue. Her answer showed me a side of her I never knew existed.

She explained that she was just as afraid of him as I was, that he beat her and threatened her too, and that he was always very careful not to let anyone else know about it. She was so sorry, she said, but at the time she was totally incapable of giving me the love I needed because she was in fear for her own safety.

She started to cry when she told me the details. I felt such compassion for her, laying there in her bed like that, waiting to die any day. But, most of all, I felt sorry because we'd never talked like this before. When her tears stopped, and as I was wiping them from her cheeks, she touched my arm with her frail hand and asked me to forgive her for not being a good mother. She said she really loved me, both then and now, and that it would mean a lot to her if I could find forgiveness in my heart for her.

I didn't move except to brush away the tears from my own eyes. Suddenly, a very emotional experience when I was a teenager came to mind. My mother was in a bad mood and had punished me for something I was innocent of. It was in that moment that I had decided, resolutely, to put her out of my life. Now, however, as I recalled that highly-charged event, I was able to see the unhappiness in her face that I didn't see before. I never knew she was that unhappy.

As my vision of the past receded, she looked up at me from her bed, our eyes met, and I told her that I forgave her, not just for that instance, but for everything uncaring she'd ever done to me. Then I leaned down to hug her, and as I did, it felt like a great weight was lifted from my chest. We both wept some more that night, and, after that, something shifted in me . . . and in her. From then on, until the time she passed away, she was much calmer and at peace. The way I see it, our forgiveness healed us both.

—ALAN MATOUSEK, Birmingham, AL

Assessing Where You Are

I thought we would start with some good assessment exercises. These will help you determine where you are in the forgiveness process and where you are with a number of different issues related to forgiveness, such as happiness, well-being, and general life satisfaction. I don't advise skipping this chapter. The questionnaires here can offer you much insight into your life and frame of mind and will also help you later to measure your progress.

Please copy the checklists and scales so you can retake them as you wish.

Exercise Checklists

The following two checklists will give you a general sense of how forgiving you are. You may think you already know this, and you may be very surprised.

DISTRESS CHECKLIST

Next to each item, I would like you to put a number from 0 to 4: 4 indicates very much, 3 indicates a great deal, 2 indicates somewhat, 1 indicates a little bit, and 0 indicates not at all. In the past week, I experienced the following:

_____ Overall Psychological Distress

_____ Depression

_____ Guilt

_____ Anger and Resentment

_____ Hostility

_____ Vengeance

_____ Vulnerability and Fear

_____ Negative Attitudes and Beliefs

_____ Anxiety in General

_____ Death Anxiety

_____ Ruminating (dwelling on things) and Obsessing

_____ Interpersonal Sensitivity (e.g., your feelings being easily hurt)

_____ Physical or Health Problems

_____ Tendency toward Revenge
_____ Tendency toward Avoidance
_____ Distrust
_____ Paranoia
_____ Emotional Instability
_____ Irritability
_____ Trauma

Now add up the 20 numbers on this checklist to get your
Total Negative Score _____ (the total score ranges from 0 to 80).

WELL-BEING CHECKLIST

Now try this one. Next to each of these items, put a number from 0 to
4: 4 indicates very much, 3 indicates a great deal, 2 indicates somewhat, 1 indicates a little bit, and 0 indicates not at all. In the past week,
I experienced the following quality, feeling, or attitude:

_____ Gratitude and Appreciation
_____ Positive Quality of Life
_____ Happiness
_____ General Sense of Well-Being
_____ Satisfaction with Life
_____ Hope
_____ Optimism
_____ Positive Beliefs and Attitudes
_____ Peace
_____ Joy
_____ Self-Worth and Self-Esteem
_____ Warmth
_____ Friendliness
_____ Positive Mental Health
_____ Sense of Meaning and Purpose in Life
_____ Trust
_____ Empathy
_____ Love of Others
_____ Love of Self
_____ Attentiveness

Now add up the 20 numbers on this checklist to get your
Total Positive Score _____ (the total score ranges from 0 to 80).

Now subtract your **Total Negative Score** from your **Total Positive Score** to get your
TOTAL SCORE _____ (this score will range from -80 to 80).

The higher your score, the more likely you are a very forgiving person. The lower your score, the more likely it is that you are holding on to unforgiveness. As you know by now, being chronically unforgiving has a number of negative effects in our lives. The correlations are summarized in diagram 1.

Diagram 1. Summary of Relationship between Forgiveness, Beliefs, and Emotions and Well-Being

Gratitude and Appreciation	Psychological Distress
Positive Quality of Life	Depression and Guilt
Happiness and Well-Being	Anger and Resentment
Life Satisfaction	Hostility and Vengeance
Hope and Optimism	Vulnerability and Fear
Positive Beliefs and Emotions	Negative Attitudes and Beliefs
Peace and Joy	Anxiety and Death Anxiety
Self-Worth and Self-Esteem	Ruminating and Obsessing
Warmth and Friendliness	Interpersonal Sensitivity
Positive Mental Health	Physical and Health Problems
Meaning and Purpose	Revenge and Avoidance
Trust and Empathy	Distrust and Paranoia
Love and Self-Love	Emotional Instability
Attentiveness	Irritability and Trauma

Forgiving people tend to be much more optimistic, hopeful, and trusting and have high levels of self-worth and positive beliefs. Forgiving people are also much likelier to be warmer, friendlier, loving, peaceful, and joyful. They have a greater self-esteem and self-worth, are more empathetic, and have a greater sense of meaning and purpose in life.

On the other hand, people who are unforgiving are much more likely to experience emotional distress in general and, specifically, higher levels of depression, anxiety, guilt, anger, and resentment. They are also more likely to be hostile, vengeful, and vulnerable and to frequently ruminate and obsess over perceived hurts. Unforgiving people also have more physical symptoms, according to the scientific research, and are more interpersonally and emotionally sensitive than forgiving people.

You may experience all or some of these negative feelings and beliefs and some or all of the positive ones. *Wherever you are is okay.* We're just trying to identify your starting point. This says nothing about your character or whether you are a good person. It is so important not to judge yourself.

I encourage you to come back to these checklists and fill them out weekly or monthly to see where you are and how much progress you have made as we go through the exercises in the book together.

Subjective Happiness Scale (SHS)

This scale was developed by Sonya Lyubomirsky and is widely used by happiness researchers. For each of the following statements and/or questions, please circle the point on the scale that you feel is most appropriate in describing you.

1. In general, I consider myself to be:

1	2	3	4	5	6	7
Not a Very Happy Person						A Very Happy Person

2. Compared to most of my peers I consider myself to be:

1	2	3	4	5	6	7
Less Happy						More Happy

3. Some people are generally very happy. They enjoy life regardless of what is going on, getting the most out of everything. To what extent does this characterization describe you?

1	2	3	4	5	6	7
Not at All						A Great Deal

4. Some people are generally not very happy. Although they are not depressed, they never seem as happy as they might be. To what extent does this characterization describe you?

1	2	3	4	5	6	7
A Great Deal						Not at All

Add up the numbers from the four items to get your
Subjective Happiness Total Score _____

An average score on the SHS questionnaire is 19 or 20. A low score is in the range of 12 to 15. A very low score is less than 12. A high score is in the range of 24 to 26. A very high score would be 27 or 28. The higher the number, the greater your overall happiness.

Lyubomirsky, S., and H. Lepper, "A Measure of Subjective Happiness: Preliminary Reliability and Construct Validation," *Social Indicators Research* 46, no. 2 (February, 1999): 137–155. Adapted slightly with kind permission from Springer Science+Business Media.

Satisfaction with Life Scale (SWLS)

This scale was developed by Ed Diener and his colleagues. It has been very widely used for many years by researchers in the field of subjective well-being. I recommend you take it weekly or at least every four or five weeks. My clients retake it every five weeks.

Please write down the number that most accurately reflects your opinions in the space next to each item.

1	2	3	4	5	6	7
Strongly Disagree	Disagree	Slightly Disagree	Neutral	Agree	Slightly Agree	Strongly Agree

_____ 1. In most ways my life is close to ideal.
_____ 2. The conditions of my life are excellent.
_____ 3. I am satisfied with my life.
_____ 4. So far I have gotten the important things I want in life.
_____ 5. If I could live my life over, I would change almost nothing.

Add up the numbers from the five items to get your
Satisfaction with Life (SWLS) Total Score _____

Your score will be a gauge of your overall satisfaction: 31 to 35 is Extremely satisfied, 26 to 30 is Satisfied, 21 to 25 is Slightly satisfied, 20 is Neutral, 15 to 19 is Slightly dissatisfied, 10 to 14 is Dissatisfied, and 5 to 9 is Extremely dissatisfied. The higher the number, the greater the life satisfaction.

Diener, E., R. A. Emmons, R. J. Larsen, and S. Griffin, "The Satisfaction with Life Scale," *Journal of Personality Assessment* 49, no. 1 (1985): 71–75. Reproduced by permission of Taylor and Francis, LLC, *www.taylorandfrancis.com*.

The Gratitude Questionnaire (GQ6)

This scale was developed by Michael McCullough and Robert Emmons and their colleagues. Again, it is widely used by researchers in the field of subjective well-being, happiness, and positive psychology. I recommend retaking it weekly or at least every four or five weeks. My clients retake it every five weeks.

Using the scale below as a guide for questions 1 through 4, write a number beside each statement to indicate how much you agree with it.

1	2	3	4	5	6	7
Strongly Disagree	Disagree	Slightly Disagree	Neutral	Slightly Agree	Agree	Strongly Agree

_____ 1. I have so much in life to be thankful for.

_____ 2. If I had to list everything in life I had to be grateful for, it would be a very long list.

_____ 3. I am grateful for a wide variety of people.

_____ 4. As I get older, I find myself more able to appreciate the people, events, and situations that have been part of my life history.

Using the scale below as a guide for questions 5 and 6, write a number beside each statement to indicate how much you agree with it.

7	6	5	4	3	2	1
Strongly Disagree	Disagree	Slightly Disagree	Neutral	Slightly Agree	Agree	Strongly Agree

_____ 5. When I look at the world, I don't see much to be grateful for.

_____ 6. Long amounts of time go by before I feel grateful to something or someone.

Add up your scores for questions 1 through 6 to get your
Gratitude Questionnaire (GQ6) Total Score _____ (this number
should be between 6 and 42).

An average score for the GQ6 Scale is 37. A low score is 29 to 30. A
very low score is below 29. A high score is 40 to 41. A very high score
is 42. The higher the number, the more grateful you are. The lower the
number, the less grateful you are.

Copyright 2002 by the American Psychological Association. McCullough, M. E., R. A. Emmons, and J. Tsang. "The Grateful Disposition: A Conceptual and Empirical Topography," *Journal of Personality and Social Psychology* 82, no. 1 (2002): 112–127. Adapted with permission.

How Forgiving Are You?

The next questionnaire is very important because it measures how
forgiving you are in general, not just how well you can forgive a
particular person or yourself on one particular occasion. It is called
the Heartland Forgiveness Scale and it was developed by Laura
Thompson and her colleagues to help people discover how forgiving they are in three important areas: forgiving themselves, forgiving someone else, and forgiving uncontrollable circumstances.

**Because I will be asking you to fill it out again later you will
want to make a number of copies of it before filling it in.**

You can also take the Heartland Forgiveness Scale on the Inter-
net by going to *www.forgivenesssolution.com.* Click on the link for
"questionnaires" and then on the link for the Heartland Forgiveness
Scale. You will not only be able to fill out the Heartland Forgiveness Scale online but also have it scored automatically for you.

The Heartland Forgiveness Scale (HFS)

Directions: In the course of our lives, negative things may occur
because of our own actions, the actions of others, or circumstances
beyond our control. For some time after these events, we may have
negative thoughts or feelings about ourselves, others, or the situation. Think about how you <u>typically</u> respond to such negative events.

On the line next to each of the following items, write the number (from the 7-point scale below) that best describes how you <u>typically</u> respond to the type of negative situation described. There are no right or wrong answers. Please be as open as possible in your answers.

1	2	3	4	5	6	7
Almost Always False of Me		More Often False of Me		More Often True of Me		Almost Always True of Me

☐ _____ 1. Although I feel bad at first when I mess up, over time I can give myself some slack.

◯ _____ 2. I hold grudges against myself for negative things I've done.

☐ _____ 3. Learning from bad things that I've done helps me to get over them.

◯ _____ 4. It is really hard for me to accept myself once I've messed up.

☐ _____ 5. With time, I am understanding of myself for mistakes I've made.

◯ _____ 6. I don't stop criticizing myself for negative things I've felt, thought, said, or done.

◯ _____ 7. I continue to punish a person who has done something that I think is wrong.

☐ _____ 8. With time, I am understanding of others for the mistakes they've made.

◯ _____ 9. I continue to be hard on others who have hurt me.

☐ _____ 10. Although others have hurt me in the past, I have eventually been able to see them as good people.

◯ _____ 11. If others mistreat me, I continue to think badly of them.

☐ _____ 12. When someone disappoints me, I can eventually move past it.

◯ _____ 13. When things go wrong for reasons that can't be controlled, I get stuck in negative thoughts about it.

☐ _____ 14. With time, I can be understanding of bad circumstances in my life.

◯ _____ 15. If I am disappointed by uncontrollable circumstances in my life, I continue to think negatively about them.

☐ _____ 16. I eventually make peace with bad situations in my life.

◯ _____ 17. It's really hard for me to accept negative situations that aren't anybody's fault.

☐ _____ 18. Eventually, I let go of negative thoughts about bad circumstances that are beyond anyone's control.

Heartland Forgiveness Scale Scoring and Interpretation

There is a square or circle next to each of the blanks where you have written your responses to each item. You will now write a score for each item in the circle or square that is next to that response.

1 **Score the Items with Squares Next to Them:** For each item with a square next to it (items 1, 3, 5, 8, 10, 12, 14, 16, and 18), your score is the same as the number that you wrote. To score each of these items, simply write the same number for your score that you already wrote for your response. For example, if you wrote the number 6, your score would be 6, and you would write the number 6 in the square next to your response for that item.

2 **Score the Items with Circles Next to Them:** For each item with a circle next to it (items 2, 4, 6, 7, 9, 11, 13, 15, and 17), the scores are not the same as the number you wrote. For these items, the scores are "reversed" (e.g., a response of 1 is scored as 7 and a response of 7 is scored as 1). Use the list of scores given below to write the correct score next to the number that you wrote in response to each of these items. For example, if you wrote the number 6, your score would be 2, and you would write the number 2 in the circle next to your response for that item.

The Number You Wrote	Your Score
1	⑦
2	⑥
3	⑤
4	④
5	③
6	②
7	①

3 **Calculate and Interpret Your HFS Subscale Scores and HFS Total Scale Score**

FORGIVENESS OF SELF SUBSCALE

Calculate Your Score: Add together your scores for items 1 to 6. The result is your **Forgiveness of Self** score. _____

Interpret Your Score: Your score on the Forgiveness of Self subscale indicates how forgiving you tend to be of yourself, with higher scores indicating higher levels of forgiveness, and lower scores indicating lower levels of forgiveness.

- A score of 6 to 17 means that you are usually unforgiving of yourself.
- A score of 18 to 29 means that you are sometimes forgiving and sometimes unforgiving of yourself. That is, you are about as likely to forgive yourself as you are not to forgive yourself.
- A score of 30 to 42 means that you are usually forgiving of yourself.

FORGIVENESS OF OTHERS SUBSCALE

Calculate Your Score: Add together your scores for items 7 to 12. The result is your **Forgiveness of Others** score. _____

Interpret Your Score: Your score on the Forgiveness of Others sub-scale indicates how forgiving you tend to be of other people, with higher scores indicating higher levels of forgiveness, and lower scores indicating lower levels of forgiveness.

- A score of 6 to 17 means that you are usually unforgiving of other people.
- A score of 18 to 29 means that you are sometimes forgiving and sometimes unforgiving of others. That is, you are about as likely to forgive others as you are not to forgive others.
- A score of 30 to 42 means that you are usually forgiving of other people.

FORGIVENESS OF SITUATIONS SUBSCALE

Calculate Your Score: Add together your scores for items 13 to 18. The result is your **Forgiveness of Situations** subscale score. _____

Interpret Your Score: Your score on the Forgiveness of Situations subscale indicates how forgiving you tend to be of negative circumstances, events, or situations that are beyond anyone's control (such as an illness or a natural disaster). Higher scores indicate higher levels of forgiveness, and lower scores indicate lower levels of forgiveness.

- A score of 6 to 17 means that you are usually unforgiving of uncontrollable situations.
- A score of 18 to 29 means that you are sometimes forgiving and sometimes unforgiving of uncontrollable situations. That is, you are about as likely to forgive uncontrollable situations as you are not to forgive uncontrollable situations.
- A score of 30 to 42 means that you are usually forgiving of uncontrollable situations.

TOTAL HEARTLAND FORGIVENESS SCALE

Calculate Your Score: Add together your three scores for the **Forgiveness of Self, Forgiveness of Others,** and **Forgiveness of Situations**

subscales (or add together your scores for items 1 to 18). The result is your **Total Forgiveness** scale score. _____

Interpret Your Score: Your score on the **Total Heartland Forgiveness** scale indicates how forgiving you tend to be of yourself, other people, and uncontrollable situations. Higher scores indicate higher levels of forgiveness, and lower scores indicate lower levels of forgiveness.

- A score of 18 to 53 means that you are usually unforgiving of yourself, others, and uncontrollable situations.
- A score of 54 to 89 means that you are sometimes forgiving and sometimes unforgiving of yourself, others, and uncontrollable situations. That is, you are about as likely to forgive as you are not to forgive.
- A score of 90 to 126 means that you are usually forgiving of yourself, others, and uncontrollable situations.
- You can write your subscale and total scale scores in the boxes below.

Heartland Forgiveness Scale

Scale / Subscale	Your Score
Forgiveness of Self (Items 1 to 6)	
Forgiveness of Others (Items 7 to 12)	
Forgiveness of Situations (Items 13 to 18)	
Total Forgiveness (Items 1 to 18)	

Thompson, L. Y., C. R. Snyder, L. Hoffman, S. T. Michael, H. N. Rasmussen, L. S. Billings, L. Heinze, J. E. Neufeld, H. S. Shorey, J. C. Roberts, and D. E. Robert, "Dispositional Forgiveness of Self, Others, and Situations: The Heartland Forgiveness Scale," *Journal of Personality* 73, no. 2 (January 2005): 313–359. Reproduced with permission of Blackwell Publishing, Ltd.

On the following page you will find a summary sheet that you can use to record your initial scores on these four scales. I recommend you copy the summary sheet so you can use it again later.

Summary of Scores: Initial Assessment Scoring

Heartland Self-Forgiveness Subscale Score   _____

Heartland Forgiveness of Others Subscale Score   _____

Heartland Forgiveness of Circumstances Subscale Score   _____

Heartland Forgiveness Scale Total Score   _____

Subjective Happiness Scale (SHS) Score   _____

Satisfaction with Life (SWLS) Total Score   _____

Gratitude (GQ6) Total Score   _____

A client of mine named April responded to all of the exercises in this book. You will read her comments a little later on. Here are her scores at the initial assessment. (Her scores at the fifth and tenth sessions are presented at the end of the book.) Your scores may be higher or lower than hers. Whatever they are is okay.

SUMMARY OF ALL OF APRIL'S SCORES: INITIAL ASSESSMENT SCORING

Heartland Self-Forgiveness Subscale Score   25

Heartland Forgiveness of Others Subscale Score   33

Heartland Forgiveness of Circumstances Subscale Score   17

Heartland Forgiveness Scale Total Score   75

Subjective Happiness Scale (SHS) Score   10

Satisfaction with Life (SWLS) Total Score   21

Gratitude (GQ6) Total Score   29

CHAPTER 2

Identifying Who You Feel Has Harmed You

"[Forgiving] your enemies... is crucial. It's one of the most important things. It can change one's life. To reduce hatred and other destructive emotions, you must develop the opposites—compassion and kindness.... Forgiveness allows you to be in touch with these positive emotions."
—DALAI LAMA, *The Wisdom of Forgiveness*

"The weak can never forgive. Forgiveness is the attribute of the strong."
—MAHATMA GANDHI

EVERETT WORTHINGTON IS ONE of the most prolific research-ers and writers in the field of forgiveness and generously gave me permission to use this powerful forgiveness story.

"I wish the youth who murdered Mama were here now."
I pointed to a baseball bat. "I'd beat his brains out."
It was late and very dark outside. What a New Year's Day.
I could feel the hatred almost radiating from my face. Mike

had just told Kathy and me what he had observed when he walked into Mama's house that morning—a frail, crumpled, lifeless, and abused body. The blood was spattered on the walls and two small pools of blood, one beneath her head and the other beneath her hips, were visible. The house was a complete shambles—broken mirrors, articles thrown everywhere, destruction all around. I was stunned. Numb. I could hardly take it in.

We recalled the struggles and the good times. I was reminded of being interviewed on a radio call-in show. At the end of the interview the host said, "I think we have time for one more call and I think you're going to like this."

The soft, East Tennessee drawl of my mother came through the telephone to my ears.

"Sonny," she said using my boyhood nickname, "I've been listening to your interview. You're a good boy, Sonny." I was forty-eight. It was a wonderful, warm affirmation from a woman who had put so much into my life. Now I knew I would never hear such affirmations from her again.

When we arrived in Tennessee, the police could tell us little. "It looks like a burglary by some youth that went wrong. The youth probably did not know your mother was at home and she surprised them. She was struck three times by a crowbar," said the police detective. "We're so sorry for your loss."

Suddenly an irony struck me. Less than a month before, I had delivered to our publisher a book on forgiveness written by Mike McCullough, Steve Sandage, and myself called To Forgive Is Human. *I couldn't help asking myself, Who did I write that book for? Was the book for other people? Did its lessons apply to me as well? My anger didn't like the answers.*

Uncomfortably, I began to try to apply the five lessons (REACH) we had taught others about the difficult work of forgiveness. At the heart of forgiveness is a feeling of empathy for the person who has wronged a victim. Could I for a moment put my rage on hold and recall the hurt more objectively? Could I experience a sense of empathy for the youth who had murdered my mother? I knew I couldn't merely conjure up a feeling of empathy. Empathy develops out of vivid recall of the circumstances, but from the point of view of the wrongdoer instead of the person harmed.

So, I began to imagine what it must have been like for two youths to stand outside a suburban home and think about the perfect robbery they intended to commit. It was New Year's Eve. Dark house. No car in the driveway. They could be assured that no one would be back until after midnight.

Suddenly prickles of fear might have raced up his spine. "What are you doing in here?" my mother might have said, voice taut with outrage and fear. He probably wheeled around and thought, Oh no, I've been seen. This wasn't supposed to happen. This was supposed to be a perfect robbery. This old woman is going to put me in jail.

In the grasp of his own emotions, he probably struck out quickly with the crowbar still resting in his hand, striking her on the cheek. She spun as she fell back. He struck her across the back and shoulders. She rolled onto her back, and consumed with fear and anger he delivered the third blow to her temple.

He might have thought What have I done? *"This was supposed to be a perfect robbery," he might have whined plaintively to his buddy. "Now I've killed this old lady." Frustration and anger replaced the shock and fear. He began to act out his rage. He assaulted her with a wine bottle. Then he began to throw objects. With the crowbar, he shattered the mirror above the bookcase—the mirror that had seen his shameful act. Every mirror in the house was shattered.*

I could understand and even feel with the youth the horror of what he had done.

Follow-Up to the Story: Helping Oneself Heals Others

So, I began to talk about forgiveness at conventions. At one convention, one woman hung back. She said, "I am the mother of a youth who broke into a woman's house and murdered her when the robbery was discovered." She looked so forlorn that my heart went out to her. She said "They hold my husband and me accountable for what our son did. We raised him as a Christian boy. But his crowd at school led him down a dark path." I murmured an inadequate understanding. "Our friends have rejected us. Frankly, when you began to talk I expected more condemnation. I almost walked out. I've been pretty disillusioned with people." She was close to tears. Bitterness was barely below the surface. "I think the forgiveness you demonstrated today may have turned my life around. When I heard you describe what the robbery might have been like from the point of view of the boy who committed the murder, I felt that it is possible that people might someday understand. My faith in humans is restored. I think I can begin to forgive the people who hurt me."

Writing can be a very powerful way of opening channels within yourself for forgiveness. It can help you become clearer about what's blocking you and even help you identify who is unforgiven and why. Please get some paper and a pen or go to your computer, and let's begin.

Exercise: Who Did Something within the Past Year That Hurt or Harmed You?

This is the first of many forgiveness exercises that will help you begin to release negative feelings, grudges, hurts, guilt, and resentments and to shift your perspective. You may think you already know who you need to forgive, but as you work you may be very surprised at who and what you hold a grievance toward.

Journaling Experience 1: Last Year

Choose one person within the past year that did something that you felt hurt or harmed by and whose actions (or inactions) triggered feelings of anger, guilt, resentment, sadness, or anxiety. It could also be a circumstance that happened seemingly beyond your control. Please spend five or more minutes writing down your feelings, beliefs, and experiences in your journal.

Throughout the book I have included sample responses and journal entries from my client April, so you can see how someone else worked through the exercises. Here's April's first contribution:

APRIL'S RESPONSE

I would say in the last year the person who hurt me most was my grandmom. I had always been pretty close to her, and when my dad died, I began to see a different side. Perhaps it was something I never noticed before, or maybe my dad's death was too much for her. Things just changed. It seemed she wanted less and less to do with my sisters and me. When I finally moved out of my old house, she barely wished me well, and I haven't heard from her since. She even told my sister that I was a thief for taking my dad's bed that I had been using for two years and said, "We'll all have our judgment day." That hurt. I never took anything from her. I did whatever she needed me to do to help her, and in the end I guess it wasn't enough.

Journaling Experience 2: Earlier in Life

Now choose another person who did something that you felt hurt or harmed by, but this time when you were much younger, perhaps in your childhood or teenage years, and whose actions (or inactions) triggered feelings of anger, guilt, resentment, sadness, or anxiety. It could also be a circumstance that happened seemingly beyond your control. Please spend five or more minutes writing down your feelings, beliefs, and experiences.

This is something I've brought up a few times, but my mom is someone who hurt me when I was a child. I was too young to fully understand, but I knew she was leaving and I knew how sad it made my dad, so that made me sad, too. We didn't have a very good relationship when I was growing up. I always felt like if I didn't make the [effort], I didn't see her. I used to get mad because she always seemed to put down my dad and my older sisters, which I didn't think was right. I have come a long way with her since then.

Journaling Experience 3: Yourself

Now I would like you to focus on yourself. Pick a situation or circumstance, preferably from the past year, though earlier would be all right, too, in which you did something for which you judged yourself harshly, criticized yourself, or just held a grievance or attack thought against yourself. Please spend five or more minutes writing down your feelings, beliefs, and experiences.

APRIL'S RESPONSE

It has been a little more than a year, but this is one specific time I think about often, the day my dad died. I always replay everything in my head from that day. I blamed myself for a very long time. I felt like if I pushed him to go to the doctors more, or pushed him to eat better, he would still be here. I thought that maybe if I came downstairs just a few minutes sooner, he would be here. I know I shouldn't think this way, but I have for a long time.

Using Affirmations

Now I want you to go back and reflect on any *positive benefits* you may have experienced because of these experiences, interactions, and circumstances. Sometimes this is very hard to do; the whole experience has become clouded with negativity. But I urge you to try it. This is a very important step in the forgiveness process.

While you are doing that, it would be helpful to contemplate some affirmations. *Affirmations are the second set of exercises that you will be using in this book to help you forgive.* Affirmations are powerful beliefs with powerful energy connected to them. I encourage you to contemplate, learn, and practice the affirmations in this book in a consistent way. Here is one way I recommend.

Write each affirmation down on a 3 x 5 card and contemplate the cards for a few minutes four to five times each day, beginning in the morning and ending in the evening before sleep. *Save these cards.* The affirmations in the book can, in themselves, catalyze a great deal of change. When used along with the other exercises, they will be even more powerful. You might want to make up several cards, and, to help you remember and repeat them, post them on your bathroom mirror, on your refrigerator, on the dashboard of your car, or in another convenient place. Throughout the day, repeat them whenever you experience a challenge or grievance.

Exercise: Affirmations 1 and 2

AFFIRMATION 1

"Inherent in every difficulty or challenge is the seed of an equal or greater benefit. I will look for that seed and nurture it."

AFFIRMATION 2

"Inherent in every grievance, judgment, and attack thought is the seed of the opportunity for practicing forgiveness. I will look for that seed and nurture it."

Exercise: Journaling Positive Benefits of Experiences 1–3

After you have contemplated these affirmations for a little while, write about each of the three previous experiences and how each one activated strengths in you; how you became a better, stronger, wiser person in some way; and how you experienced some positive outcomes from the experience or strengthened a relationship because of the perceived harmful experience. Focus not only on the positive benefits to you in the past but also on the potential benefits for you in the future.

APRIL'S RESPONSE ABOUT LAST YEAR

After everything that happened with my grandmom, I realize the importance of being dependent on myself and no one else. I think that maybe she has things going on in her own life that are causing her pain. I also realized that I don't want to surround myself with negativity because it won't help me have a positive attitude.

APRIL'S RESPONSE ABOUT EARLIER IN LIFE

My relationship with my mom has come a long way. I decided the only way to have her in my life was to forgive her for the past. I learned how to communicate with her better. I now understand that part of the reason we didn't get along was because we were so much alike.

APRIL'S RESPONSE ABOUT HERSELF

From this experience, I learned that there are many things in my life that are sometimes beyond our control. I've tried to stop blaming myself for that day and realize that even if I came downstairs a few minutes sooner, it wouldn't have mattered. It was my dad's choice not to create a healthy lifestyle for himself.

Keep on Journaling

As you go through all the steps to forgiveness outlined in this book and practice different exercises and processes, write about your experiences of doing these exercises in your journal. Make sure to note what exercises and processes have had the most positive, beneficial, and healing effects on you. If you do this regularly, you will be able to look back at the earlier entries and notice the significant changes you have made in your ability to forgive and in your level of happiness and well-being.

CHAPTER 3

Discovering What Hurts:
One Core Problem (Unforgiveness) and One Core Solution (Forgiveness)

*"Before we can experience the pure and serene state
of love, there is one priceless gift we must learn how
to give—to ourselves and to others.... The gift I am
speaking about is* forgiveness. *To heal the split between
our dark side and our higher self, we must learn how
to forgive ourselves for our imperfections,...for our
judgmental minds.... We also must find the willingness
to forgive those who have hurt us, lied to us, disappointed
us, and betrayed us.... Ultimately, we have to...forgive
the presence that we think of as God."*

— DEBBIE FORD, *Why Good People Do Bad Things*

---

*"Forgiveness takes away what stands between your
brother and yourself.*
It is the wish that you be joined with him and not apart
. . .
*The holiest place on earth is where an ancient hatred has
become a present love."*

— *A Course in Miracles*

I MET ELLEN MANY years ago. I knew her and her husband and
some of the personal, marital, and family struggles she has had
over the years. She is a courageous and loving woman and was kind
enough to share this story with me. It demonstrates the kind of
healing transformation that can take place in family relationships
when you are ready and willing to forgive. It also shows how forgiveness can bring about love and an open heart.

> *I never really understood my father; he was a distant, harsh
> man who ruled our home with an iron fist. With a houseful of
> women, he would complain about the fact that he had three
> daughters and no sons. My whole life I tried to please him. As
> a youngster, I was a tomboy—as close as he was going to get to
> having a son. He would often refer to me in masculine terms
> calling me boy, son, or Paco. When I approached puberty
> and decided I preferred dresses and dancing to climbing
> trees and playing soccer, our relationship—if you can call it
> that—ended.*
>
> *Eventually, I married, had a baby boy, and I could see
> that his baby grandson brought him enormous pleasure.
> Unfortunately, two weeks after my son was born my father
> had a massive stroke. The doctors never understood how he
> survived, but I knew his determination to live would not let
> him go so easily. After he was released from the hospital, his
> left side was paralyzed, his speech was slurred, and he needed
> someone to care for him while my mother was at work.*
>
> *Every morning my husband dropped our son and me at my
> parents' home on his way to work. I would care for my father,
> bathe him, shave him, feed him. I even had to deal with
> bedpans and cleaning him afterward. I went there day after
> day, hoping, praying that just once he'd say, "thank you" or
> "good job"—something, anything positive. Instead, day after
> day I got, "You don't know how to make oatmeal" or "I hate
> the way you bathe me."*

"You're going to cut me with that razor"; "You're stupid"; and "You can't learn anything."

Day after day I came home in tears. This went on for about two years until my mother's union switched insurance companies. The new company covered a nurse's aide for my dad for up to six hours a day. So now, I only had to cover two hours a day but nothing else changed. I still went there every day, and all I wanted to hear was that I was loved and appreciated for all I was doing and giving up, and every day I was disappointed, heartbroken, and tearful. After about ten years, my husband said to me, "Enough is enough; either you find a way not to be upset or stop taking care of your dad."

I had a difficult decision and I prayed for guidance. Could I continue to care for my dad, because he was my dad and sacrificed to support us, without ever expecting him to change or say thank you? Could I give up my hope that we could have a different relationship and accept that the way he showed love was through his years of work? Could I forgive him for not being the dad I wanted? Could I just walk away from him and live with myself? I decided that I could not walk away—that in spite of everything I loved him. I chose to forgive him and love him, faults and all.

A funny thing happened, though. Within a year of this decision—suddenly my dad was saying, "No one takes care of me as good as you" and even he said, "I love you" to me regularly. A year later he died, but for a glorious year I had the father I always wanted, because I opened my heart first and forgave him.

One Core Problem, One Core Solution

As you know by now, at the core of my work is the belief that lurking underneath almost all of the other problems we have there is *one core problem:* unforgiveness.[1] In other words, if you are depressed or angry or anxious or having any number of other psychological, emotional, or interpersonal issues, a grievance, judgment, should, or attack thought is at the heart of it all, being used consciously or unconsciously by you against yourself or another person. A grievance or attack thought is any thought with the intent to harm, injure, hurt, threaten, offend, disparage, diminish, blame, judge critically, or judge harshly someone else or oneself. *Attack thoughts always separate us from our true selves and from others.* Attack thoughts include phrases or tones of voice that say or imply: you are wrong, bad, incompetent, inadequate, sinful, not good enough, stupid, worse than, and foolish. Phrases that include *always* and *never* are usually attack thoughts as well, such as "you always drive too fast" or "you never remember to put away your clothes." Attack thoughts against oneself include the same kinds of thoughts directed against oneself: "I am wrong, bad, incompetent, inadequate, sinful, not good enough, stupid, worse than, and foolish." *Shoulds* include statements such as "you should do something differently" or "I should do something differently," said or thought with a judgmental tone.

For that one core problem, there is also one core solution: *forgiveness.*[2] Forgiveness is the letting go of the grievance, judgment, should, and attack thought that you use (consciously or unconsciously) against another person or yourself. Forgiveness is a shift in perception and attitude. It is also about seeing the inner light or goodness in yourself and in other people. For some of you, this may be quite challenging to understand at first. I know it took me a while to see and understand that *unforgiveness* could be such a powerful force and that it was underneath so many other problems. This is why forgiveness is often said to be the key to happiness and peace. Forgiveness removes the blocks and barriers to the presence of love, peace, happiness, and light. Fortunately, however, forgiveness is inherent within the problem and can be learned.

The next set of exercises is designed to help you discover what grievances, judgments, and attack thoughts you hold against yourself, other people, groups, or God so that you can then begin to learn how to forgive yourself and others.

Exercise: Identifying Your Grievances and Attack Thoughts

1 In your notebook or journal, write down any grievance, judgment, should, or attack thought that you are holding against *the people you live with*. (If you don't live with anyone, think about the person you are closest to.) It doesn't matter how large or small the grievances, judgments, shoulds, or attack thoughts are or how strong or weak your feelings are toward this person or persons.

APRIL'S RESPONSE

People you live with—Because I have a lot of unresolved feelings from my past, I take a lot of my emotions out on Brian because we live together. Most of the time I am upset or angry about something that he doesn't have anything to do with, but I don't know where to place those feelings.

2 Now write down any grievances, judgments, shoulds, or attack thoughts that you have against *someone you work with*, including your boss, supervisors, colleagues, clients, customers, employees, and supervisees. Again, it doesn't matter how large or small the grievances, judgments, shoulds, or attack thoughts are or how strong or weak your feelings are.

APRIL'S RESPONSE

For the most part, I enjoy my job. There are, however, many clients that come in [who] aggravate me. The ones I have the biggest problem with are those [who] walk in when we are about to close. It seems like the same three or four people that do this frequently, and I think it's rude. It's as if any time is less valuable than theirs. I feel it is disrespectful toward the employees.

3 Now write down any grievance, judgment, should, or attack thought that you are holding against *your parents, siblings, in-laws, aunts, uncles, grandparents,* etc. Again, it doesn't matter how small or large you consider the grievance, judgment, should, or attack thought to be or how strong or weak your feelings are.

APRIL'S RESPONSE

The time I was angry at my mom for leaving was when I was five. I felt like she should've been there a lot more throughout my life. She said things that hurt me and made me feel bad about the person I was. My uncle is also someone who made me feel bad. He said, "You're a worthless clone of your father." That's hard to hear, especially from a family member.

4 In your journal, write down any grievance, judgment, should, or attack thought that you are holding against *yourself*. It doesn't matter how large or small the grievances, judgments, shoulds, or attack thoughts are or how strong or weak your feelings are toward yourself.

APRIL'S RESPONSE

I am insecure about myself. I constantly wonder if I'm living up to the standards of other people. I tend to be hard on myself when things go wrong. I put myself down a lot. Sometimes I think I'm not good enough for anyone.

5 Now write down any grievance, judgment, should, or attack thought that you are holding against *someone from another ethnic, religious, national, or international group*. Again, it doesn't matter how small or large you consider the grievance, judgment, should, or attack thought to be or how strong or weak your feelings are.

6 Finally, write down any grievance, judgment, should, or attack thought that you are holding against *God, nature, the Universe, or* *any Higher Power.* Again, it doesn't matter how small or large you consider the grievance, judgment, should, or attack thought to be or how strong or weak your feelings are.

APRIL'S RESPONSE

I don't feel like this so much anymore, but when my dad died I kept thinking, "Why? Why would God do this to me?" I questioned my belief in God at one point.

Soon you will be learning some techniques to help you release these grievances, judgments, shoulds, and attack thoughts, and I will explain more about the role they play in your healing process. For now, we are just identifying the limiting and attacking thoughts that cause you emotional pain and distress and helping you begin to see the glass as half full rather than half empty. In other words, there is always a silver lining within these upsetting experiences that trigger unforgiving thoughts and feelings and another way of looking at them.

CHAPTER 4

Choosing Love over Fear

"Love is what we were born with. Fear is what we learned here.... The practice of forgiveness is our most important contribution to the healing of the world."
—Marianne Williamson, *A Return to Love*

"'Complete forgiveness' is different from what is usually called forgiveness in the world. Complete forgiveness starts by our realizing that whatever is happening we have asked for. We then offer our perceptions and thoughts about the reality of the grievance to the Holy Spirit and ask for a new perception to be given us. Once the Holy Spirit gives us this new perception we must choose it as ours. This is how grievances are let go. Since our brothers and sisters bring us those forgiveness lessons, our relationships are actually our salvation."
—Rev. Tony Ponticello, *After Enlightenment*

"Forgiveness is the fragrance the violet sheds on the heel that has crushed it."
—Mark Twain

ONE OF THE FIRST times Jerry [Jampolsky] and I lectured together was at the opera house in Seattle. We were backstage waiting to be announced, and Jerry looked through a peephole in the curtain. "Wow," he commented, "the house is packed."

This must have made him nervous because suddenly he expressed an overwhelming desire to urinate! Even though we knew that they were going to introduce us in a few minutes, he had to go, so he asked the stagehand where the bathroom was and raced toward it. Later, he told me that he ran as fast as he could, but as he started back, he realized that he'd exited from a different door into an adjoining building. He had to find his way back to the restroom and go out the correct door before he could locate me. He arrived just as we were being announced.

Meanwhile I was having my own anxieties. We'd only lectured together a few times, and I knew that people really came to hear Jerry. My anxiety quickly turned to anger. I said to myself, I will never forgive Jerry for this. Then I began fantasizing about what would happen if he didn't get back in time and the curtain rose and I was standing onstage alone. I decided that I'd tell the truth and say, "Sorry, Jerry went to the bathroom and he'll be right back."

We were out of the sight of the master of ceremonies as he began to introduce us. Just as he finished, Jerry came tearing across the stage with literally a second to spare. The curtain went up and we opened our lecture with the title of our talk, "Forgiveness Is the Key to Happiness!"

While onstage, I actually shared the fact that we were giving a talk on forgiveness, yet here I'd been just moments before thinking I'd "never" forgive Jerry, who was full of his own self-condemnation! Never more than that night did we recognize the truth of the old saying: "You teach what you need to learn."

Awareness of the ego is essential if we're to attain a peaceful mind and a happy heart. Forgiveness requires us to look honestly at our thoughts and emotions and see how destructive judgment and anger are: before we turn on the light, we have to see that it's dark.
—from GERALD JAMPOLSKY and DIANE V. CIRINCIONE, *Finding Our Way Home: Heartwarming Stories That Ignite Our Spiritual Core*

Forgiveness Is a Bridge

Forgiveness can be likened to a bridge that connects one path that you can travel in life to a second.[1] At any given time, you and I are traveling down one of these two paths. Very few people travel exclusively down one path all the time. The first path is a path of low vibrational frequency or energy. This path can be thought of as the fearful path.[2, 3, 4] The second path is a path of high vibrational frequency or energy sometimes thought of as the positive path—the path of light or the path of the Self.[5, 6] It is not bad or wrong to be on any path at any given time. The positive path is, however, the Truth of who we are, that which we all, consciously or subconsciously, strive for. Please be kind to yourself when you read these words. The purpose of this book is to help you travel across the bridge of forgiveness—from the lower path to the higher one—using the most effective tools that have been developed.

The bridge of forgiveness crosses from the path of fear, negativity, guilt, blame, unhappiness, hate, and weapons of self-destruction (i.e., the path of the ego-mind) to the positive path of light, love, peace, happiness, joy, and well-being. Forgiveness allows you to release the past and to cross the bridge from the path of fear and negativity to the positive path of light and love.[7] In the process, a shift will take place in your attitudes, beliefs, perceptions, choices, decisions, habits, relationship patterns, and energy.

What you and I experience in life is the result of which path we choose to travel. When you or I are traveling the fearful path, we are separated from our sense of oneness with our true Self, the Truth of who we are. When we are traveling the path of happiness, love, and light, we are united, aligned, or connected with our true Self, the Truth of our Being. As you can see in the diagram, a line connects the two paths. At any moment you and I are somewhere along that line. Most people move back and forth across the line at different moments in their life, and at any given moment our attitudes, beliefs, choices, and energy level determine how far we are on either side of the line.

The more forgiving you are, the more likely you will be on the positive path.

Diagram 2. The Two Paths

Ego-Mind	Self/Truth/Being
Separation	Oneness/Unity
Fear	Love
Unhappiness	Happiness
Sadness	Joy
Anger	Contentment
Guilt	Innocence
Conflict	Peace
Darkness (Absence of Light)	Light

Diagram 2 contrasts the extremes of the two paths. In actuality, there are plenty of shades of gray between the two contrasting points of view, and we all move back and forth between them. As you work your way through this book, you will find yourself spending more of your time aligned with the path of love, peace, happiness, contentment, and joy, which is ultimately your true or core nature.

Happiness Is Found in the Present

One of the most pernicious obstacles in our path to happiness is a tendency to dwell in regrets over the past or anxieties about the future. In actuality, "now" is the only time there is. You can think about the past or the future, but this very moment is the only moment that exists. When the future arrives it will be the present moment. It will be the "now." So if you or I spend too much time focusing on the past or focusing on the future, we are not going to be happy, because life does take place right now, *right now,* **right now.**

At any given moment in time, life is a choice between happiness and unhappiness, between negative and positive, between love and fear, and therefore between the "ego-mind" and the "Self/Truth/Being." At any moment in time, you and I can choose which path we are going to travel. The process of forgiveness lets us stay centered in the present most of the time rather than dwelling on the distressing past or projecting our fears and worries into the imagined future. It is only in the present that happiness can be found.

Shoulding on Ourselves

In the previous exercise, you wrote down your grievances, judgments, shoulds, and attack thoughts. Anytime we "should" on ourselves, we have emotionally backed expectations and obligations for ourselves based on some standard rules of conduct. For example, you might say to yourself: "I should earn X dollars a year" or "I should have gotten that promotion" or "I should make my spouse or mother happy all the time" or "I should be able to get an A in chemistry." When we operate from these shoulds, we tend to judge ourselves harshly, and we fall below our own expectations and standards of conduct. Judging ourselves in this way is a form of attack. Anytime we "should" on another person, we are having expectations for that person based on some standard or rules of conduct. When the other person doesn't live up to that expectation or standard, we tend to judge them harshly. That judgment is also an "attack thought." You can learn to identify these attack thoughts and let them go. There is nothing bad or wrong with having them.

But when you learn to release them through the process of forgiveness, you will experience more love, peace, happiness, and joy in your life.

In addition, if you look closely, when another person with whom you are interacting is expressing attack thoughts and grievances—for example, expressing blame or judgment and getting angry—you will discover that underneath the anger, grievances, and attack thoughts are hurt and disappointment. Furthermore, if you look even more closely, you will discover that underneath the hurt and disappointment is fear. Fear, in turn, is a call for help and for love.

The fear operates on two levels. First, there is the other person's fear that you do not love, care, appreciate, or value them. Second is the fear that they are disconnected from the love within themselves. So hurt and disappointment cover up fear, and fear is a call for help and for love. Therefore, an "attacking person" is a fearful person calling for help and love. Moreover, when you are attacking or angry at another, you will discover the same process working within you; that is, you are experiencing hurt and disappointment, and that hurt and disappointment cover up fear. The fear within you is, in turn, calling for help and for love.

You can learn, with practice, to shift your perceptions and perspective to see that an attacking or critical person is a fearful person calling for help and for love. Learning to shift your perception and your attitudes is a key aspect of forgiveness. It is also a choice that you can make. Making that choice *empowers* you. Not making that choice *disempowers* you.

This is one of the most powerful decisions you can make and has the ability to transform the quality of your life. Part of the work of this book is to help you *re-empower* yourself by helping you *return* to your core self, that place that always exists within you, of love, peace, happiness, strength, and joy.

The next set of exercises, which I have adapted from *A Course in Miracles* and the work of Gerald Jampolsky, can help you release your shoulds.[8, 9]

Exercise: Affirmations 3 to 7

If you have been reading the book straight through, bear with me. I will repeat my introduction to affirmations for those who are just coming into the conversation.

Affirmations are powerful beliefs with powerful energy connected to them. I would like to encourage you to contemplate, learn, and practice the affirmations in this book in a consistent way. Here is one way I recommend: Write each affirmation on a 3 × 5 card. Read the cards three to four times a day, starting in the morning and ending before bedtime. Repeat the affirmations throughout the day, especially when you experience any emotional distress such as sadness, anxiety, hurt, guilt, or anger. You may want to make several copies of the affirmations and tape them to your bathroom mirror, refrigerator, or the dashboard of your car.

Memorizing each affirmation is not necessary but would certainly be beneficial. Keep in mind that you do not have to believe in the affirmation at first. I encourage you to repeat the affirmation anyway, and do it with as much conviction as possible. Contemplate its meaning. Allow yourself to feel its positive energy.

As we practice affirmations, we shift from fearful, lower vibrational energy to a positive, higher vibrational energy path. Later in the book, you will learn to combine some of these affirmations with energy techniques that will make them even more powerful for you.

AFFIRMATION 3

"I can elect to change all thoughts, beliefs, attitudes, and negative energies that hurt."

AFFIRMATION 4

"I can elect to change all thoughts, beliefs, attitudes, and negative energies that cause emotional distress."

AFFIRMATION 5

"I can escape from the emotional distress I experience by giving up grievances and attack thoughts."

AFFIRMATION 6

"I am determined to see and experience things differently."

AFFIRMATION 7

"I can learn to see that attack and anger cover up fear, and fear is a call for help and for love."

APRIL'S COMMENTS ON USING THE AFFIRMATIONS

From my personal experience, the affirmations were more effective when I wrote them each down on an index card and read over them a few times a day. With each affirmation, I was able to see the way I viewed situations and events in my life in a negative way, and by applying each one to my life it allowed me to shift my thought process to a more positive one. There are things that happen every day that one of these affirmations can apply to.

From Fear to Love

A lifetime of personal and spiritual growth and practicing psychotherapy has led me to understand that underneath *all* distressing emotions is the core emotion of fear, which is itself a lack of love. Love is the core positive emotion that we experience when we are connected to our inner Being or true Self. When we feel separate from our inner Being or true Self, we experience fear. All other distressing emotions are secondary to fear. The essence of our Being is love, and our journey through life is a quest to return to our core, which is love.

Whenever we experience distressing emotions, we are, in fact, calling for love. On one level, we are calling for love from other people, but on a deeper level we are calling for love from and toward ourselves. So it follows that whenever someone else is expressing negative or distressing emotions, feelings, judgments, or complaints toward us or toward themselves, they are calling for love. *Therefore, it can be said that every communication is either an expression of love or a call for love.* Forgiveness allows you and me to remove the blocks and barriers to the experience of that love. For example, if your spouse, lover, friend, parent, sibling, or child is expressing a lot of negativity, anger, resentment, bitterness, or frustration, rather than seeing it as a sign of disrespect you can learn to see it as a call for help and a call for love. In fact, you can learn to see that underneath the negativity are hurt and disappointment, and underneath the hurt and disappointment is fear. By forgiving these people you care about and by staying calm and centered, you can learn to respond in a more resourceful, compassionate, and beneficial way to their calls for help and for love.

Identifying Stressors

In life, we're often going along, doing fine, when we encounter a *stressor,* either:

1. something that *is* happening that you *don't* want to happen or
2. something that *isn't* happening that you *do* want to happen.

When we encounter stressors, we tend to judge them negatively and react automatically with a grievance, attack thought, or should, as in "that shouldn't have happened" or "something else should have happened."

The next set of exercises will help you identify the stressors in your life (if you don't happen to know what they are!).

Exercise: Stressors

1 In the space below, write down a list of stressors you have experienced in the last year that you didn't want to happen. Let's call them Disappointment Stressors. These can be small stressors, such as the washing machine breaking down, or large ones, such as your father, mother, or pet dying. Make a chart in your journal like the one you see below. After each stressor, write a number from 1 to 10 that indicates how strong your emotional reaction was to that stressor, with 1 being no reaction at all and 10 being a very strong emotional reaction. For example, the washing machine stressor may have triggered an emotional intensity reaction of 3 out of 10, and the death of a parent may have triggered an emotional intensity reaction of 9 out of 10. If you need more space, copy the form below or use a blank sheet of paper.

Disappointment Stressors	Number

APRIL'S RESPONSE

Donald (ex-boyfriend) died	10
Someone tried to interfere in my relationship	7
My mom, stepdad, little sister, and brother moved to Texas	6
Moved out of the only house I had ever lived in	6
Lost relationship with my grandmom	5

2 Now list those stressors that had to do with things you wanted to happen and didn't. Let's call them Expectational Stressors. Again, these can be small stressors, such as you wanted to get a small promotion at work and didn't get it, or large ones, such as you wanted your partner to propose to you and it didn't happen. After each stressor, write down a number from 1 to 10 that indicates how strong your emotional reaction was to that stressor. Let 1 be no reaction at all and 10 a very strong emotional reaction. If you need more space, copy the form below.

Expectational Stressors	Number

APRIL'S RESPONSE

I wanted to go back to school	3
I wanted a job I could advance in	4
I wanted my family to move back here	5

Discovering Your Old Films and Old Tapes

If you are like many people, you will have an automatic emotional reaction in response to the stressor. Usually this is because there are some old films and tapes playing inside your head in the form of unresolved grievances, judgments, complaints, hurts, guilt, fears, and anger; that is, negative emotions that have not been released. These old films and tapes are always from the past—for example, when you were young, you were poor, or one of your parents died suddenly when you were eight. Maybe when you applied to be in the school play, you were turned down, or when you were hoping to be invited by a certain boy or girl to the school prom, they invited someone else.

Exercise: How Stressful Are Your Old Films and Tapes?

In your journal, write about some of the old films or tapes from your past that were triggered by the stressors you wrote about in the previous exercise. Most of the time, these will be events from your childhood or adolescence, but they may also have been from previous relationships postadolescence or from previous jobs. We will call them Old-Tape Stressors. After each Old-Tape Stressor, write down a number from 1 to 10 that indicates how strong your emotional reaction was to that stressor. Let 1 be no reaction at all and 10 a very strong emotional reaction. You can either photocopy the form below or use a blank sheet of paper and add the headings yourself.

Old-Tape Stressors	Number

APRIL'S RESPONSE

When I was thirteen, I walked out and saw my best friend kissing the boy I liked	8
My mom putting me down most of my childhood	8
My mom left when I was five	7
I didn't get the main part in a play at school	3

These two types of stressors usually trigger a moderate to strong emotional intensity reaction. In other words, you usually experience distressing emotions.

If you observe yourself closely, you will also notice that you tend to ask yourself unforgiving questions all the time. We all do: Whose fault is it? Why am I such a failure? Why are they so dumb or stupid? What is wrong with me? What is wrong with them? Why am I always making mistakes? Why am I so inadequate? Why am I not good enough? Who is to blame?[10]

For example, a client of mine, Jim, went out to dinner with his in-laws. He thought his in-laws were making fun of his wife because she had had a stroke and was having difficulty communicating. He blamed them, thinking they were insensitive to his wife's feelings and made some critical, nasty comments to them. His in-laws became very upset, and one of them stormed out of the restaurant. Jim became even angrier and more insulting, which was out of character for him. His in-laws felt humiliated. His wife was very upset with him and commented on his unruly behavior. He then became very self-critical, judging himself harshly and felt terribly guilty.

Jim believed he was stupid for behaving that way and that there must be something very wrong with him. He felt inadequate, and it reminded him of the many times he had felt inadequate and guilty as a child. This lowered Jim's already low level of self-esteem even further. When he came to see me, he was extremely unforgiving toward himself, his in-laws, and his parents and was feeling very guilty, depressed, angry, and anxious. Jim was clearly calling for help and love.

How Are Your Old Tapes Clouding How You See Others?

Old tapes and films from the past (in particular the past hurts, disappointments, anger, guilt, fears, and attack thoughts *that you inflict upon yourself*) not only generate emotional distress within yourself, but if they have not been released or let go, you will automatically project them onto other people. You won't see other people clearly. You will see them through a distorted filter or lens, which will cloud your perception of them. These perceptions will then bounce back at you, as if reflected in a mirror, and most of the time you will see or experience the other people as attacking and judging you. Thus, perception is not a fact. It is a mirror.[11, 12] Because of this process of projection, the judgments, grievances, and attack thoughts that you have been holding, consciously or unconsciously, against yourself and other people from the past now lead to your feelings of being attacked, judged, and criticized by other people. The result is that you will often experience attacking, critical, judgmental, and unforgiving thoughts toward others in the present. This is reflected back at you because you have not forgiven yourself and others from the past.

As you continue to practice the forgiveness exercises in this book, you will increasingly discover the core of love that is the essence of your being. You will discover that you are not guilty or sinful but innocent, loving, peaceful, and joyful by nature. You may have made mistakes or errors in your life, but those errors can now be seen differently through a new lens. In other words, the perceptions can be corrected. You will begin to see that all those so-called mistakes and errors were just calls for love and healing—in disguise.

Exercise: Releasing Yourself from Past Mistakes

Reflect on your past to some of the mistakes you made, choices or decisions you made, or actions you took that with hindsight you might have done differently. In your journal, write down these mistakes and reflect on how you can now see that these mistakes were just errors or just awkward attempts on your part to give or receive love, caring, or understanding.

APRIL'S RESPONSE

I think my biggest mistake is my reaction to a situation I don't like or that I am uncomfortable with. My emotions sometimes get the best of me, and I am unable to take a step back and look at a situation for what it is. I also make the mistake of taking out things on the wrong people because I have a hard time shutting those negative emotions off once I begin to feel them.

You have had the opportunity in this chapter to review many current and past stressors and mistakes. Although just reading about them might discourage some people, in practice I have found that writing about these stressors in your journal, as April and many of my clients have done, seems to be very helpful, clarifying, and releasing. It also further prepares you to begin to make the healing changes that are recommended and described in the following chapters.

CHAPTER 5

Seeing Beyond Judgment and Blame:

The Path of Transformational Forgiveness

*"The basic difference between [false forgiveness and
true forgiveness] is that false forgiveness sees sin as* real,
while true forgiveness sees sin as unreal. *False forgiveness
assumes that sin is real and then attempts to overlook it;
this doesn't work, because it only ends up reinforcing the
'reality' of the sin. True forgiveness recognizes that sin is
unreal, and thus* truly *overlooks it; this works, because
it reawakens us to the truth that God's Son is sinless.
We can exchange false forgiveness for true forgiveness by
allowing the Holy Spirit to teach us how to forgive."*
　　—Greg Mackie, *How Can We Forgive Murderers?*

---

*"Let's say Jennifer was unkind to you. She betrayed a
confidence or lied about you to a coworker, though now
she has apologized. You might not have been forgiving
toward her, though that certainly would have been
the highest expression of your essential self. You might
have understood the need for forgiveness, perhaps, but
it was still too much of a stretch for you emotionally.
The fact that you* might *have forgiven her—that in an
enlightened state you* would *have forgiven her—means*

that the choice for forgiveness will be waiting for you until you're ready. You will now meet Jennifer, or someone just like her, no matter where you go. For forgiving the particular issue she represents in your life is the lesson your soul needs to learn. That issue will be scripted into the curriculum of your life's journey."
—MARIANNE WILLIAMSON, *Everyday Grace*

WHAT FOLLOWS IS A *true account*, summarized from various journalistic accounts of the events that took place of *how one entire community forgave.*

In October 2006, a gunman, not Amish, stormed into an Amish one-room schoolhouse in Pennsylvania, killed five girls and seriously wounded five others, then killed himself. In notes he left behind, he said he was tormented by the fact that twenty years earlier he had molested two very young female relatives. But when these women were contacted, they said there was never any molestation. Clearly the man was deeply disturbed, fearful, tormented, and in need of help he never received.

Amazingly, the members of the Amish community forgave the murderer and even more amazingly reached out with compassion to the widow of the murderer. How did they do this? The answer seems to lie in the religious and cultural beliefs of the Amish.

They truly believe the Christian doctrine of "forgive our trespasses as we forgive those who trespass against us." They donated money to the killer's widow and went to the killer's burial service. In fact, some of the Amish families, who had buried their own daughters the day before, attended the service and even hugged the widow and other members of the killer's family.

Forgiveness has a history of hundreds of years among the Amish, and *they believe that it eliminates feelings of emotional pain, hatred, and revenge.* They are publicly dedicated and committed to unconditional forgiveness.

Toward Transformational Forgiveness

Conventional approaches to forgiveness focus on seeing that another person did something wrong; committed a sin; did something bad or evil; or was a perpetrator, victimizer, injurer, or attacker in some way. The transformational forgiveness approach, on the other hand, emphasizes that there is nothing bad, wrong, evil, harmful, or sinful that happened, even though you may have experienced it that way. For most of you, this may be a difficult idea to grasp at first. Once you do, however, everything will change for the better.

Be patient with yourself and use the Psychological Uplifters described in subsequent chapters. That will help you as you grapple with this powerful idea and attitude. For those of you who have experienced a lot of trauma, it is natural to resist this idea at first. That is okay.

In the *transformational forgiveness approach,* other people are seen as making mistakes or errors that are missing the mark or off target and thus are obvious or disguised calls for help and love. In this approach, everyone is seen as equal and, figuratively, as your brother or sister. No one is seen as better or worse than you. Everyone's essence or true Self is seen equally as a holy, blessed child of the divine. In the transformational forgiveness approach, a correction is needed, not judgment, grievances, punishment, or blame.

The same thing applies to yourself. You can and will make mistakes, errors, and unwise choices and decisions from time to time and no doubt have done so in the past. This too is a call for love and help but from the core of your own Self/Truth/Being. In this case, you can learn how to make a correction to your attitudes, beliefs, choices, and energy to forgive and love yourself more. You can learn how to release self-judgments, grievances, and attack thoughts. In the process, you will return to the voice of love and light within you, this inner teacher who already loves you unconditionally.

Looking beneath the Anger

Every time you interact with another person, that person is consciously or unconsciously pressing your happiness (positive emotions) or unhappiness (negative emotions) buttons. Your "happy buttons" include happiness, peace, joy, or love; your "unhappiness or fearful emotional distress buttons" include anger, guilt, fear, hurt, and resentment. You, of course, are also consciously or unconsciously pressing the other person's happiness or unhappiness buttons, as well as your own. The truth is that *every second of every minute of every hour of every day we are, unconsciously or consciously, pressing our own happiness or unhappiness buttons.*

However, beneath the emotional distress, anger, resentment, guilt, sadness, fear, and anxiety you and the other person experience lie some limiting, judgmental, unforgiving belief, attitude, or thought and some negative energy that is generating the emotional distress. When you forgive yourself and others—by choosing to *release* the limiting, judgmental, unforgiving belief, attitude, or thought and *replace* it with a more compassionate, understanding, and forgiving thought, attitude, or belief—you will begin to see the beauty, worth, innocence, and love inside yourself and inside the other person.

For example, once many years ago, my wife was upset and angry at me for coming home late. At first I became defensive and angry. She became angrier. Then I asked for inner guidance and heard the words inwardly, "Be quiet and listen." I then saw her hurt and disappointment and realized she was calling for love. I forgave her and then saw her beauty, worth, innocence, and love. I also saw it in myself. She cried as I expressed understanding and empathy. I hugged her. We quickly made up. Then we enjoyed the rest of the day together.

Releasing Yourself from Four Key Words That Undermine Forgiveness

No matter how deep our wounds or how strong the feeling of unforgiveness, any one of us can learn how to release the limiting attitudes, beliefs, thoughts, and negative energies that keep us locked in the past. It starts with looking at the words we use. **There are four key words that just about everyone experiencing emotional distress and unforgiving thoughts and feelings uses.** In fact, these are not only words, but also *emotional mind-sets.*

The four key words are:

1. **can't**
2. **should**
3. **shouldn't**
4. **impossible**

Let's just take the word *can't.* How often do you say to yourself or someone else, "I can't change the way I think, feel, or act"? How often do you think, "I can't change this unforgiving, critical, judgmental thought" or "I can't let go of the sadness, hurt, anxiety, guilt, or anger"? When you say this to yourself or to someone else, it is as if you put yourself into a psychological prison and throw away the key. You start feeling helpless, hopeless, powerless, and depressed—and you disempower yourself.

By paying careful attention, you can also learn to release the words *should* and *shouldn't.* When you "should" on yourself, you judge and attack yourself, which generates guilt and depression and lowers your self-esteem. When you "should" on someone else, you judge that person, you attack that person, and you experience anger and relationship, marital, and family problems. When you say to yourself or someone else, "You 'shouldn't' be saying or doing that," the same process occurs. Notice in the next few weeks how often you do this.

The fourth word is *impossible,* as in, "It's impossible for anything to change." Again, observe how often you say or think to yourself it's always been this way and it's impossible for anything to change.

These four key words or emotional mind-sets when said to yourself or others disempower you. Just noticing how often you think or say them begins to *re-empower* you. Then you can begin, one small step at a time, releasing them and letting them go.

Setting an Intention, Having Willingness

In order to shift from the path of negative affect, fear, and emotional distress to the path of love, peace, happiness, and joy, you will want to have a clear-cut <u>intention</u> *and a little* <u>willingness</u>. A clear-cut intention directs you to your goal of love, light, peace, joy, and well-being. It is like a psychological laser beam. An intention aims you in the direction you want to go. A little willingness indicates that you intend to begin the journey toward reaching your goal. A little willingness starts the ball rolling in the direction of your goal and begins the process of helping you shift from the path of fear to the path of love. A little willingness also calls upon the power of the Higher Self within you. The Higher Self, also called Higher Power, Infinite Intelligence, or Higher Intuition, is that part of your mind that is wiser, more intuitive, loving, compassionate, integrated, and whole. In later chapters, we will discuss the use of the Higher Self.

Listening to the Voice of Love, Not Fear

Following on the idea that life is a choice between love and fear, we all have two voices within us: the voice of fear and the voice of love. The inner voice of fear and of the ego-mind tends *at its most extreme* to be critical, judgmental, harsh, negative, belittling, disrespectful, uncompassionate, unsympathetic, divisive, scornful, sarcastic, comparing, blaming, confused, arrogant or self-deprecating, self-centered, and fault-finding. It wants to be "right." The inner Voice of the Self/Truth/Being tends to be caring, compassionate, kind, harmonious, wise, intuitive, positive, peaceful, joyful, light, joining, giving, visionary, purposeful, grateful, and appreciative. It wants to be "happy." Your inner Teacher on the path of fear will encourage you to listen to the Voice of the ego-mind. Your inner Teacher on the path of light and love will encourage you to listen to the Voice of the core of your Self/Truth/Being.

Your inner Teacher on the path of light and love knows that your highest goal is not only to experience happiness and well-being but also to ultimately awaken to and realize your true or core Self, the truth of your Being.

There is a natural resistance on the part of our ego-mind to learning forgiveness. In fact, it would be accurate to say that our ego-minds do not want us to learn how to forgive. This is because if we learn how to forgive, we will be undermining the entire mind-set and way of being of the ego-mind. Forgiveness then becomes a learned process, a process that requires a strong intention, a little willingness, and help from our Higher Self. The Higher Self is that part of our mind that can objectively observe our thought pro-cesses, attitudes, beliefs, emotions, choices, and behavior patterns and can help us make a switch or shift from the path of fear and the ego-mind to the path of love and the core of our Self/Truth/Being. The Higher Self, which is aligned with unconditional love and light, can also help us learn to forgive and to align ourselves with our highest good and highest purpose and vision in life. The Higher Self is a wise and compassionate place within us that is al-ready connected with our Self/Truth/Being. You and I can access our Higher Self by calling upon it at regular intervals. Later in the book, you will learn more about how to do this.

Thorny and Nurturing Teachers

Just as there are two Voices within us, we will also encounter nur-turing teachers and thorny teachers. But unlike the voice of fear, these thorny teachers have something very important to teach us.

Perhaps it goes without saying that nurturing teachers are the people we all like to encounter and experience. These are the people who care about us, nurture us, support us, guide us, are compas-sionate and empathetic with us, and love us. We like to be around nurturing teachers, and most of us try to attract them into our lives. On the other hand, there are those thorny teachers who press our "emotional buttons," especially the fearful, hurtful, angry, sad, disappointing, resentful, shameful, inadequate, and guilty ones. By pressing our emotional buttons, they reach the places within us that are unhealed and need healing.

These "thorny teachers" are like personal and spiritual growth exercise machines. They can show up as parents, siblings, friends, colleagues, bosses, employees, acquaintances, volunteers, supervisors, neighbors, clergymen, and politicians. By pressing our emotional buttons, they trigger our fearful ego-mind and can catapult us onto the path of emotional distress for some period of time.

It is, however, no accident that they are in your life. Seen from the perspective of the Higher Self, these perceived "thorny teachers" provide the maximum opportunity for personal and spiritual growth. They give you the opportunity to forgive them (your mirror) and yourself so that you can heal your unhealed emotional wounds and return to the path of light, love, and happiness. Then you will be able to see the light, love, and magnificence in these people and also in yourself. From this perspective, the "thorny teachers" are teachers of love in disguise. Although they may not be the only emotional triggers to unforgiveness, they are the major ones you are likely to encounter in your life. In addition, you will learn that even the "thorny angels" are your saviors.

Later in the book, I will teach you some "energetic" forgiveness techniques for rebalancing your own energy fields from the disruptions these thorny teachers can cause. For now, I just want you to open up to the idea that the most disruptive experiences or people are often also the most instructive.

CHAPTER 6

Discovering What You Don't Want and What You Do:
The Process of Setting Goals

"The moment that one sincerely and freely forgives another, something wonderful and good happens to both the forgiver and the forgiven. The capacity for both to love one another is increased and strengthened."
—ARLY PRIOR

"I can have peace of mind only when I forgive rather than judge."
—GERALD JAMPOLSKY, *Love Is Letting Go of Fear*

By the time I was in my twenties, I had become an expert at attacking or belittling others.... My ego was like an automatic pilot... God help anyone who happened to be in the line of fire! I would go instantly into my attack-and-defend mode.

In 1973, my first wife, Pat, and I divorced after a twenty-year marriage, and I found myself in emotional quicksand. I thrashed around in a mire of pain, shame, anger, blame and frustration, exhausting me. . . . I became an alcoholic and had a preoccupation with suicide. During those painful years, I believed that my relationship with Pat could never be healed. . . .

I had been an atheist for many years. The idea that I might one day be on a spiritual path seemed as unlikely as Pat and I ever being friends again. Then, in 1975, I became a student of the teaching of A Course in Miracles. *I noticed my belief system changing. Where once I had struggled to affix blame, guilt, and shame, all of that faded away. Soon I noticed that I was seeing myself and Pat very differently and was taking responsibility for all my thoughts and actions.*

Every day I concentrated on seeing Pat in this new light. Rather than looking for who was to blame, I asked for God's help in forgiving myself and my now ex-wife. I woke up each day with a single purpose—to have peace of mind, peace of God, as my only goal. Miraculously and unexpectedly, I soon noticed that the tension about Pat and our relationship was fading.

Pat remarried about a year later and moved to Seattle. Time passed, and one day, I was booked to give a lecture at the Opera House in that city. Pat, her father, and her new husband came to hear my talk.

We met for breakfast the next morning, and Pat said she loved everything I had said. How very different our lives had become since our marriage!

Upon my return to San Francisco, I told everyone, "You know, this forgiveness stuff really works!" About six months later, I learned that Pat and her new husband were moving to Tiburon, where I lived.

*My first response...was, "Oh, no!" It had been easy to
be forgiving of Pat and myself when she was living several
hundred miles away. But I wondered what would happen if
we were bumping into each other from time to time at the
grocery store.*

*During the years that followed, I realized how important
it is to make forgiveness a continuous daily practice. I am
happy to say that today, Pat and I are dear friends. The
animosity of years past is gone. When Pat remarried, she asked
that I take photos of her wedding and my wife, Diane, do the
videotaping. We did so with much pleasure. That day I was
once again grateful for the miraculous impact of forgiveness
that had touched all of our lives.*

—from GERALD JAMPOLSKY, *Love Is Letting Go of Fear*

The Magic Wand and Miracle Goals

On any journey, and especially the forgiveness journey, the setting
of positive and constructive goals is very important. Goals allow
you to set a clear-cut course, a direction in which you are headed.
They give you something to aim for and they let you know when
you have arrived. Goals are what you strive for when you know
what you want.

Sometimes, however, you may find that you don't know clearly
what you want. You are miserable, unhappy, and focused at first
more on what you don't want than what you do want. I developed
the following exercise to help you get clearer about what you *do*
want.

First, list specifically the five to ten major negative feelings, attitudes,
beliefs, judgments, grievances, attack thoughts, and hurts you have
toward yourself, someone else, or some set of circumstances. *This
indicates what you don't want to achieve or experience in your life.*
Write these down in your journal or notebook.

Exercise: What You Don't Want

1. *To be unhappy*
2. *To feel sad all the time*
3. *To be alone*
4. *To be pessimistic about the future*
5. *To be so self-conscious*

Exercise: What You Do Want

Now list and then focus on the opposite; that is, what you *do* want to achieve and experience in the next three, six, and twelve months. Write these positive goals, such as peace, love, joy, harmony in relationships, in your notebook or journal. Take into account the feedback you received from filling out the self-assessment scales in the previous chapters.

One version of this exercise that frequently helps the clients I work with I call the "Miracle Goal" question. It works like this: Imagine you have a Magic Wand. (I usually ask my clients to pick up a pencil and imagine it turned into a Magic Wand.) Then imagine that you waved the magic wand right before you fell asleep at night and woke up the following morning three months later and found that a miracle had happened. How differently would you think, feel, act, and behave? How differently would you perceive things? How differently would other people see you? Then imagine that you fell asleep again and woke up six months later. Imagine that a bigger miracle had happened. How differently would you think, feel, act, and behave? How differently would you perceive things? How differently would other people see you? Then finally imagine you waved the magic wand and woke up one year later and a very big miracle happened. How differently would you think, feel, act, and behave? How differently would you perceive things? How differently would other people see you? In your journal, write down your "Miracle Goals."

APRIL'S RESPONSE
   1. To be happy
   2. To have peace
   3. To enjoy every moment of life
   4. To feel fulfillment in everyday activities
   5. To be optimistic
   6. To feel good about myself

Now try the following Psychological Uplifter Technique. If you do it correctly and often, this technique can, on its own, help you feel emotionally uplifted. It will also reduce your barriers and blocks to forgiving and, because it helps create such a positive mind-set, help you accept yourself as you are.

Exercise: Psychological Uplifter 1

I developed the following technique as an expansion upon the "setup" used by Gary Craig in his groundbreaking Emotional Freedom Techniques (EFT).[1] It also stems from my own Miracle Acupressure Tapping Technique (MATT).[2] Done alone, consistently, and regularly, it can, in itself, be considered a powerful tool of transformation.

1 Find a quiet place where you won't be disturbed, such as a bedroom, office, bathroom, or car. Go there.

2 Now, choose three to four words that apply to your situation (for example, fear, anxiety, sadness, frustration, guilt, shame, marital problems, etc.) and circle them.

3 Put one hand on your heart while repeating out loud the following Psychological Uplifter. Within reasonable limits, the louder you say it, the better. If you absolutely aren't able to say it out loud because of the limitations of your surroundings, say it to yourself with high intention.

4   Now say, *"Even though I have this problem or negative emotion (name the emotion; e.g., fear, anxiety, hurt, anger, depression,
sadness, frustration, guilt, shame, low self-esteem, or marital, family,
relationship, or work problems, etc.), I accept myself deeply and profoundly, and I am a good and magnificent person."* Repeat this three
times.

Then say, *"I love and forgive myself unconditionally despite my
problems, limitations, and challenges"* (repeat three times). Then say,
"I am entitled to miracles" (repeat three times). If at all possible, say
this louder and with more conviction each time.

Try to do this exercise ten to twenty times per day *or* as often as you
can, until you feel relief. Be kind to yourself. If you miss a day or two
or if, on some days, you do the Psychological Uplifter less often, don't
judge yourself.

Copy down Psychological Uplifter 1 on a separate sheet of paper
or a 3 × 5 card so that it will be easier for you to remember.

CHAPTER 7

Knowing When to Let Go

"Forgiveness reduces stress, blood pressure, muscle tension, and depression. Forgiveness is sometimes the missing ingredient in a complete healing.... We forgive for ourselves, to transcend judgment, increase our life energy, and experience love and joy.... Forgiveness allows us to find peace and create an environment where love can flourish."
—PHILLIP AND JANE MOUNTROSE, *The Heart & Soul of EFT and Beyond*

"Today, Creator, grant me the courage and the will to forgive the people I love the most. Help me to forgive every injustice I feel in my mind, and to love other people unconditionally. I know the only way to heal all the pain in my heart is through forgiveness."
—SHARI ROSENTHAL AND SUSYN REEVE, *With Forgiveness*

CHARLENE WAS A THIRTY-EIGHT-YEAR-OLD married woman with two children when she came in to see me for therapy. She was clearly struggling with depression, anger, hurt, and some suicidal thoughts. Charlene was the second person to complete *The Forgiveness Solution* and do all the exercises. Here is her forgiveness story.

> *I came in for therapy because I had been depressed for about two and a half months. I wished that I wasn't here anymore. It took all I could do to get up to go to work. When I came home, I lay down on the bed and just wanted to go to sleep. I didn't care about eating or doing anything. I wanted to sleep and not wake up until everything was better. I hadn't been able to let go of past experiences. I thought my sister, Mary, did things that hurt and that angered me. I had been holding on to a lot of that resentment and anger. This deep hurt and anger was compounded by my dad's declining health and his transfer to a nursing home from his own house near me. My sister, who lived in Texas, seemed all of a sudden to want to be a part of my life and my father's life. She wanted to know the details of everything, after what I perceived as being hurtful to me. I resented this.*
>
> *I had strong negative feelings and low self-esteem. I felt frustrated with the situation. My husband and I talked about it and felt therapy would be beneficial in helping to pull me out of my depression. I wanted to feel better about myself and to deal better with my sister.*
>
> *During weekly therapy sessions, I learned forgiveness tools and letter-writing exercises that gave me insight into my problems. These powerful exercises helped me to release the anger, hurt, and bitterness that I had been holding on to for so long.*
>
> *In frequent e-mails to my sister, I have been able to share with her the details of my father's life as his health declines. I hope and look forward to the day that my sister and I will be a part of each other's lives again.*

The therapy sessions have helped me to feel worthwhile. I have been able to accept myself and to choose a better path to happiness.

Reading The Forgiveness Solution *workbook helped me to learn about different areas and ways to achieve forgiveness, and the different experiences made me feel that I wasn't alone. Doing the exercises in the workbook, in particular, helped me to relax and to become a lot calmer and much more forgiving. Some of the forgiveness tools that I feel really helped me are the Psychological Uplifters, which I typed up on the computer. I laminated them as well and put them up around the house. I also carried one in my wallet. This way I was always reading it. If I was feeling a little down I could always take one out of my wallet and read it. The tapping, using the Positive Pressure Point Techniques and the light imagery exercises, which allowed the light to come into me, were very helpful.*

The forgiveness tools had a significant part in helping me to become a more relaxed, calm, forgiving person with a much better outlook on my day-to-day life. Now I look forward to the future. I am a lot more peaceful and happier.

In this chapter, I will recount some classic teaching stories and introduce some powerful affirmations that will help you shift your perspective, perception, and attitude. Some people find that these stories and affirmations in themselves catalyze substantial positive change within them. All these stories demonstrate that it is not the circumstances of our lives that determine our well-being but the attitude we have toward those circumstances, the choices we make, and our willingness to let go and forgive.

I suggest you read and perhaps reread them a few times and just contemplate their meaning as it applies to your life.

I will also introduce some affirmations that go along with the themes in these stories particularly well.

Exercise: Teaching Stories

THE ALLIGATOR AND HOLDING ON

Once there was an alligator and some hunters who wanted to capture the alligator for the alligator's skin. The hunters knew that the alligator loved meat, so they set up a trap for the alligator with meat in it. The hunters would place the trap on the beach and hide in the woods nearby. The alligator would smell the meat and come out of the water onto the beach. He would then reach into the trap and grasp the meat. The trap would shut down around the alligator giving the huntsmen time to come out of the woods safely and approach the alligator. The alligator could escape easily by opening his mouth, which was grasping the meat. This would release the trap. But the alligator always held on tightly to the meat, giving the huntsmen time to get close to the alligator and shoot him. If the alligator had only let go, he would have escaped. We humans are often like alligators. We hold on to our anger, resentments, bitterness, grievances, and attack thoughts and then we get killed. By letting go, we would be free.

THE TWO MONKS AND LETTING GO

Once there were two monks who had been friends for twenty years and were traveling for a long time through the desert. After many hours of traveling one day, they approached a wide river. One monk noticed that the bridge across the river was broken just as the other monk noticed that a beautiful woman was standing next to the bridge looking quite distressed. The second monk asked the woman if he could help. She said yes, that she had been traveling a long distance in the desert but couldn't swim. She said the bridge was broken, and she needed to get to the other side so she could continue her journey. The second monk generously offered to carry her across the river on his back. Both monks then waded across the river. The second monk let the woman down, and the two monks continued on their journey. The first monk, however, was furious with the second monk and got madder and madder for three hours. Finally, he couldn't contain himself any longer and said angrily to his dear friend, "How could you do that? How could you break the vows of celibacy we took twenty years ago and the vows to never have any physical contact with a woman? How could you betray our fellow monks and our sacred lineage?" The second monk looked at the first monk and said, "I agree, I carried the woman on my back for five minutes but then I put her down, while you have been carrying her on your back for three hours." In the same way, when we hold on to our anger, we carry a grudge like the first monk, and we are unwilling to let it go and release it. We could choose instead to put it down within five minutes and let it go like the second monk. Then we would be at peace.

THE RAT AND CHEESE STORY: DISCOVERING ALTERNATIVES[1]

I first heard this story many years ago in the "est training." Many others have used various versions of it over the years.

Once there was a rat, some cheese, a maze with five alleys, and an experimenter. Imagine that the experimenter put a rat at the bottom of the maze in front of the five alleys. Imagine that the experimenter then put cheese at the end of alleyway number four. The game consisted of a number of trials in which the rat had to find the cheese. On each trial the rat will explore the alleys, looking for the cheese. He will typically first run down alleyway number one. No cheese. He will run down alley number one a number of times and still find there is no cheese there. So he will run down alley number two. No cheese. He will try alleyway number two several times. No cheese. He will try alleyway number three many times. No cheese. He may jump over to alleyway number five and explore that alleyway a number of times. No cheese. If the experimenter puts the cheese down alleyway four each time he does the experiment, eventually the rat will discover that the cheese is down alleyway number four and go there to get the cheese. In other words, the rat will stop looking for the cheese in the other four alleyways.

If the experimenter then decides to change alleyways and puts the cheese down the second alleyway, the rat will initially go down the fourth alleyway, notice there's no cheese there, and then go back down. The rat may do this two or three more times, but it will eventually figure out that the cheese is no longer there and start exploring the other alleyways again until it finds the cheese.

The major difference between rats and humans is that rats will stop going down alleyways that have no cheese. Humans, on the other hand, will go down the fourth alleyway forever, even if there is no cheese there. Humans will carpet alleyway number four, they will paint alleyway number four, and they will do cartwheels in alleyway number four. They may even buy comfortable chairs to put in alleyway number four because alleyway number four feels familiar to them. In fact, sometimes they will spend weeks, months, even many years going down empty alleyways with no cheese in them.

Even when they are in emotional pain, humans will often continue to hold on to their grievances, judgments, guilt feelings, sadness, anger, attack thoughts, fear, and unforgiveness and continue to go down alleyway number four, even though there is no cheese there. Rats, however, know that if they are not getting any cheese in an alleyway to explore different alleyways until they finally find the cheese. They know they need to explore other alternatives and options in order for there to be cheese in their life. The cheese, in the case of humans, is peace, happiness, joy, love, and harmony in relationships.

PINK AND WHITE DOORS: CHOICE AND EMPOWERMENT

A client once came in to see a therapist and related his problems to the therapist. The therapist listened patiently for a long time. At the end of the session, the therapist said to the client that he could leave the office through either of the two white doors. The client insisted, however, that he wanted to leave the office through a pink door. The therapist gently pointed out to the client that there was a pink wall but no pink doors. The client didn't want to hear what the therapist said and insisted on leaving through a pink door. The therapist was very understanding but gently reminded the client that there were only white doors and one pink wall. The client was determined, however, and went over to the pink wall and banged his head against it. No matter how much the client tried to get out of the office through the pink wall, it wouldn't budge, and the client became increasingly frustrated and in pain.

Finally, the therapist pointed out to the client that his problems were like the white doors and the pink wall. The client could let go of the hope for a different and better past, forgive, and move on (exit through the white doors), or the client could hold on to the past, hold on to resentments, hurts, and grudges, and knock his head against the pink wall. This, of course, would only perpetuate the client's emotional pain. The choice was up to the client. One choice empowered the client and one choice disempowered the client. Most clients then decide to leave the office through a white door.

In your journal, write down your thoughts, feelings, reactions, images, sensations to these teaching stories. In particular, write down any insights, shifts in points of view, and perspectives that you may have had from reading and contemplating these stories. You may want to reread them over the next few weeks or months.

APRIL'S RESPONSE

I enjoyed each of these stories, but I like the rat and cheese story the best. I think the story is saying that even though we continue to go down the same path or "alleyway" knowing that it will hurt or upset us, we do so because we become comfortable with that choice, and we don't know how to go about choosing the better "alleyway" for us in order to experience something better.

The next simple exercise is a kind of metaphor for life. In life, wisdom occurs when you know what to hold on to and when, and what to let go of, when, and how.

Exercise: A Fist and Releasing

Make a fist with one hand. Imagine that all your anger, hurt, resentment, guilt, disappointment, bitterness, blame, grievances, and attack thoughts are in that hand. Make the fist tighter and tighter. If you keep holding the fist very tight, after a while it will become numb. Then, at some time in the future, if you should choose to open it slowly you will notice you start to feel pain at first. Keep holding the fist very tight, imagining that all your distress is in that fist. Keep holding the fist very tight until you are ready to release the anger, hurt, resentment, guilt, disappointment, bitterness, blame, grievances, and attack thoughts. Walk around with that fist very tight. Try driving with the fist very tight.

When you are finally ready to open the fist and release all those feelings, do it slowly. Notice the sensations you have. Notice the difference between holding on and letting go. Do this little exercise once a day for seven days. Then write down your responses in your journal.

APRIL'S RESPONSE

Holding on continues to cause pain, discomfort, and upsetting feelings, but once they are let go, there is a strong sense of peace and calmness that happens very quickly.

Thirty Useful Affirmations

Once again, here are the instructions for using affirmations. If you read these instructions earlier, you can skip down to Affirmation 1.

Affirmations are powerful beliefs with powerful energy connected to them. I would like to encourage you to contemplate, learn, and practice the affirmations in this book in a consistent way. I recommend writing each affirmation on a 3 x 5 card. Read one card a day three to four times starting in the morning and ending in the evening. Repeat the affirmation for the day throughout the day, especially when you experience any emotional distress, such as sadness, anxiety, hurt, guilt, or anger.

You may want to make several copies of each affirmation and tape them to your bathroom mirror, refrigerator, or the dashboard of your car. Memorizing the affirmations is not necessary but would certainly be beneficial. You do not have to believe in the affirmations at first. Repeating the affirmations, especially with some conviction and contemplating their meaning, will help you shift from the fearful, lower vibrational energy to the positive, higher vibrational energy path. The affirmations are like lessons. It takes time to master and apply an affirmation or lesson. *Be kind and patient with yourself.* Learning the affirmations and applying them successfully to your life is like learning a new skill. No one masters a skill the first time they learn it. It takes practice, persistence, and patience. Once learned, however, your life will be transformed.

AFFIRMATION 1

"Inherent in every difficulty or challenge is the seed of an equal or greater benefit. I will look for that seed and nurture it."

AFFIRMATION 2

"Inherent in every grievance, judgment, and attack thought is the seed of the opportunity for practicing forgiveness. I will look for that seed and nurture it."

AFFIRMATION 3

"I can elect to change all thoughts, beliefs, attitudes, and negative energies that hurt."

AFFIRMATION 4

"I can elect to change all thoughts, beliefs, attitudes, and negative energies that cause emotional distress."

AFFIRMATION 5

"I can escape from the emotional distress I experience by giving up grievances and attack thoughts."

AFFIRMATION 6

"I am determined to see and experience things differently."

AFFIRMATION 7

"I can learn to see that attack and anger cover up fear, and fear is a call for help and for love."

AFFIRMATION 8

"I can choose forgiveness, peace, and contentment instead of this: anger, guilt, fear, sadness, resentment, bitterness, hurt, anxiety, embarrassment, etc."

AFFIRMATION 9

"I can choose to see things from the other person's perspective."

AFFIRMATION 10

"I can choose to forgive rather than judge others and myself."

AFFIRMATION 11

"Forgiveness is my key to happiness and peace."

AFFIRMATION 12

"Forgiveness is my key to freedom and release."

AFFIRMATION 13

"Whatever I give (forgiveness or judgments), I give to myself."

AFFIRMATION 14

"When I am healed (of this guilt, depression, anger, anxiety, and relationship problems), I am not healed alone."

AFFIRMATION 15

"Without judgment, I am willing to allow everything to be as it is."

AFFIRMATION 16

"Without judgment, I am willing to see that everything that happens to me is happening for my personal, relationship, and spiritual or overall growth."

AFFIRMATION 17

"Under all circumstances, I can choose love over fear and peace over conflict."

AFFIRMATION 18

"Under all circumstances, I can learn to let go of grievances and heal."

AFFIRMATION 19

"Under all circumstances, I can transform the quality of my life by forgiving and giving up attack thoughts."

AFFIRMATION 20

"Under all circumstances, I can choose to appreciate rather than judge."

AFFIRMATION 21

"I am the light. I am surrounded by light. I am protected by light. I forgive in the light."

AFFIRMATION 22

"The light has come. I forgive and bless and honor all things (including myself) in the light."

AFFIRMATION 23

"When I forgive, I am blessed and honored. When I am blessed and honored, I bless and honor others."

AFFIRMATION 24

"When I forgive, I am aligned with the light. When I am aligned with the light, I am blessed."

AFFIRMATION 25

"When I forgive, I see my innocence. When I see my innocence, I see the light."

AFFIRMATION 26

"More miracles come from forgiveness and gratitude than anything else."

AFFIRMATION 27

"Miracles come in the light. Blessings come in the light. Forgiveness comes in the light. Love comes in the light."

AFFIRMATION 28

"Forgiveness is my function in the light. Blessings are my function in the light. Love is my function in the light."

AFFIRMATION 29

"My forgiveness brings me happiness, peace, joy, blessings, and love."

AFFIRMATION 30

"I am grateful for the opportunity to forgive, love, and be happy in the light."

APRIL'S COMMENTS ON USING THE AFFIRMATIONS

From my personal experience, the affirmations were more effective when I wrote them each down on an index card and read over them a few times a day. With each affirmation, I was able to see the way I viewed situations and events in my life in a negative way, and by applying each one to my life, it allowed me to shift my thought process to a more positive one. Things happen every day to which one of these affirmations will apply.

Experiment with these affirmations in all circumstances that you find challenging and where you might otherwise have the tendency to hold on to grudges and grievances.

CHAPTER 8

Making New Choices through Relaxation, Imagery, and Forgiveness Afformations

*"Forgiveness sings the glory of the heart.... The ability
to extend complete forgiveness does not come quickly or
easily. It is a great virtue that must be cultivated for a
long time.... Forgiveness is a great blessing, not just to
give but to receive"*
—SWAMI CHIDVILASANANDA, *Enthusiasm*

*"Forgiveness is a doorway to freedom and this freedom
serves to move you into higher consciousness.... The
moment the mind chooses to forgive, in that place where
resentment is felt, the heart forgives.... Of course,
forgiving yourself is a must, and asking for forgiveness
brings humility.... Keep forgiving. Train your mind to
shift.... This means that if you choose now to plant a
seed of positivity, it will begin to grow, and when your
Higher Self sees what you are doing, it will support you.*
—SAI MAA LAKSHMI DEVI, *Petals of Grace*

Hiraldo was very distressed when he came to see me for therapy. He was still hoping his wife would reconcile with him. She had other plans, as you will see. He was confused, bewildered, guilty, angry, depressed, and hurt. One of the many interventions I used with him focused on helping him let go of the hope for a different and better past. It is constructive and beneficial to be hopeful about the future. But hoping you can change the past is self-defeating. It leads to self-judgment and helpless feelings. And yet many of us do it. Accepting the past allows you to move on. Using the techniques I present in this chapter (as well as others from the rest of the book), Hiraldo was able to do that, and his life changed for the better.

As a Hispanic and a Catholic, divorce is not a word that is used very often. I went to college, got a job, got married, and worked hard to provide the American dream for my family. Until one day, after sixteen years of marriage and four kids, my then wife asked me for a divorce—she told me that it was not me, I was a great father, a great provider, and finally I was a great husband, just not for her—she did not love me anymore.

The first six months of the divorce, I struggled with thoughts of being alone, thinking of what is it exactly I did to be in this position. Could I have done something different with my job, could I have provided something better for my family? I could not sleep or eat. This is something that I was not expecting—my parents had been married for fifty-three years. They had ups and downs, but they always found a way to work things out. Her parents have been married for over forty years—so how could this happen to me?

My professional career taught me to deal with the toughest unions in America. This, I could not deal with. I even thought, "What if I was not here anymore?"

*I became very withdrawn, depressed. My biggest frustration
was from trying to figure out what I did. I was faithful, I
provided a great environment for my wife and kids, could not
wait until they went to college. My wife kept assuring me that
there was nothing that I did—it was all her. She wanted to be
independent.*

*Finally, I listened to my family and sought help from a
therapist—reluctantly I made an appointment. I struggled at
the beginning, explaining to a stranger what had happened
and how I was feeling. My first thought was to ask him for a
pill, the magic wand that is going to make all this go away.
Obviously, this did not happen; what my therapist offered was
a structured method, which helped me to understand what
I was feeling and helped me to forgive myself. Within the
first two meetings, with his guidance, I set goals for myself:
three months, six months, and one-year goals. In addition,
he explained and offered a variety of forgiveness-related
literature, real-life examples, affirmations, the Psychological
Uplifter, exercises, and a series of forgiveness-oriented analogies
that helped me to understand my role and the different choices
I needed to make. One of the most important choices was
to decide to forgive and love myself, to look at myself in the
mirror and know that I did and continue to do the right
things for my kids.*

*The bottom line is this: The methods, processes, examples,
exercises, affirmations, whatever you want to call them, helped
me to get my life back. This may not seem to be such a big
deal for a lot of folks, but for someone that was used to solving
every problem under the sun, I was very happy to have my life
back and start feeling really good about myself again.*

*P.S. The relationship with my kids has been enhanced; my
career change has been one of the best decisions I have made.
They [the kids] spend 80 percent of the time with me; my
oldest has finished her freshman year in college, and my other*

kids are also looking forward to attending. Finally, my oldest daughter has told me how much of a role model I have been to her . . . at the end of the day this is what really matters.

One of the key tools I taught Hiraldo was relaxation. Relaxation exercises of one kind or another have been around for a long time. Edmund Jacobson, in his book *Progressive Relaxation,* developed one of the first of these widely used exercises.[1] Joe Wolpe and Arnold Lazarus used relaxation exercises extensively in their early book *Behavior Therapy Techniques,* a part of their systematic desensitization procedure.[2] Relaxation helps to quiet the mind and relax the muscles. For many people, learning to relax makes it easier to practice forgiveness. I created the following relaxation procedure for my first book, *Creating Well-Being: The Healing Path to Love, Peace, Self-Esteem, and Happiness,* which was published back in 1989.[3] It can be used in conjunction with many of the other exercises in this book, as it will help you to be more receptive to both visualization and affirmation exercises. In addition to relaxation, the exercises take you on an inner journey to a safe place that we call an *inner sanctuary.*

Exercise: Relaxation and the Inner Sanctuary

This is a guided-imagery exercise, so you might want to record it first or have someone else read it out loud to you. You might, however, prefer to purchase the CD at *www.integrativehelp.com* or *www.forgivenesssolution.com.*

Close your eyes. Relax. Get in a comfortable, open body position, with your arms and legs uncrossed, so the energy can flow more easily and smoothly. Pay attention to your breath. Be aware of your breath as you breathe in and out slowly and deeply, slowly and deeply. Breathing in and out slowly and deeply, slowly and deeply. Focus on your breath. Breathing slowly and deeply. Now allow yourself to repeat the word "calm" on the in-breath and "relax" on the out-breath. "Calm" on the in-breath and "relax" on the out-breath. Breathing in "calm" and breathing out "relaxed." Breathing in "calm" and out "relaxed." Now continue to breathe slowly and deeply on the in-breath and out-breath, but this time hold your breath for a count of three between the in-breath and the out-breath. So, you are breathing in "calm," holding your breath for a count of three, and breathing out "relaxed."

In just a few moments, you're going to take an elevator ride down from the tenth floor to the first floor. As you go down the elevator from the tenth floor to the first floor, you're going to become even more calm and relaxed...deeper and deeper...calmer and calmer... more and more deeply relaxed. Now picture yourself on the tenth floor of an elevator. Slowly the elevator descends from the tenth floor to the first floor. From ten to nine, nine to eight, eight to seven, the elevator slowly descends, and, as it does, you become so calm, so deeply relaxed, deeper and deeper...calmer and calmer.... The elevator continues to descend further, from seven to six, six to five, five to four, and, as it does, you continue to descend further and further inside yourself to the core, the center of your Being, the place of deep calm, peace, joy, strength, light, love, and well-being.

Relaxing even further...calmer and calmer...more and more deeply relaxed...deeply at peace...deeply in touch with your sense of well-being, descend from four to three, three to two, two to one; the elevator continues to descend further, and, as it does, you go deeper and deeper inside yourself, closer and closer to the core of your Being...more and more deeply relaxed...calmer and more deeply relaxed...so calm...so peaceful...so deeply relaxed. Such a deep sense of well-being.

In just a few moments, you'll find yourself in a safe, peaceful, beautiful, nurturing, and loving environment of your own choosing. It is so safe, so peaceful, so beautiful, and so loving. You experience such a deep sense of well-being. So now the door of the elevator opens and you find yourself walking out into a safe, peaceful, beautiful, nurturing, and loving environment of your own choosing, your own "inner sanctuary." Look around, walk around this safe, peaceful, beautiful, nurturing, and loving inner environment of your own choosing, your "inner sanctuary." Feel the safety, the peace, the beauty, the love of the "inner sanctuary." Sense it. Smell it. Touch it. Feel it. So safe, so peaceful, so beautiful, so nurturing, and so loving. Your own "inner sanctuary."

In just a few moments, you will leave the "inner sanctuary" and return to the elevator. Take a few slow, deep breaths and walk over to the first-floor elevator. Enter the elevator. When the elevator returns to the tenth floor, your eyes will be open, and you will feel deeply relaxed and refreshed, with your consciousness back in the room. Now the elevator begins to rise from the first to the second to the third floor. Gradually, you begin to move your body around a little bit. The elevator continues to rise to the fourth, fifth, and sixth floors, and you begin to awake more and more. The elevator rises to the seventh, eight, and ninth floors. Gradually, you begin to open your eyes. Finally, the elevator rises to the tenth floor, and you are fully awake with your consciousness back in the room.

It will help make the relaxation and "inner sanctuary" experience a vibrant and powerful part of you if you take a few moments each time you do this exercise to write down what you experienced. You can write down your experiences in your journal.

APRIL'S RESPONSE

This experience really helped me feel calm and relaxed. I could really imagine the elevator going down each floor and helping me relax. I felt much better after this exercise.

The next simple exercise expands on the basic relaxation exercise. You can do it immediately after doing the relaxation exercise or separately if you want.

Exercise: Imagery of Seeds and Weeds

This simple exercise helps to plant forgiveness seeds in your subconscious mind that begin to grow over time, even while you are unaware of it. You can do it while practicing the relaxation exercise when you are in the "inner sanctuary" or on its own if you feel even a little relaxed. This is another guided-imagery exercise, so you might want to record it first or have someone else read it out loud to you. Before you start, close your eyes and take three slow, deep breaths. Do each step slowly.

- Picture a tiny forgiveness seed being planted in rich, fertile soil.
- Notice some nurturing fertilizer being placed around the tiny forgiveness seed.
- Notice some water being sprinkled around the forgiveness seed in order to further nurture this tiny little life.
- Visualize the warmth and light of the sun shining down upon the seed and the soil surrounding it, warming and nurturing the little forgiveness seed.
- Picture the right amount of rain falling upon the soil, giving the earth the right amount of moisture to further the forgiveness seed's growth.
- See a gardener plucking out any weeds surrounding the forgiveness seed as it slowly begins to grow.
- Imagine the weeds being released from the soil, freeing the forgiveness seed to grow fuller and stronger.
- Picture the sun, rain, and soil nurturing the forgiveness seed day after day as it sprouts, grows, and blossoms.
- Visualize the forgiveness seed growing into a magnificent and beautiful plant or flower.
- Picture the magnificent and beautiful plant or flower radiating healing energy to everyone and everything that encounters it.
- Take three slow, deep breaths and then open your eyes.
  Now write down your experiences in your journal.

APRIL'S RESPONSE

This experience showed me that even the smallest amount of willingness to forgive can grow into something much stronger and more powerful than I thought possible.

Exercise: Opening the Way for Change

This exercise has many steps, but I have found it to be one of the favorites of my clients, especially if used over time. This simple but powerful technique allows you to open the way for change. It can be used after practicing the relaxation technique above or it can be done on its own. Again, you may want to record the exercise first or have someone else read it to you.

Put one hand on your heart. Take three slow, deep breaths. Repeat the words "calm" on the in-breath and "relax" on the out-breath slowly to yourself three times.

Repeat the following phrases *out loud*, preferably with your eyes closed.

- The past is over (repeat four times).
- I release the past (four times).
- The future is not here yet (four times).
- Now is the only time there is (four times).
- Now is the most important moment of my life (four times).
- Right now, I release all judgments and grievances against myself (four times).
- Right now, I release all judgments and grievances against other people (repeat four times while thinking of specific people).
- Right now, I release all judgments and grievances against God or the Universe (four times).
- Right now, I choose to forgive everyone in my life, including myself (four times).
- Right now is the key to the future (four times).
- Right now, I am the predominant creative force in my life (four times).
- Right now, I choose to be happy (four times).
- Right now, I choose to be at peace (four times).
- Right now, I choose to be joyful (four times).
- Right now, I choose to be healthy (four times).
- Right now, I choose to be free (four times).

- Right now, I choose to be true to my Self (four times).
- Right now, I choose to be true to my deepest Self (four times).
- Right now, I choose to be loving (four times).
- Right now, I choose to create (fill in the blank). Imagine yourself, right now, having successfully created something you want in your life because of having forgiven yourself or someone else. Picture yourself experiencing this right now, with all the positive feelings and sensations along with it.
- Right now, I choose to allow (fill in the blank) into my life. Picture yourself having allowed something you want to happen in your life because of having forgiven yourself or someone else. Imagine, in other words, that you are a magnet and have effortlessly drawn that experience into your life right now. Picture yourself experiencing all the positive feelings and sensations along with it.
- Right now, I choose to receive (fill in the blank) in my life. Picture yourself having completely received what you want right now because of having forgiven yourself or someone else. Imagine yourself experiencing right now all the positive feelings and sensations along with it, including peace, joy, happiness, love, and other positive emotions.
- Right now, I choose to appreciate. Focus on all the things in your life you have to appreciate over the (a) last month, (b) last six months, (c) last year, (d) last five years, and (e) your whole life. (Do slowly, one at a time.) The more you appreciate things and experiences in your life, the easier it is to forgive.

Take three slow, deep breaths again, in through the nose and out through the mouth. Then slowly open your eyes.

In your journal, write about your experiences.

APRIL'S RESPONSE

This exercise taught me how to live in the present. If I focus on the present time, I feel much more calm and at peace.

Also, if I show gratitude for all the things I've had or have, I appreciate everything that much more.

Exercise: Preprogramming Yourself for Forgiveness

All of the exercises and processes that you have done so far emphasize forgiving yourself, someone, or some circumstance in the present, based on some experience you have had in the past, either the recent past or the distant past. In this exercise, which I have come to call the *carpet of forgiveness,* you first practice a relaxation technique, such as the one at the beginning of this chapter, or a meditation technique, if you know one. Then you imagine a carpet laid out in front of you. The carpet represents your future. You imagine yourself walking down the carpet into your future. As you walk down that carpet, something is going to happen at some point that you don't want to happen, or something you want to happen is not going to happen. Unless you are a very liberated being, in many cases you will start to judge that person or experience negatively, or you will judge yourself negatively. You will begin to hold a grievance or grudge and to feel hurt, angry, guilty, fearful, and/or sad.

In this exercise you will consciously choose to practice forgiveness. In other words, you will be programming yourself to practice forgiving almost as soon as the upsetting event or experience takes place in which you begin to judge. By prepaving forgiveness along the carpet of forgiveness, you will empower yourself. You will program your mind to forgive in *advance* situations that would ordinarily lead you to hold on to grievances and anger or guilt for some period of time. By practicing in advance, you will find yourself returning to a peaceful and happy state of consciousness much more quickly.

Imagine that you are walking into the future on the carpet of forgiveness. In your journal, write down some possible scenarios where you might ordinarily get quite upset and would benefit from forgiving as quickly as possible.

APRIL'S RESPONSE

1. When I'm driving and someone cuts me off

2. Someone walks in my work right when we're about to close

3. My boyfriend tells me at the last minute he has a hockey game (softball, basketball)

Now write down some ways you could practice forgiveness in those situations, based upon the information you have learned so far.

APRIL'S RESPONSE

1. By getting mad, I would only be hurting myself, and I would look at the other person's perspective.

2. Be more understanding of other people. Maybe they have something difficult going on in their life that takes up their day, so it's the only time they can come in.

3. I understand that he is passionate about and really enjoys doing these sports, and I shouldn't get mad when he has a game.

The next exercise is an extension of the carpet of forgiveness exercise.

Exercise: Future Self

Now imagine that the carpet extends five years into the future, and you are meeting your *future self*. Imagine, moreover, that you have been diligently practicing the forgiveness techniques in this book for five years and that you are a much happier, more loving, and peaceful person. Have a conversation between your *future self* and your present self. Let your *future self* explain to you (your current self) how it has managed to learn forgiveness so successfully over the past five years. Ask your *future self* why it has succeeded at learning to forgive so masterfully when you were struggling with it so much five years earlier.

In your journal, carry on the conversation between your *future self* and your current self. If you are doing these exercises with a partner, you can pair up, and one of you can play the role of your current self and one can play the role of your *future self*. Then switch roles. Be sure to write about both: current self and *future self*.

APRIL'S RESPONSE

Current Self: For a long time, it seemed very difficult to practice forgiveness; how has that changed?
Future Self: I can now see things from a much more positive, healthy perspective.

Current Self: Is this something that just happened overnight?
Future Self: No, it has been an everyday process to understand forgiveness. Using many affirmations and the Psychological Uplifter helped a great deal.

Current Self: Is that all that it takes?
Future Self: No, I also had to be open and willing to change. I had to make the ultimate decision to experience peace and love in my life, and that starts with forgiveness.

Afformations[4]

Afformations spelled with an "o" differ from affirmations spelled with an "i." Unlike affirmations, which you repeat over and over again to bring about a certain experience or event, afformations assume a certain experience or event has already occurred and you are asking yourself why it did. In the future self exercise above, you used a kind of afformation in which your *future self* explained to your current self why it had mastered forgiveness.

Exercise: Eleven Forgiveness Afformations

I want you to try this exercise over the course of a week. Read each afformation four times a day: once in the morning upon awakening, once at night, and twice more during the day. Contemplate the afformation for two to three minutes each time, and then go about your day. Let your subconscious mind work on the afformation. For most people, first writing the afformation down on a 3 × 5 card or a sticky note works best. Select five afformations from the list below and contemplate each one for a week at a time, or use all of them. You can also make up your own afformations.

1. Why have I been able to forgive so easily when at first it appeared to be so difficult?
2. Why have I learned to release judgments and grievances so quickly when before I held on to them for long periods of time?
3. Why do I find it so much easier to see things from the other person's point of view so effortlessly when previously I rarely did it?
4. Why am I able to see the goodness in other people when something unfortunate happens when I never could before?
5. Why am I capable of being so much kinder to myself now when I make mistakes when before I was so critical and harsh?
6. Why am I able to shift perspectives so easily now when someone else is angry with me when before I just got angry or guilty very quickly?
7. Why am I capable of seeing that anger covers up hurt and disappointment when I couldn't before?
8. Why am I able to see so easily now that hurt and disappointment cover up fear, and fear is a call for love?
9. Why am I able to see now that the core of all human beings irrespective of their behavior is love?
10. Why am I able to see now that whenever I forgive, I forgive only myself?
11. Why am I willing and able to see now that forgiving always brings me closer to my loving core self, the truth of my being?

In your journal, write about your experience of using these afformations or the ones you created yourself. You may find it helpful to write the afformations down in your journal as well.

APRIL'S RESPONSE

The afformations exercise allowed me to reflect on situations that have already occurred in my life, and I was able to see that I could now shift to a more positive perspective than I had before.

This chapter has been about learning how to make new choices using relaxation, imagery, and afformation techniques. By learning to self-regulate mentally and emotionally with these tools, you are learning how to greatly re-empower yourself and forgive more easily. The next two chapters will introduce you to some very powerful energy techniques. These will help you to rapidly and effectively (and for some people dramatically) shift the energy around your hurt, pain, guilt, resentments, grievances, disappointments, anger, fear, and anxiety.

CHAPTER 9

Energetic Forgiveness and Releasing:

Positive Pressure Point Techniques 1–4

"Holding on to anger is like grasping a hot coal with the intent of throwing it at someone else; you are the one who gets burned."
—BUDDHA

"Resentment is like taking poison and waiting for the other person to die."
—MALACHY MCCOURT

"It is just as necessary to forgive ourselves as it is to forgive others, and the principal reason why forgiveness seemed so difficult is because we have neglected to forgive ourselves."
—CHRISTIAN D. LARSON

A FORMER CLIENT OF mine, Ted, wrote this story. As he mentions, he had one of the highest distress scores on my assessment scales that I had ever seen. In addition to a lot of physical pain, he was experiencing high levels of depression, anxiety, guilt, and anger. He also had substantial marital and family problems and had not worked in a few years. Naturally, he was skeptical of therapy, as his previous therapy experiences had not worked very well for him. Nevertheless, he was quite motivated. On his own, he started a journal to report on his experiences during therapy and to keep track of the assignments I gave him. The change that took place during our sessions was unusually fast, so be kind to yourself if you find yourself changing more slowly. Nevertheless, it shows how rapidly change can take place, sometimes even with extremely high levels of distress. Here is part of his story *in his own words.*

I remember the very moment I decided to seek help. I just got the [Yellow Pages]... and opened it without looking. It was quite a miracle that it would open to the page of a therapist who would help me through all this mess I had in my life. When I made the call to his office to set the appointment, I could feel that this would be the one to really help me. In our first therapy conversation, we spoke of all the evaluation sheets I had completed. I was off the chart for most of them. My stress symptom level was in outer space. He said it was 279, the second-highest score he had ever seen. There were things that made me cry. There were hopes, dreams I once had that were no longer part of me, and I wanted them back. He instructed me through the Psychological Uplifter (see p. 103), which worked a miracle the very first day. I learned how to rid myself of negative thoughts, feelings, and other emotions. That Psychological Uplifter is now part of my daily life, and I know if more people would use it, they would soon notice results. I put it on my cell phone, so I could read it when I was stuck in traffic or at the mall.

Here is the beginning of my Psychological Uplifter: "Even though I have anger, depression, grief, guilt, low self-esteem, marital and family problems, I accept myself deeply and profoundly, and I am a good and magnificent person." The words are so powerful for me, and I do think they could be powerful for all who are searching for peace and inner forgiveness. Later he taught me the Positive Pressure Point Techniques, which were also very powerful for me. Depression is nothing to play with. It will bring you to the lowest of lows. You will find that you don't even know yourself or can feel yourself.

Forgiving all things in my life is not an easy job; understanding the past of why I was treated in such a negative manner and the continued connection with the people who made me feel so bad about life and myself seemed so sick. How could I love/like the people who hurt me? How could I continue to have a relationship with them? Trust me, it wasn't easy, but it had to be done. I went into therapy to learn how to love, forgive, understand, and move forward in my life. My life is very important to me and I desire to have wonderful things, people, and events in it.

I set a goal to seek peace in my life and relationships. Having a positive relationship was something I have always wanted with friends and family. The willingness to forgive came from within my deepest self. I knew that my Higher Power would love me and forgive me, no matter what. So, I found in my heart that through all of my pain, I could forgive others. It was going to take time to reach the total goal of forgiveness and peace. Some days I had to remind myself to "Let Go and Let God." I knew in my heart I wanted to. But there were times when I would become so angry. I also realized that I could only change and heal myself. Those around me had to make their individual changes.

Forgiveness is an everyday test, and I work on forgiveness every day of my life. Moving toward the better things of the heart: love, peace, joy, laughter, positive attitude, and forgiveness. I want my soul to be free of the heartache I know so well. That's why I choose forgiveness.

In this chapter, I'll be introducing you to some energy therapy techniques. There are many different energy therapy techniques, such as Emotional Freedom Techniques (EFT), Energy Tapping (ET), the Tapas Acupressure Techniques (TAT), Touch and Breathe (TAB), and others.[1] Briefly, the theory behind energy therapies is that negative emotions occur as a result of a disruption or restriction in the flow of energy in and around the human body. The approach that I use to eliminate that disruption, which is an adaptation of a number of these techniques, is called the Positive Pressure Point Techniques, or PPPT. These techniques will teach you how to eliminate the emotional distress generated by unforgiving attack thoughts (anger, guilt, frustration, anxiety, hurt, etc.) by either tapping gently on key pressure points on the body or holding these pressure points and engaging in slow, deep breaths. While using some of these techniques, you will also repeat certain powerful affirmations.

Positive Pressure Point Technique Level 1: Use of Pressure Points and Tapping with No Affirmations (PPPT-L1)

Step 1 Select one area of emotional distress, such as anger, hurt, guilt, sadness, or fear, that you experience when you think about the person, circumstance, or self that you are having a challenging time forgiving. Rate it on a 10-point scale, with 10 being very distressed (i.e., experiencing a lot of anger, hurt, guilt, sadness, or fear) and 1 being not distressed at all. Your result is called SUDs (subjective units of distress).

Step 2 Briefly think about the particular form of emotional distress you are feeling. This is called attuning to the negative feelings. Do not dwell on it, however. Just briefly think about it.

Step 3 Using the index and middle fingers of your right hand, rub continuously on the neurolymphatic point, also called the "sore point" because it often feels weaker or sorer than other points on the chest, while repeating the Psychological Uplifter 2. You will find the "sore point" on the diagram below (see diagram 3 and figure 1).

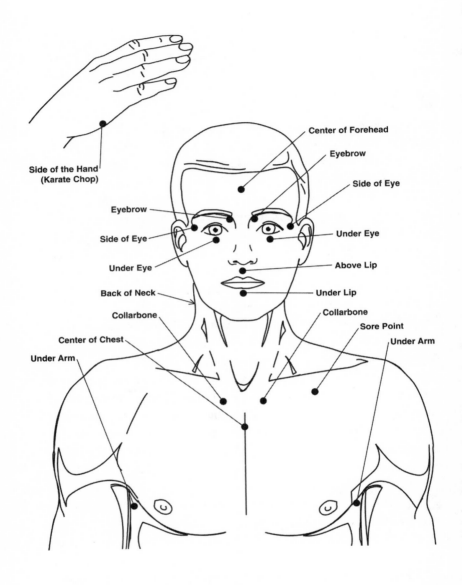

Diagram 3

Figure 1   **Figure 2**

Within reasonable limits, the louder you say the Psychological Uplifter, the better. Find a quiet place to do this where you won't be disturbed. If it is impossible to say it out loud, say it to yourself.

Psychological Uplifter 2

Repeat the following three times. **"Even though I have this problem or negative emotion (name the emotion, e.g., fear, anxiety, hurt, anger, depression, sadness, frustration, guilt, shame, low self-esteem, or marital, family, relationship, or work problems, etc.), I accept myself deeply and profoundly, and I am a good and magnificent person."**

Now, three times, while rubbing continuously on the sore point, say, **"I love and forgive myself unconditionally, despite my problems, limitations, and challenges."**

Now, while rubbing on the sore point, that is, the neurolymphatic point (diagram 3), say three times: **"I am entitled to *miracles.*"** If at all possible, say this louder and with more conviction each time. Many people find it beneficial to write the Psychological Uplifter 2 on a card, their cell phone, their computer, an organizer, or something else of your choosing and post it in various places at home, at work, etc.

Step 4 With two fingers, tap gently on the fleshy side of your other hand (see figure 2).

This conventionally is called the "karate chop" point because it is the place from which you would give a karate chop. Say the following phrases:

1. **Anything is possible**
2. **I am entitled to miracles.**
3. **Miracles are happening.**
4. **Miracles come from love.**

Repeat this step two times.

Step 5 Using two fingers, continue tapping on the side of the hand on the fleshy area (figure 2) and say: **"I release this (fill in the name of the emotional distress or limiting belief here, such as, anger, hurt, guilt, disappointment, judgment, grievance, attack thoughts) and all of its roots and causes and all of its effects on me and everyone else in my life."** (Repeat two times.) Then say, **"Instead, I choose to feel calm, relaxed, at peace, and confident."** (Repeat two times.)

Step 6 Again, reflect briefly on the one area of emotional distress, such as anger, hurt, guilt, sadness, or fear, you feel when you think of the person, circumstance, or self that you are having a challenging time forgiving. Again, rate it on a 10-point scale with 10 being very distressed (i.e., experiencing a lot of anger, hurt, guilt, sadness, or fear) and 1 being not distressed at all.

Step 7 Attune to the emotional distress. Briefly think about the emotional distress, anger, hurt, guilt, sadness, disappointment, fear, etc. Do not dwell on it, however. Just think about it briefly.

Step 8 Using two fingers of either hand, tap gently and consistently fifteen to twenty times on each of the following eight pressure points:

Figure 3

Figure 4

1. Center of the forehead (figure 3). Use one hand and two fingers.
2. Inside corner of the eyebrows, just below the eyebrow (figure 4). Using two fingers of both hands is preferable.

Figure 5

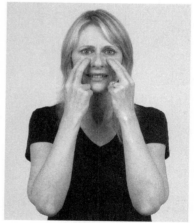

Figure 6

3. Just outside the side of the eye (figure 5). Using two fingers of both hands is preferable.
4. Under the eye on the bony part of the eye in the center (figure 6). Using two fingers of both hands is preferable.

Figure 7

Figure 8

5. Above the lip (figure 7). Using two fingers of one hand is preferable on this pressure point.

6. Below the lip and above the chin (figure 8). Using two fingers of one hand is preferable on this pressure point.

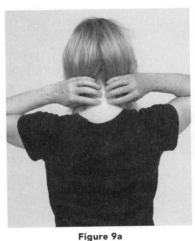

Figure 9a

Figure 9b

7. Behind the neck (figures 9a and 9b). When tapping behind the neck, use all the fingers of both hands. Tap up, down, and all around thirty-five times on the back of the neck points, as this

area is especially beneficial. Make sure when tapping on the back of the neck to go down the center, up, and around while covering all the muscles, arteries, and veins in the back of the neck.

Figure 10

8. The collarbone-chest area (figure 10). Using two or more fingers of both hands is preferable on these pressure points.

After tapping on the first four points, stop briefly and give yourself another SUDs (subjective units of distress) rating from 1 to 10. In most cases, the numbers will have dropped as many as two to six points, and very occasionally all the way to 1. After tapping on all eight pressure points, give yourself another SUDs rating. In many cases, the SUDs rating will have dropped to 1. If the SUDs rating has not dropped to 1, repeat Level 1. If you are having difficulty, read the troubleshooting instructions at the end of the last section of this chapter, Positive Pressure Point Technique Level 4 (see p. 115).

In your journal, write about your experience using this positive pressure point technique.

See figures 11 and 12 for typical pictures of before (distressed) and after (happy) doing the PPPTs.

Positive Pressure Point Technique Level 2: Pressure Points with Holding and Breathing with No Affirmations (PPPT-L2)

Follow the instructions for the first seven steps of Positive Pressure Point Technique Level 1.

Step 8 Using two fingers of either hand, hold each pressure point while breathing in slowly through the nose and breathing out slowly

| Figure 11 | Figure 12 |

through the mouth. Breathe in and out slowly through the nose and out through the mouth three times for each the following eight pressure points:

1. Center of the forehead (figure 3). Use one hand and two fingers.
2. Inside corner of the eyebrows, just below the eyebrow (figure 4). Using two fingers of both hands is preferable.
3. Just outside the side of the eye (figure 5). Using two fingers of both hands is preferable.
4. Under the eye on the bony part of the eye in the center (figure 6). Using two fingers of both hands is preferable.
5. Above the lip (figure 7). Using two fingers of one hand is preferable on this pressure point.
6. Below the lip and above the chin (figure 8). Using two fingers of one hand is preferable on this pressure point.
7. Behind the neck (no figure). Put one hand on the back of the neck and one hand on the forehead. Do the holding and breathing as usual.
8. The collarbone-chest area (figure 10). Using two or more fingers of both hands is preferable on these pressure points.

After holding and breathing on the first four pressure points, stop briefly and give yourself another SUDs rating from 1 to 10. In most cases, the numbers will have dropped as many as two to six points, and occasionally all the way to 1. After holding and breathing on all eight points, give yourself another SUDs rating. In many cases, the SUDs rating will have dropped to 1. If the SUDs rating has not dropped to 1, repeat Level 2 and retest yourself. If you are having difficulty, read the troubleshooting instructions at the end of the last section of this chapter, Positive Pressure Point Technique Level 4 (see p. 115).

In your journal, write about your experience using this positive pressure point technique.

Positive Pressure Point Technique Level 3: Pressure Points with Tapping, Holding, and Breathing with No Affirmations (PPPT-L3)

Level 3 of the Positive Pressure Point Technique is identical to Levels 1 and 2 except that you alternate a round of tapping on the eight pressure points with a round of holding and breathing.

Start with the first seven steps of PPPT-L1 (see p. 101).

Step 8 Using two fingers of either hand, tap gently and consistently fifteen to twenty times on each of the eight pressure points. After you have tapped on the pressure point fifteen to twenty times, again using two fingers of either hand, hold each pressure point while breathing in slowly through the nose and breathing out slowly through the mouth two times for each of the following eight pressure points:

1. Center of the forehead (figure 3). Use one hand and two fingers.
2. Inside corner of the eyebrows, just below the eyebrow (figure 4). Using two fingers of both hands is preferable.
3. Just outside the side of the eye (figure 5). Using two fingers of both hands is preferable.
4. Under the eye on the bony part of the eye in the center (figure 6). Using two fingers of both hands is preferable.

5. Above the lip (figure 7). Using two fingers of one hand is preferable on this pressure point.

6. Below the lip and above the chin (figure 8). Using two fingers of one hand is preferable on this pressure point.

7. Behind the neck (figures 9a and 9b). When tapping behind the neck, use all the fingers of both hands. Tap up, down, and all around thirty-five times on the back of the neck points, as this area is especially beneficial. Make sure when tapping on the back of the neck to go down the center, up, and around while covering all the muscles, arteries, and veins in the back of the neck. Then, when you hold and breathe, put one hand on the back of the neck and one hand on the forehead. Do the holding and breathing as usual.

8. The collarbone-chest area (figure 10). Using two or more fingers of both hands is preferable on these pressure points.

After both tapping, holding, and breathing on the first four pressure points, stop briefly and give yourself another SUDs rating from 1 to 10. In most cases, the numbers will have dropped from two to six points, and occasionally all the way to 1. After tapping and holding and breathing on all eight points, give yourself another SUDs rating. In many cases, the SUDs rating will have dropped to 1. If the SUDs rating has not dropped to 1, repeat Level 3 of the Positive Pressure Point Technique; that is, do the tapping, holding, and breathing again on all eight points, giving yourself a SUDs ratings after four points and again after all eight points. In most cases the SUDs level will have dropped to 1. If you are having difficulty, read the troubleshooting instructions at the end of the last section of this chapter, Positive Pressure Point Technique Level 4 (see p. 115).

In your journal, write about your experience using this positive pressure point technique.

Three Frames of Reference, Analogies, or Metaphors

Three metaphors can be helpful here in making all levels of the Positive Pressure Point Technique work most effectively for you.

1. TREES AND THE FOREST

All of your problems can be seen as a forest with an unknown number of trees. Each problem is like a tree, and each time you use the PPPT, you cut down one tree in the forest. After a number of trees are cut down (and we don't know how many trees there are in advance), the trees cut down will fall over and knock down the rest of the forest. (In other words, you will be able to generalize, and all your problems will be solved.)

2. RIVER AND THE OCEAN

Under ordinary circumstances, water will flow smoothly down a river to the ocean, unless the flow of water to the ocean is dammed up or blocked by trees, debris, garbage, etc. In this case, there is a blockage in the flow of the water to the lake. In the same way, you have lines of energy that flow through and around your body. In Chinese medicine, these flows or energy are called meridians and vessels. (There are twelve major meridians and two major vessels.) When energy is blocked from flowing freely along these lines, emotional distress occurs. By tapping on the pressure points and/or breathing deeply while holding the pressure points (while attuned to the distressing emotion), the energy begins to flow freely (the water flows back to the lake) and the emotional distress is released. This brings about peace, calm, and healing.

3. STACKED CAFETERIA PLATES

In this analogy, your emotional distress (anger, hurt, guilt, sadness, fear) is compared to a series of plates stacked one above another in a cafeteria. Each problem represents one plate. When one problem is resolved using the Positive Pressure Point Technique (PPPT), a plate is removed from the pile. Underneath the first plate (problem) is another one that you can't see/feel until the first stacked plate/problem is removed. It is important to be aware of this analogy because sometimes when one problem is being released another one pops up, and unless you realize this is natural, you may mistakenly think the technique is not working when in fact it is working perfectly.

I encourage you to practice Levels 1, 2, and 3 of the Positive Pressure Point Technique ten to twenty times a day, or as often as you can, for a few weeks before learning the next levels and experiment with using it on all kinds of distress related directly or indirectly to issues of unforgiveness.

Positive Pressure Point Technique Level 4: Pressure Points with Tapping, Holding, and Breathing with Affirmations (PPPT-L4)

Level 4 of the Positive Pressure Point Technique is identical to Level 3 except that you alternate a round of tapping on the eight pressure points with a round of holding and breathing and also add certain affirmations.

Start by doing the first seven steps of the Positive Pressure Point Technique Level 1 (see p. 101). Then using two fingers of either hand, tap gently and consistently fifteen to twenty times on each the eight pressure points (see below).

In Level 4 of the Positive Pressure Point Technique, when tapping on each pressure point, use the following generic affirmation formula two to three times (usually three at first):

I release X, I want Y.
I release X, I choose Y.
I release X, I am Y.

More specifically, say, "I release anger, I want to be at peace," "I release anger, I choose to be at peace," and "I release anger, I am at peace"; or "I release guilt, I want to be at peace," "I release guilt, I choose to be peace," and "I release guilt, I am at peace"; or "I release hurt, I want to be at peace," "I release hurt, I choose to be at peace," and "I release hurt, I am at peace."

This set of affirmations focuses on what you want to release, what you want to experience—empowerment (I choose) and acknowledgment/remembrance of one's true nature (peace). In general, it reinforces what you have been learning in other ways; that is, releasing darkness and choosing/acknowledging light. Sometimes it is also beneficial to add "I release X, I intend Y" and "I release X, I focus on Y" after you say, "I release X, I choose Y," where X is the anger, guilt, hurt, or other distressing emotion, and Y is "be at peace."

1. Center of the forehead (figure 3). Use two fingers of one hand.
2. Inside corner of the eyebrows, just below the eyebrow (figure 4). Using two fingers of both hands is preferable.
3. Just outside the side of the eye (figure 5). Using two fingers of both hands is preferable.
4. Under the eye on the bony part of the eye in the center (figure 6). Using two fingers of both hands is preferable.
5. Above the lip (figure 7). Using two fingers of one hand is preferable on this pressure point.
6. Below the lip and above the chin (figure 8). Using two fingers of one hand is preferable on this pressure point.
7. Behind the neck (figures 9a and 9b). When tapping behind the neck, use all the fingers of both hands. Tap up, down, and all around thirty-five times on the back of the neck points, as this area is especially beneficial. Make sure when tapping on the back of the neck to go down the center, up, and around while covering all the muscles, arteries, and veins in the back of the neck.
8. The collarbone-chest area (figure 10). Using two or more fingers of both hands is preferable on these pressure points.

After you have done the tapping with the affirmations on each pressure point, I encourage you to practice the holding and breathing process two times on each pressure point, with the idea that you are breathing in peace on the in-breath and breathing out whatever distress you are attuned to on the out-breath. For example, you want to imagine that you are breathing in peace and breathing out anger or guilt or sadness or fear or hurt. Sometimes you may find it beneficial to use more than one word while doing the tapping. For example, you may want to say: "releasing anger, hurt, and disappointment," instead

☺ You are strong and brave. ☺

of releasing only anger. You may want to say "I want" or "I choose to be calm, relaxed, and at peace" rather than "I want" or "I choose to be at peace." The main point is that you are reducing or releasing the negative distress and increasing or strengthening the positive feelings and attitudes.

In your journal, write about your experience using this positive pressure point technique.

You may find that you prefer either the tapping method or the hold and breathe method, and you may find after practicing them both that you prefer doing the Positive Pressure Point Technique process with or without affirmations. Everyone is unique, and there is no right or wrong way to do it. I do, however, encourage you to try the different versions on all kinds of unforgiveness issues, both small and large, and to practice it frequently, such as ten to twenty times a day. Practicing even a few times a day, however, can give great relief for many people. It is often very beneficial to write the affirmations or the whole process on note cards, your computer, PDA, or in a journal.

APRIL'S RESPONSE

I was twenty-two and living with my boyfriend. I was angry at my father for not taking care of his health, not going to the doctor for checkups, and for dying suddenly when he was fifty-two and I was twenty. I also blamed myself for not being able to convince him that he should exercise more, eat healthier, and get regular medical checkups. As a result, I felt resentful, guilty, and hurt, even though I loved my father a great deal. I used the Positive Pressure Point Technique (PPPT) Levels 1 and 2 to deal with my strong feelings, which had SUDs ratings of 10 and 8. I responded very well and quickly. My SUDs level dropped on anger and hurt from 10 to 7, 7 to 5, 5 to 3, and 3 to 1 toward my father. Then I used PPPT Levels 3 and 4 for dealing with my guilt, unforgiveness toward myself, and self-blame. Once again my SUDs level dropped rapidly from 8 to 5, 5 to 2, and 2 to 1. At this point I felt much calmer and peaceful and much more forgiving and accepting of both my father and myself. Just then, I started to feel some grief and sadness over my father's death. Another round of PPPT and my SUDs level on grief went down from 8 to 1. This time I felt a deep sense of calm, peace, acceptance, and contentment.

Troubleshooting

If you get stuck using any of the above Positive Pressure Point Techniques, I have two recommendations. Most of the time it won't be necessary to use these, but if you do run into trouble, they can be very helpful.

1. **Tap the karate-chop point.** In this approach, you tap the padded side of one hand, also known as the karate chop point, with two fingers of the other hand, tapping continuously while repeating: "Even though I still have this problem (fill in the blank; for example, anger, hurt, resentment, guilt, sadness, fear, anxiety, etc.), I accept myself deeply and profoundly and I am a good and magnificent person." Do this three times and then return to the Positive Pressure Point Technique you are using.

2. **Access an earlier or deeper upset/feeling.** In this approach, which I find is the most powerful, you close your eyes and look within until you find an earlier or deeper feeling inside you that you didn't notice before, one that was underneath the feeling you were working on. For example, suppose you were using the PPPT to release hurt and the SUDs numbers came down from 10 to 8, then 8 to 6, and then became stuck; that is, the numbers either didn't get any lower, or they moved very slowly from 6 to 5 and 5 to 4. Close your eyes and look inside. You might then discover that there were some strong angry feelings underneath the hurt feelings. Switch over to the angry feeling, give it a SUDs number

(for example, a 9 out of 10), and then do the Positive Pressure Point Technique on angry feelings. When the SUDs on the angry feelings have come down to 1, check back to see what the SUDs number was on hurt feelings. Sometimes the SUDs number on the hurt feelings will also have come down to 1 (the hurt will be gone). At other times, some of the hurt will still be there. At that point, give it a new SUDs number from 1 to 10. Then do the Positive Pressure Point Technique you are using for hurt feelings until it comes down to 1.

EXAMPLES

Linda was feeling a lot of anger and unforgiveness toward her husband, Bob, for having an affair. We started doing the Positive Pressure Point Technique Level 1, using the tapping method without any affirmations on the pressure points. She did the Psychological Uplifter *"Even though I have this anger, I accept myself deeply and profoundly, and I am a good and magnificent person. I love and forgive myself unconditionally, despite my problems, limitations, challenges, and anger. I am entitled to miracles"* three times while rubbing on the sore point; that is, the neurolymphatic point. She gave herself a SUDs rating of 10 on her angry feelings. She attuned herself briefly to the angry feelings. After tapping the first four points, her anger went down to 8 and then didn't move any further. She tapped on the side of one hand (karate chop point) with two fingers of the other hand, and said, *"Even though I still have this anger, I accept myself deeply and profoundly, and I am a good and magnificent person."* She did this three times and then returned to the Positive Pressure Point Technique Level 1. Her SUDs number only went down to 7 after tapping on four more pressure points.

She then closed her eyes and discovered that she was experiencing a lot of sadness in her heart and face areas. She gave herself a SUDs number of 9 on sadness and started doing the PPPT Level 1 from the beginning. This time, her SUDs level dropped quickly from 9 to 6, 6 to 4, 4 to 2, and 2 to 1. She then went back and checked the SUDs level for the angry feelings, which was now 4. She decided to use PPPT Level 2 (hold and breathe on the pressure points) and found her angry feelings quickly released. She had a SUDs level of 1 after doing the technique on just a few pressure points.

Cliff was feeling very guilty and unforgiving toward himself over his son's death. He had been watching the boy swimming in their backyard pool and had taken his eyes off him for just a few moments. In just those few minutes, his son drowned.

We used the PPPT Level 3, which included the tapping and hold and breathe method. He did the Psychological Uplifter *"Even though I have this guilt, I accept myself deeply and profoundly, and I am a good and magnificent person. I love and forgive myself unconditionally despite my problems, limitations, challenges, and guilt. I am entitled to miracles"* three times while rubbing on the sore point; that is, the neurolymphatic point.

He gave himself a SUDs rating of 8 on his guilty feelings. He attuned himself briefly to the guilty feelings. After tapping and holding and breathing on the first four points, his guilt went down to 5 and then didn't move any further. He tapped on the side of one hand (karate chop point) with two fingers of the other hand and said, *"Even though I still have this guilt, I accept myself deeply and profoundly, and I am a good and magnificent person."* He did this three times and then returned to the Positive Pressure Point Technique Level 3.

After tapping and holding and breathing on the next four points, Cliff's SUDs level only dropped one more point to 4. When he closed his eyes and looked inside, he discovered that he had some intense resentful/bitter feelings toward his wife that he had been suppressing. He gave this a SUDs number of 10. He then did the Positive Pressure Point Technique Level 3 on his bitter/resentful feelings, and they dropped quickly from a SUDs number of 10 to 7 to 4 to 1 in one round. When he went back to the guilty feelings, he was surprised to discover they were also at a SUDs number of 1.

Ava felt deep grief and unforgiveness over her husband's drinking and doing drugs. She told herself many times to leave him but didn't when he pleaded with her to give him another chance. Now they were having financial problems and had lost a lot of money. In addition to her grief, she felt guilt, anger, and disappointment, both with her husband and herself.

Ava did the Psychological Uplifter on her anger toward her husband: *"Even though I have this anger, I accept myself deeply and profoundly, and I am a good and magnificent person. I love and forgive myself unconditionally, despite my problems, limitations, challenges, and anger. I am entitled to miracles."* She repeated these words three times while rubbing on the sore point; that is, the neurolymphatic point. She gave herself a SUDs rating of 7 on her angry feelings. She attuned herself briefly to the angry feelings. Using the hold and breathe technique (PPPT Level 2), her anger went down to 4 and then to 1 quickly. Then she decided to use it on her guilty feelings. She attuned herself briefly to the guilty feelings. Using the hold and breathe technique (PPPT Level 2), her guilt, which started at a SUDs level of 8, went down to 6 and then didn't drop any lower.

She tapped on the side of one hand (karate chop point) with two fingers of the other hand and said, *"Even though I still have this guilt, I accept myself deeply and profoundly, and I am a good and magnificent person."* She did this three times and then returned to the PPPT Level 2. The SUDs numbers went down to 4 after tapping on four more pressure points. She repeated the PPPT Level 2, but the SUDs level only dropped to a 3 after using it for four more pressure points. She then closed her eyes and looked within.

Ava discovered that she was experiencing a lot of fear that if she left her husband, she wouldn't be able to survive with two kids and a low-paying job. Ava gave her fear a SUDs level of 8 and then did the Psychological Uplifter on fear. She also decided to switch over to PPPT Level 4, using the affirmations. Her SUDs level dropped fairly rapidly from 8 to 6, 6 to 4, 4 to 2, and 2 to 1.

Ava used Level 4 to release her grief, which had measured a 7 on her SUDs test. One round of PPPT Level 4 reduced the grief from a 7 to 5, 5 to 3, and 3 to 1. At that point, Ava was feeling much more relaxed, calm, confident, cheerful, and at peace with herself.

The first four levels of the Positive Pressure Point Technique are very powerful. In my experience, if you use them consistently and persistently, they will usually trigger substantial positive changes in your distressed feelings and greatly help with the forgiveness process. Any one of them alone can also catalyze major changes in you; together they provide a set of tools that have the ability to dramatically improve the quality of your life.

Of course, if you have tried using the Positive Pressure Point Techniques on your own for a while and are having difficulty making them work, you might want to consult an experienced therapist, healer, or coach skilled in their use. The Positive Pressure Point Techniques described in the next chapter build on the skills learned in this chapter, though they can also be used as stand-alone techniques.

CHAPTER 10

Energetic Forgiveness and Finding Peace:

Positive Pressure Point Techniques 5–8

"We must develop and maintain the capacity to forgive. He who is devoid of the power to forgive is devoid of the power to love. . . . There is some good in the worst of us and some evil in the best of us."
—MARTIN LUTHER KING, Jr., sermon, 1957

"The forgiving state of mind is a magnetic power for attracting good."
—CATHERINE PONDER

M ANY YEARS AGO, I saw a client named Ben, a large, forty-five-year-old, African-American man who had just been released from jail after serving three years for armed robbery. He had a slight limp. On the outside, Ben had a tough appearance, but there was something very sweet about him that I saw in his eyes. He called to make an appointment after seeing an ad in the telephone book. Ben came to see me in my suburban office from a rough neighborhood in North Philadelphia, which was quite unusual. He had no insurance, so he was paying quite a bit out of his own pocket for these therapy sessions. In the initial interview, he said he was out of work, was not on drugs, and was involved in a conflict-filled relationship with his girlfriend. He was coming to see me because one month earlier, his mother, whom he lived with, had died. He had been very close to his mother emotionally, he said. Ben's mother had serious asthma problems in the past. For many years and on many occasions, he had to call an ambulance for his mother because of her asthma.

One month earlier, he had called an ambulance for his mother. On this occasion, the white ambulance attendant came, and for some reason Ben and the attendant got into an argument at the front door over some racist-tinged remarks, according to Ben—or, at least, that was how Ben saw it. In any case, the ambulance then took Ben's mother to the hospital, except this time the attendant didn't give Ben's mother any oxygen, and she died on the way to the hospital. Ben felt extremely sad, grief stricken, angry, and guilty. He was angry at the ambulance attendant for not giving his mother oxygen. He was feeling very guilty for arguing with the attendant. Ben believed this was the reason his mother did not get the needed oxygen in the ambulance. He was feeling very sad and grief stricken about his mother's death.

After the usual intake interviews, I slowly taught Ben an earlier version of the Positive Pressure Point Technique. I taught it to him very slowly, as it was new to me at the time. Within twenty minutes in the third session, Ben said his subjective units of distress (SUDs) on his guilt dropped from 10 to 1.

The following week, his SUDs level on guilt was still at a 1. We then worked on his sadness and grief, which was also at a SUDs level of 10. Again, within twenty minutes, his SUDs level dropped to 1, using an earlier version of the Positive Pressure Point Technique. He felt extremely good at the end of the sessions. At the beginning of the fifth session, he said his SUDs level was at 2 on his sadness/grief. His explanation was that his mother had only recently died, and he still missed her a little bit. By that time, his SUDs score on anger had spontaneously dropped to 1. Ben was feeling very forgiving at this point of both himself and the ambulance attendant, and his grievances and judgments had essentially dissolved.

When I asked Ben in the sixth session how he could afford the therapy sessions, he told me that he had lied to me in the first therapy session. I was quite surprised, of course. He said that he had been using cocaine, but the therapy sessions were so helpful that he stopped using the cocaine and was now using the money to pay for the therapy sessions. By this time, Ben had forgiven himself and the ambulance attendant, and the therapy sessions switched to focusing on his relationship problems with his girlfriend and helping him find a job. We terminated after twelve sessions, and he was very appreciative. Frankly, I was amazed and grateful for the opportunity to work with and help Ben.

Positive Pressure Point Technique Level 5: Use of Pressure Points with Tapping, Holding, and Breathing with Forgiveness Affirmations (PPPT-L5)

In Level 5, we add forgiveness affirmations. After doing all the steps of Level 4, you then tap continuously about a hand's width beneath your armpit, first under the right arm and then under the left (figures 13a and 13b). Finally, you tap on the center of the chest (no figure). The forgiveness affirmations are used to further emphasize that forgiveness is a key to happiness, to strengthen your connection with the path of light, and to further connect you with your true identity.

| Figure 13a | Figure 13b |

Forgiveness Affirmations[1]

Repeat these phrases while tapping continuously under the right arm.

- I forgive myself for my contribution to this problem.
- I forgive myself. I am doing the best that I can.
- I forgive myself. I release all judgments against myself.
- I forgive myself. I release all criticisms against myself.
- I forgive myself. I release all grievances against myself.
- I forgive myself. I release all attack thoughts against myself.
- Forgiveness is the key to happiness.

Then, while tapping under the left arm, repeat these phrases.

- I forgive him/her (use the person's name) for his/her (pick one) contribution to the problem.
- I forgive him/her (use the person's name). He/she is doing the best that he/she can.
- I forgive him/her. I release all judgments against him/her.
- I forgive him/her. I release all criticisms against him/her.
- I forgive him/her. I release all grievances against him/her.
- I forgive him/her. I release all attack thoughts against him/her.
- Forgiveness is the key to happiness.

Now, while tapping in the center of the chest, repeat these phrases.

- Forgiveness is the key to happiness. (Say twice.)
- There is forgiveness in my heart for myself and for him/her. (Say twice, usually using the person's name.)
- There is love in my heart for myself and for him/her (use their name). (Say twice.)
- Deep down, I am the Presence of Love. (Say twice.)
- I thank God or the Universe (choose one) that all my problems have been solved, and I am at peace.
- I thank God or the Universe (choose one) that I am at peace, and all my problems have been solved.
- I thank God or the Universe (choose one) that I am healed and at peace.
- I thank God or the Universe (choose one) that I am at peace and healed.
- I thank God or the Universe (choose one) that I am out of darkness and experiencing light.

Now put your hand on your heart and close your eyes. Then say silently and slowly to yourself:

- I am grateful for all the experiences in my life in the last week, the last month, the last three months, the last six months, and the last year. (Say three times and reflect on those experiences.)
- I am at peace. (Say two times, slowly.)
- I am calm, relaxed, and at peace. (Say two times, slowly.)

Take three more slow, deep breaths. Gradually, very gradually, open your eyes and bring your consciousness back into the room.

Give yourself a SUDs number. If it isn't down to 1, repeat the PPPT-L5 from the beginning. If you are having difficulty, read the troubleshooting section that follows PPPT-L4 (see p. 115).

In your journal, write about your experience using this Positive Pressure Point Technique.

APRIL'S RESPONSE

I also had some unresolved feelings toward my ex-boyfriend, Donald, who was my first love. In many ways, he taught me how to love. I was very puzzled, angry, and hurt when he broke up with me unexpectedly. Although I stayed in contact with him, it was not that long after that when he died in a motorcycle accident. The accident was one year earlier and just one year after my father died. Needless to say, two deaths in two years, of males I loved, generated a lot of sadness and grief. I wanted to focus on Donald's funeral and all the feelings I had at that time. We did PPPT Levels 4 and 5 on my hurt, sadness, grief, and anger while at the funeral. Within a short time, I felt much calmer, relaxed, and at peace with myself and my ex-boyfriend.

Positive Pressure Point Technique Level 6: Pressure Points, Tapping, Holding, and Breathing and Reporting on Internal Experiences with No Affirmations (PPPT-L6)

Level 6 uses both the tapping and the holding and breathing method on the pressure points used in Level 3, but it differs from Level 3 in that it allows you to report on your internal experiences and assess whether each intervention increases, decreases, or creates no change in your distress level.

First follow steps 1–7 from Positive Pressure Point Technique Level 1, p. 101.

Step 8   Place two fingers in the center of the forehead for five seconds. Ask yourself: does this make the emotional distress better, worse, or is it the same? (Just tell the truth to yourself.) Then tap on the center of your forehead for fifteen to twenty seconds with the same two fingers and ask yourself: does this make the emotional distress better, worse, or is it the same? Then hold two fingers in the center of the forehead and take two slow, deep breaths. Ask yourself: does this make the emotional distress better, worse, or is it the same? Then notice what thoughts, feelings, images, and body sensations are coming up for you. (If none, notice that also.) Finally, give yourself a SUDs number from 1 to 10.

Step 9 Do the same thing for each of the seven other pressure points (see below); that is, first hold the pressure point for five seconds, then tap on the pressure point for fifteen to twenty seconds, and finally, hold your fingers on the pressure point or points and take two slow, deep breaths. After each one of these processes, ask yourself: does this make the emotional distress better, worse, or is it the same? Then notice what thoughts, feelings, images, and body sensations are coming up for you. (If none, notice that also.) Finally, give yourself a SUDs number from 1 to 10.

1. Center of the forehead (figure 3). Use one hand and two fingers.
2. Inside corner of the eyebrows, just below the eyebrow (figure 4). Using two fingers of both hands is preferable.
3. Just outside the side of the eye (figure 5). Using two fingers of both hands is preferable.
4. Under the eye on the bony part of the eye in the center (figure 6). Using two fingers of both hands is preferable.
5. Above the lip (figure 7). Using two fingers of one hand is preferable on this pressure point.
6. Below the lip and above the chin (figure 8). Using two fingers of one hand is preferable on this pressure point.
7. Behind the neck (figures 9a and 9b). First put one hand on the back of your neck and one hand on your forehead. Then, when tapping behind the neck, use all the fingers of both hands. Tap up, down, and all around thirty-five times on the back of the neck points, as this area is especially beneficial. Make sure when tapping on the back of the neck to go down the center, up, and around while covering all the muscles, arteries, and veins in the back of the neck. Then put one hand on the back of your

neck and one hand on your forehead again when you hold and breathe.

8. The collarbone-chest area (figure 10). Using two or more fingers of both hands is preferable on these pressure points.

In most cases, the SUDs will come down to 1 after one round. If they do not, repeat the steps above or use the troubleshooting examples at the end of the previous chapter.

Write about your experiences in your journal.

Positive Pressure Point Technique Level 7: Use of Pressure Points and Extensive Imagery (PPPT-L7)

Level 7 begins with the same seven steps used in Level 1, with step 5 omitted. See p. 101.

Step 7   Hold one hand on your heart and say slowly, preferably with your eyes closed.

1. I have a problem. The problem is_____ (be brief and specific in terms of your feelings and/or beliefs; for example, anger, resentment, guilt, sadness, grievance, judgment, fear, anxiety, shame, etc.).
2. The problem can change.
3. There is a solution to the problem. The solution is inherent within the problem.
4. I want the problem to change. I want _____(describe briefly exactly what you want to experience; that is, the opposite of the problem described at number 1; for example, peace, love, joy, contentment, happiness, etc.).
5. I choose to find a solution to the problem.

Tap ten times *each* on the top of your head (see diagram 4 below), in the center of your forehead, on the inside corner of both your eyebrows, under your eyes, above your lip, below your lip, and on your two collarbone points. (See the earlier figures in chapter 9 if needed.)

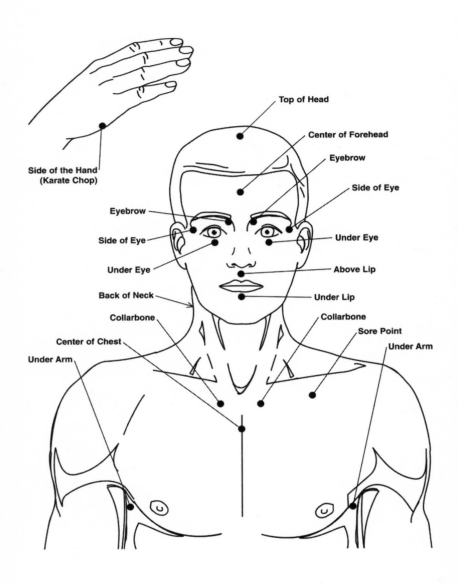

Diagram 4

Keep your eyes closed and find a picture or image that represents in some way the problem-solution template. Allow the image or picture of the <u>solution</u> to just bubble up in your awareness. Describe the image. Change the image in some way so it is enhanced and even more positive. Describe the changed image.

Give yourself a SUDs number from 1 to 10.

If the SUDs number has not dropped to 1, repeat the seven steps above until it does.

In your journal, write about your experiences.

Positive Pressure Point Technique Level 8: Use of Pressure Points, Holding, and Unforgiveness and Forgiveness Affirmations (PPPT-L8)

This technique was inspired by Tapas Fleming's excellent Tapas Acupressure Technique or TAT.[2] It was previously called the ACT technique.[3]

Figure 14

This technique is usually done by placing the palm of one hand on your heart and the palm of the other hand on your solar plexus/stomach area (ACT holdings; see figure 14).

You can use other hand positions as well, such as the top of the head, the back of the head, the back of the neck, and the forehead. Most of the time, though, placing the palm of one hand on your heart and the other on your solar plexus/stomach area works very well.

1 Think of an area of unforgiveness toward yourself, someone else, or some circumstance and your feelings about it. Give yourself a SUDs number from 1 to 10. Put your attention on the unforgiveness problem (grievance, judgment, anger, resentment, guilt, sadness, fear, etc.) and do the ACT holdings. Hold that position for two minutes while contemplating the problem. Notice what thoughts, feelings, images, and body sensations come up.

2 Put your attention on the opposite condition (what you would consider opposite to that unforgiveness problem) and do the ACT holdings; that is, focus on a positive condition or experience you would have if the problem were resolved (for example, peace and contentment). Do the ACT holdings for one to two minutes while contemplating the opposite condition. Notice what thoughts, feelings, images, and body sensations come up.

3 Do the ACT holdings and repeat slowly to yourself for one to two minutes: *"God (or Universe, whichever word you like), thank you for healing all the roots and causes (known and unknown) of this unforgiveness problem."* Notice what thoughts, feelings, images, and body sensations come up.

4 Do the ACT holdings and repeat slowly to yourself for one to two minutes: *"God (or Universe), thank you for healing all ego-based thoughts, feelings, judgments, and separation connected to this unforgiveness problem."* Notice what thoughts, feelings, images, and body sensations come up.

5 Do the ACT holdings and repeat slowly to yourself for one to two minutes: *"God (or Universe), thank you for removing all the darkness related to this distress and unforgiveness and bringing in the light."* Notice what thoughts, feelings, images, and body sensations come up.

6 Do the ACT holdings and repeat slowly to yourself for one to two minutes: *"God (or Universe), thank you for helping me forgive everyone I held a grudge, grievance, or attack thought against re-*

lated to this problem, including God, my family, my friends, and my-self." Notice what thoughts, feelings, images, and body sensations come up.

7 Do the ACT holdings and repeat slowly to yourself for one to two minutes: *"God (or Universe), thank you for helping me forgive myself for every grudge, grievance, or self-attack thought I held against myself because of this problem."* Notice what thoughts, feelings, images, and body sensations come up.

8 Do the ACT holdings and repeat slowly to yourself for one to two minutes: *"I thank God (or the Universe) that I am healed and I am at peace."* Notice what thoughts, feelings, images, and body sensations come up.

9 Do the ACT holdings and repeat slowly to yourself for one to two minutes: *"I thank God (or the Universe) this unforgiveness problem has been solved and I am at peace."* Notice what thoughts, feelings, images, and body sensations come up.

10 Do the ACT holdings and repeat slowly to yourself for one to two minutes: *"I thank God (or the Universe) for everything I have to be grateful for in the past three, six, and twelve months."* (Focus on each time period separately.)

Give yourself a SUDs number from 1 to 10. Most of the time the SUDs number will be down to 1. If it isn't, repeat the ten steps above.

In your journal, write about your experiences.

APRIL'S RESPONSE

My mother had left my father and [me] when I was just five years old. I felt criticized and put down during those early years and still felt a lot of hurt and abandonment. In addition, my self-worth was quite shaken by these events at an early age. Although my relationship with my mother had improved over the years, I still felt a lot of hurt, confusion, anger, self-judgment, and self-blame. I also had a lot of hurt, frustration, disappointment, and anger at my uncle, who was very critical of me after my father's death. We used levels 6 and 7 of the Positive Pressure Point Technique on these, and my SUDs level decreased from a 7 to a 1 on my feelings around my mother and 9 to 1 on my feelings toward my uncle. Overall, I was much more relaxed and at peace, especially toward my mother. In the process, we worked on my negativity toward myself using PPPT Level 8. My SUDs level decreased from 7 to 1, and I felt a lot more self-confident.

See figures 15 and 16 below for typical pictures of before (distressed) and after (happy) doing the PPPT.

Figure 15 **Figure 16**

These two chapters on the Positive Pressure Point Techniques have introduced you to a very powerful set of energetic forgiveness tools that can greatly, and often rapidly, facilitate change for you. For some people, it will be necessary to use these tools on a variety of emotional issues relating to unforgiveness and attack thoughts.

For some people, it will also be necessary to use the troubleshooting examples to help you make the techniques work. However, for many of you, these techniques, either alone or in combination, will work dramatically when applied correctly. If you have tried them yourself a number of times and are having difficulty making them work for you, I would encourage you to locate a trained therapist, coach, facilitator, or group trained in these or related techniques to help you with them.

CHAPTER 11

Four Powerful Forgiveness Imagery Techniques

"Forgiveness is not something you do for someone else, but to free YOURSELF from the continuation of pain and anger. It is a gift to your peace of mind, your self-esteem, your relationships with others, your future."
—KENNETH CLOKE and JOAN GOLDSMITH,
Resolving Personal and Organizational Conflict

"Pray for forgiveness and an open heart."
—SONIA CHOQUETTE, *Your Heart's Desire*

"The inability to forgive comes from judgment. If one cannot forgive, it is usually themselves that they cannot forgive. They 'should' have known better. They 'should' have done better. They 'shouldn't' have allowed this or that to happen or not to happen, and so on. When one forgives themselves, they are then able to forgive another, and not before then. So how do you forgive yourself? Forgiveness starts with compassion."
—Holy Spirit's Online Message through DAVIDPAUL
and CANDACE DOYLE, 2008

As you will soon read, when Jane first came to see me, she was very troubled and traumatized and had been for some time. Her personal problems were affecting her relationship with her parents, her husband, and herself, and she was quite distressed. When I last spoke to Jane, two years after therapy ended, she was the very proud mother of two beautiful children. (When she entered therapy, she had no children.) She had changed jobs, had high self-esteem, and was doing extremely well in her new position. Her relationship with her parents and spouse had improved dramatically. Here is Jane's story in her own words:

There was a time when my life as an educated twenty-something with a promising job, supportive family, and limitless future appeared perfect to others. Sadly, my view from the inside was not nearly as ideal as many would have thought. My emotional well-being was spiraling downward as I struggled to come to peace and ultimately forgive myself and the individual who drugged and raped me.

In the months following my rape, I struggled to trust others. I feared being alone in my home and in the presence of strangers. I often lacked the self-confidence to make even the simplest, nonconsequential decisions. After suffering with feelings of anger, self-doubt, and anxiety, I turned to therapy to help me gain more control over my life.

Simple, yet powerful, therapy techniques proved beneficial to improving my emotional well-being. By appropriately naming the feelings I was experiencing, I was able to identify and confront the negativity. Deep breathing techniques that focused on allowing the positive white light to permeate my soul and push away the negative dark light helped to cleanse and invigorate my spirit. Empowering self-talk and positive-thinking exercises reinforced the concept that I had the inner strength to again become the person left behind after being raped. Practicing these techniques changed my life.

I forgave the person who raped me, not only for the crime he committed but also for the emotional devastation it inflicted. Most importantly, I forgave myself for the self-blame and disappointment I felt for so long. Therapy enabled me to harness the power within and evolve from viewing myself as a victim to becoming a self-confident and capable survivor whose wounds have healed.

Forgiveness Imagery Exercises

The four forgiveness imagery exercises below are very powerful. You may discover, like many of my clients, that you are able to make significant shifts in your ability to forgive from these exercises alone. You most likely will find them very relaxing, peaceful, healing, and uplifting. They will also help you connect with a deeper, more profound part of your self, a part often referred to as the inner light or inner Self.

These imagery exercises can be done alone or with another person reading them to you, such as a friend, peer, spouse, coach, therapist, or colleague. If you do them alone, either read them through a few times first or read them into a tape recorder or onto a CD. Many people will benefit from having soft, gentle music playing in the background. This will help you shift your consciousness so you are in a more relaxed and receptive mood. In addition, some people may benefit by *first* doing one or more of the energy forgiveness approaches in the previous chapters or by doing the Psychological Uplifter 2. In any case, like the previous exercises, the more you practice them, the more benefit you will receive from doing them. If you consistently do the forgiveness imagery exercises along with the energy exercises (i.e., the positive pressure point techniques), the affirmations, the Psychological Uplifter, and journaling, you will get the maximum benefit from this book.

Remember that forgiveness is a process that unfolds over time. Practice it on everything and everyone. Life will no doubt present you with many opportunities to practice forgiveness, so be patient yet persistent with yourself. Ultimately, the goal of forgiveness is to release the barriers between you and your true or divine Self and to dissolve the roadblocks or veil that separates you from others. It will also bring you greater peace, love, joy, happiness, gratitude, wisdom, harmony in your relationships, and blessings in your life.

Exercise 1: Creating Well-Being Forgiveness Imagery Process[1]

A. FORGIVING ANOTHER

Part I Close your eyes. Breathe deeply. Relax. Allow your attention to focus on your breath. Continue to breathe slowly and deeply. Breathing in and out slowly and deeply, slowly and deeply. Concentrate on your breath as it rises and falls, slowly and deeply. Breathing in and out. Focusing on the breath. Now, silently to yourself, repeat the words "calm" on the in-breath and "relax" on the out-breath. "Calm" on the in-breath, "relax" on the out-breath. Breathing in "calm," breathing out "relax," slowly and deeply, "calm" and "relax," slowly and deeply, "calm" and "relax." Focusing on the breath, slowly and deeply, "calm" and "relax." Now ask the creative/Infinite Intelligence, the divine, Holy Spirit to help you with the forgiveness process.

Part II Now think of someone you dislike, actively despise, or hate; someone you are angry at; or just someone you are very ill at ease or uncomfortable with. Say to that person, "I forgive you. I forgive you for anything you may have done consciously or unconsciously, intentionally or unintentionally, that I believe has caused me pain or hurt. I forgive you for any thought, feeling, act, or deed that you have done. I forgive you." Allow your heart to open to this person you have judged, you have condemned. Open your mind to doubt.

Opening . . . softening . . . softening . . . opening . . . releasing. . . . Letting go. Now, continue to breathe in and out, slowly and deeply. Calm and relax, relax and calm. Opening, opening more. Softening, softening more; releasing, releasing more; letting go, letting go more. "I forgive you (mention that person's name). I forgive you for the hurt I perceive or I think you may have caused me. I am open to doubt.

Perhaps it was just a mistake, an error. I forgive you. I release you. I release me from the pain, the hurt, the fear, the sadness, the incredible anger. I let it go, now...opening, softening, softening, opening, releasing, letting go. Breathing slowly and deeply, deeply and slowly, I allow myself to see your innocence. I allow myself to feel your pain, your hurt. I allow myself to touch your heart and be touched by your heart." It is so hard to keep oneself out of another's heart. Feel your heart opening and touching this person's heart.

Opening, softening, touching, releasing, letting go. "I forgive you for anything you did that caused me hurt or pain. I see your innocence. I see your light. I see my innocence. I see your worth. I see my worth. I release you of all judgments I have made against you. I let go of all expectations I had for you. I release all judgments or expectations I have made against myself. I release the hurt, the pain, the anger, the fear, the darkness. I forgive you. I release you. I forgive me. I am at peace. I am at peace." Opening, softening, releasing, letting go. Breathing slowly and deeply. Calm and relaxed. Calm and relaxed. At peace. At peace.

B. ASKING FOR FORGIVENESS FROM ANOTHER

Part I   Repeat part 1 of exercise A above. Once again, ask the creative/Infinite Intelligence, the divine/Holy Spirit or energy to help you. Select a person from whom you want to ask forgiveness.

Part II   Say, "I ask your forgiveness for anything I may have done consciously or unconsciously, intentionally or unintentionally, that I believe has caused you hurt, pain, or suffering. I ask your forgiveness. I ask your forgiveness (fill in the person's name) for any thought, feeling, word, gesture, or behavior that I did or contemplated doing that I perceive injured you in any way. I ask your forgiveness for any condemnation, judgment, complaint, gossip, expectation, or deed I may have had or done that I think has caused you any distress or guilt or pain. I ask your forgiveness. Opening, letting go, letting go, releasing. I ask your forgiveness! I ask your forgiveness. I ask your forgiveness."

Breathing slowly and deeply, deeply and slowly. Calm and relax. Relax and calm. Now say, "I release any judgment or condemnation, any anger or attack thoughts I may have thought or said or written toward you. I release them. I let them go, and I ask your forgiveness." Softening, opening, releasing, letting go. "I allow my mind to open, to trust. I allow my heart to open to your heart. I allow myself to be touched by your heart. I allow myself to feel your compassion, your love." Opening, softening, releasing, letting go. "I ask your forgiveness. Touching your heart, feeling your compassion, experiencing your love." Opening, softening. Breathing, slowly and deeply, calm and relax. Calm and relax. Peace and love. Peace and love.

C. SELF-FORGIVENESS

Part I   Repeat part 1 of exercise A above. Once again, ask the creative/Infinite Intelligence, the divine/Holy Spirit or energy to help you forgive yourself.

Part II   Now, repeat to yourself: "I forgive me for anything I think I did consciously or unconsciously, intentionally or unintentionally, that caused me or anyone else hurt or pain." Say to yourself, "I forgive me (use your own name). I forgive myself for any feeling, attitude, or judgment I may have contemplated, held, or experienced that I perceive caused me or anyone else anger, guilt, sadness, or pain. I forgive me." Opening, softening, softening, opening. "I forgive me (use your name) for any condemnation, criticism, or attack thoughts that I used against myself or another to diminish, demoralize, or depress myself or another. I forgive me. I forgive me. I forgive me." Releasing, letting go, letting go, releasing. "I forgive me for any self-hatred, anger, or guilt that I used to devalue myself or undermine my self-worth or my self-respect. I forgive me. I forgive me for any thought, act, behavior, or deed that I believe hurt or injured or caused distress to anyone else or to myself. I forgive me."

Softening opening, opening, softening. Releasing all doubt, all judgment, all "shoulds," all negativity, all expectations. Letting go of all the pain, all the sorrow, all the hurt, all the fear, all the anger. "I for-give me and I accept me." Allow yourself to perceive your innocence. Allow yourself to see your essential worth. Allow yourself to experi-ence your inner light and love. Say, "I forgive me" to you. Allow your heart to open to you. Opening, softening, softening, opening. Allow yourself to feel compassion for you. Touch your hurt with your incred-ible compassion. Touch your heart with your kindness and under-standing. Opening, softening. Forgive yourself. Touch yourself. Love yourself. Allow yourself to be loved. Allow yourself to love yourself.

Feel the incredible love you have for yourself. Feel your innocence. Feel your worth. See your incredible light and inner beauty. Feel your love for you. Relax and calm. Love and peace. Allow yourself to love yourself. Deeply, unconditionally love yourself. Ask the creative/Infi-nite Intelligence, the divine/Holy Spirit or energy to help you to love yourself. Deeply. Profoundly. Unconditionally. Allow yourself to love yourself. Deeply, unconditionally love yourself. Say to yourself, "I love you. You are loved. I love you. You are loved. I love you." Be at peace.

Take five slow, deep breaths, open your eyes, and in your journal write about your experiences.

Exercise 2: Light Imagery Grateful Heart Technique (LIGHT)[2]

1 Imagine a bright white light, the light of your soul, entering you through the top of your head. This white light is infinitely intelligent, wise, compassionate, and loving. This white light of your soul comes down from above, through the top of your head, through your eyes and nose and cheeks and lips, right down into your neck and shoul-ders, and then enters your *heart*.

2 Let the white light of your soul, which is so infinitely intelligent, wise, compassionate, and loving, circulate through both chambers of your *heart*, the right and left chambers of your heart. Because the white light of your soul is so infinitely intelligent, wise, compassion-ate, and loving, it knows exactly what to do and where to go to bring peace, harmony, forgiveness, and balance to your entire body, mind, and spirit. It knows what to do and where to go to heal any hurt, anger, resentment, guilt, bitterness, and pain that you may be experiencing related to unforgiveness of yourself, someone else, or some unpleasant circumstance. Feel the white light within you now.

3 Let the white light of your soul, which is so infinitely intelligent, wise, compassionate, and loving, travel into every artery, vein, tissue, and cell of your body, even into the DNA in the cells. As it does, the white light brings even more peace, harmony, forgiveness, and balance to your entire body, mind, and spirit. Once again, the white light knows what to do and where to go to heal any hurt, anger, resentment, guilt, bitterness, and pain that you may be experiencing related to unforgiveness of yourself, someone else, or some unpleasant circumstance. Feel the white light within you now.

4 Count slowly from one to ten as the white light becomes stronger and stronger and stronger. Let it become stronger and stronger as it enters every particle of your Being, every artery, vein, tissue, and cell of your body, even into the DNA in the cells.

5 Put one hand over your heart. Imagine in your heart someone or something that you love very much. Feel the warmth and compassion. Feel the love in your heart. Sense your personal inner power. Release even more of the distress, unforgiveness, hurt, anger, guilt, pain, and negativity you are experiencing, while continuing to hold your hand over your heart.

6 Focus on all the experiences you have had in the last week that you are grateful for. Review them slowly one by one.

7 Focus on all the experiences in your life you have had in the last three months that you are grateful for. Review them one by one.

8 Focus on all the experiences that you have had in the last year that you are grateful for. Review them one by one.

9 Focus on all the experiences you have had in the last five years that you are grateful for. Review them one by one.

10 Focus on all the experiences in your entire life that you are grateful for. Review them one by one.

11 Allow a very wise, compassionate teacher or being of your own choosing to enter your heart. Let this wise, compassionate teacher within your heart speak to you about the challenging person or situation you have been experiencing that you have held out of your heart. Ask this wise inner teacher how you can see things differently regarding this person or situation and how you can also see this other person or situation surrounded by loving light. See this person or situation surrounded by loving light, embraced by light, and radiating light. Feel the compassion that comes up within you now.

12 Listen within to what your heart and your loving inner teacher wants for you today, tomorrow, next week, next month, etc., regarding this person or situation. What is he/she saying to you? Allow yourself to feel grateful for the guidance you are receiving. Know that you are always guided, guarded, protected, and loved by the white light and by this loving, wise, and compassionate teacher.

Take five slow, deep breaths, open your eyes, and in your journal write about what you experienced.

Exercise 3: White Light Self-Forgiveness Exercise[3]

Find a comfortable and relaxed position. Uncross your arms and legs and close your eyes. (You may use soft, gentle music with this exercise.) Take a long, deep breath and let it out slowly. Slowly and deeply. Allow your breathing to become full and deep and relaxed. Deeper and deeper, more and more relaxed.

1 Now count down slowly from ten to zero to deepen your relaxation even more. Count down slowly and breathe deeply. As you allow your ego-mind to relax, you will become more and more receptive to the wisdom of your Higher Self and its profound healing power. You can begin counting now: 10...9...8...deeper and deeper, 7...6...5 ...calmer and calmer, 4...3...2...more and more relaxed, 1...0. You are now very, very deeply relaxed. Very calm and deeply relaxed.

2 Focus your awareness high above the top of your head. Imagine a brilliant, white, radiant light flowing down toward you from way above your head. As this brilliant, white, radiant light reaches you, imagine the energy of this brilliant, white light entering you, flowing all around you and through you, filling every particle of your body and mind. Imagine it entering every artery, vein, tissue, and cell of your body. Imagine yourself surrounded, protected, guided, and immersed in this brilliant, soft, and loving white light. This white light is infinitely wise, compassionate, and loving.

3 With each breath, inhale this light even more. Sense it gently and deeply permeating your entire being, as it enters every tissue, vein, artery, and cell of your body. Allow your awareness to focus this wise and loving white light in the middle of your heart. Breathe slowly and deeply. Slowly and deeply. Allow your heart to fill with infinite love and compassion; with light, softness, warmth, and kindness. Now visualize yourself out in front of you, as though you were seated in front of yourself. See yourself as clearly as possible, as though you were looking in a mirror or at a photograph.

4 Become aware of what you need to forgive in yourself, of all the things that keep you from self-love: your grievances, grudges, and judgments against yourself; your hurts, guilt, fears, and pains. Notice the criticisms that come up as you observe yourself. (Be gentle with yourself.) Notice where you are judging yourself. Notice how you judge and criticize your flaws and mistakes; how you judge the things you feel guilty, embarrassed, and ashamed about; how you criticize your failure to live up to your own high expectations. Take time for this part of the exercise so you have the opportunity to get in touch with all the places where you hold unforgiveness and resentments toward yourself.

5   Now take a moment to contemplate your beliefs. What does it mean that you have these shortcomings, these limitations, these grievances and judgments and criticisms against yourself? Now, connect with the energy of compassion, love, and forgiveness. Know that what you have done was through your own hurt, your own pain, your unawareness, or your limitations. Know that the judgment and criticism only serve to reinforce the limitations and shortcomings. You can choose to support your personal and spiritual growth and healing now through compassion, forgiveness, love, and acceptance.

6   Send the brilliant, loving, white light of compassion and your Higher Self's love out from your heart across to the picture of yourself in front of you. See the energy of compassion, forgiveness, and love entering your heart. See yourself receiving that love and compassion and taking it in. Feel and see this light of love flowing through you and out to the other you, entering your heart, and being fully and completely received. Allow yourself to forgive yourself. Feel the energy of forgiveness and love deep within you. Allow the love, forgiveness, and compassion to heal the hurt, the pain, and the emotional wounds of your heart.

7   Now switch roles and become the other you, the one who is being forgiven. From this position, feel the forgiveness and light entering your heart. Feel the gentle healing power of this love and forgiveness, and allow yourself to feel innocent and blessed. Allow this light and love to pour through you, through your whole body. Allow this light of love to pour through you, cleansing you, healing you, releasing you, and blessing you. Allow this forgiveness, light, compassion, and love to enter every artery, vein, tissue, and cell of your body, right down into the DNA. Feel the love, forgiveness, and compassion deeply within you. Know that you are blessed and that this light goes with you wherever you go.

8 And now, keeping your eyes closed, focus this light in your hands. Very gently lift your hands up in front of you about twelve inches apart with the palms facing each other. Relax your hands and fingers. Move your hands toward each other until you can feel the energy between your two palms. Feel this energy of healing, love, light, and forgiveness as something very real.

9 Keeping your eyes closed, bring your right hand up so the right palm is on your forehead and the palm of your left hand is on the back of your head. Feel the healing energy of love, light, and compassion entering you even more deeply. Slowly and deeply. Then gently move the palm of the left hand back behind your neck while the palm of the right hand stays on your forehead. Again feel the healing energy of love, light, and compassion even more deeply and profoundly. Then move the palm of your right hand from your forehead and put it on your heart while the palm of your left hand stays behind your neck. Again feel the warmth, the love, light, and compassion of the healing energy deeply within you. Finally, move the palm of your left hand on top of the palm of your right hand, which is on your heart. Allow all of the warmth, love, light, and compassion of the healing energy to permeate your heart. Let this healing energy flow throughout your entire body. Now breathe slowly and deeply... slowly and deeply... slowly and deeply.

10 As you sense this energy of compassion, healing, love, light, and forgiveness, know that you have the power to create profound peace and joy within your own heart, within your relationships, and within all of life. Know that you are loved and blessed. Because all minds are joined, know that you are contributing as well to the healing of the planet. Know that this energy surrounds you, guides you, loves you, and protects you and is always working for your highest good as well as the highest good of the universe.

11 Imagine that your heart is at the center of the spokes on a wheel. Imagine that the loving light in your heart goes from that center, down the spokes, and out into the hearts of everybody you know and into the hearts of everyone who is distressed in any way and needs healing. Then imagine an explosion of light and love enters the heart of all these people, bringing healing and compassion to all of them. Then imagine the light is automatically sent back from the hearts of all these people to your heart, and you experience a tremendous explosion of light and love within you.

12 Take a little time now to stay in this deep state of healing, love, light, compassion, and forgiveness, transmitting and receiving this powerful healing, light, and loving energy.

Now take five slow, deep breaths. Breathe slowly and deeply...deeply and slowly...slowly and deeply...deeply and slowly. Then slowly, very, very slowly, open your eyes, bringing your consciousness back into this room. Sense the sights and sounds around you. Bring with you the awareness, wisdom, peace, gratitude, and the blessing of this experience.

In your journal, write about your experiences.

Exercise 4: HEaling And Release Technique (HEART)[4]
Give yourself a rating from 1 to 100, with 100 being the most distressed you have ever been, 1 being the least, and 50 in the middle.

1 Close your eyes and take five slow, deep breaths, breathing in peace and breathing out release. Breathe in through your nose and out through your mouth, slowly, five times.

2 Put your right hand on your solar plexus (slightly above your stomach area), which is frequently the physical seat of many distressing and unforgiving attitudes and emotions.

3 Imagine a large garbage can inside your solar plexus and then imagine that you are dumping all your negative, upsetting, distressing, and unforgiving feelings into the large garbage can; that is, all your emotional garbage.

4 Imagine a strong cord attached to a large helium balloon lifting up the garbage can (with, of course, a strong lid on it), higher and higher into the air, farther and farther away from you. Imagine the helium balloon attached to the garbage can entering and moving through the clouds, through the stratosphere, the ionosphere, and way out into space.

5 Imagine the garbage can that is filled with anger, hurt, guilt, resentment, bitterness, disappointment, fear, etc., moving past the various planets, higher and higher into the air, farther and farther away from you, past the planets Venus and Mercury, and entering the orbit of the sun. Imagine the garbage can and the emotional garbage inside it being burnt up by the sun. Imagine the ashes dispersed in a million pieces throughout interstellar space.

6 Now take your right hand off your solar plexus and put your left hand on your heart. Imagine a bright white light, the light of your soul, entering you through the top of your head. This white light is infinitely intelligent, wise, compassionate, and loving. This white light, that is so infinitely intelligent, wise, compassionate, and loving, comes down from above, through the top of your head, through your eyes and nose and cheeks and lips, right down into your neck and shoulders, and then enters your heart.

7 Let the white light of your soul, which is so infinitely intelligent, wise, compassionate, loving, and healing, circulate through both chambers of your heart, that is, the right and left chambers of your heart. Since the white light of your soul is so infinitely intelligent, wise, compassionate, and loving, it knows exactly what to do and where to go to bring peace, harmony, and balance to your entire body, mind, and spirit. It also knows how to dissolve any unforgiveness that you are still harboring.

8 Let the white light of your soul, which is so infinitely intelligent, wise, compassionate, loving, and healing, travel into every artery, vein, tissue, and cell of your body, even into the DNA in the cells. As it does, the white light brings even more peace, harmony, forgiveness, and balance to your entire body, mind, and spirit.

9 Count slowly from one to ten as the white light becomes stronger and stronger and stronger.

10 Release your left hand briefly and then put your right hand on your solar plexus and your left hand on your heart, at the same time. Hold them there together for a slow count of ten. When both hands are placed together on the heart, and solar plexus, the light energy in the heart dispels and collapses the dark energy in the solar plexus, and the positive feelings dissolve and collapse the negative feelings and any unforgiving belief structures remaining. Let this process become stronger and stronger as you count from one to ten.

11 Release your right hand on the solar plexus (take it off). Keeping your left hand on your heart, visualize the light in your heart, circulating around both chambers of your heart again. Remember, it is infinitely intelligent, wise, compassionate, loving, forgiving, and healing and travels into every artery, vein, tissue, and cell of your body, even into the DNA in the cells. Count from one to ten again as the light brings peace, harmony, forgiveness, and balance to your entire Being.

12 Take three slow, deep breaths and open your eyes.

Give yourself another rating from 1 to 100, with 100 being the most distressed you have ever been, 1 being the least distressed, and 50 in the middle. If the rating is not down to 1 or close to it, repeat the whole heart process again.

In your journal, write about your experiences.

APRIL'S RESPONSE

This exercise helped me feel like any negative feelings were like a weight lifted off my shoulders. It quickly brings down any level of distress. It is a very relaxing technique.

These forgiveness imagery exercises have the capacity to not only help you deeply relax but also to help you shift perceptions, change your attitudes, and reconnect you with your core Self, your inner light or soul. Consequently, they work to harmonize and balance the mental, emotional, and spiritual levels of your Being. You may find yourself connecting with a place of deeper inner wisdom within yourself as well. In addition, you may find it much easier to heal your relationship struggles after practicing these processes, along with the energy exercises and the affirmations and afformations in previous chapters.

CHAPTER 12

Practicing Forgiveness in Relationship Conflicts

"Forgive your brother, that you may love him again in the joy and happiness of the Heart, and in your dance with him, you will find what righteousness is. . . . Let go of all your grievances against your brother, no matter how large or small they seem. For they are all the same, and each one has the power to keep you imprisoned from your Self. . . . Your goal now is freedom, . . . For the hellish thoughts within your mind are your prison, and only by letting them go can you be free."

—REGINA DAWN AKERS, *The Holy Spirit's Interpretation of the New Testament*

"If we pursue forgiveness, we will almost certainly not only change ourselves, but will also uncover new virtue. We will discover courage within us as we forgive even though we have been hurt. We will find altruism, mercy, and grace as we act with humility, gratitude, contrition, and love. . . . If we forgive with a pure heart, we will find the treasures we sought first—health, happiness, peace, and harmony. But the surprising treasure—the virtue that we hadn't set out to find—is the priceless gift of blessing another person through the power of forgiving."

—EVERETT WORTHINGTON, Jr., *The Power of Forgiving*

ONE OF THE MORE challenging times for practicing forgiveness occurs when one person in a close intimate relationship (married or unmarried) has been involved in another intimate relationship or affair, briefly or over a period of time. Usually, when the person not involved in the affair finds out about it, they report feeling betrayed and experiencing intense anger, hurt, frustration, disappointment, fear, distrust, and, quite often, rage, depression, and guilt. They most often blame and judge their partner and frequently blame and judge themselves. Many times, these affairs are with someone at work. Though many people would say these actions are unforgivable, it is possible to forgive and heal what is sometimes perceived as unforgivable.

Alex was a forty-five-year-old married superintendent of schools, with two children and one grandchild, when he became involved emotionally and sexually with his recently divorced and much younger secretary. His wife Jennifer, a forty-two-year-old schoolteacher, suspected something was wrong because after twenty-five years of marriage, her husband showed little interest in her sexually and was less affectionate than he had been. She thought he was depressed and going through a midlife crisis.

When she asked him if he was having an affair, he vehemently denied it. Frequent trips to the shore and stays at fancy hotels did not reassure her. Twice, he snuck off to be with his girlfriend on a yacht owned by a friend of his, while his wife was shopping for the day.

Eventually, his wife couldn't stand his denials any longer and hired a private detective, who quickly discovered what was going on between Alex and the secretary, and where and when they had their rendezvous. When Jennifer confronted Alex, he was remorseful and then extremely guilty. Jennifer, of course, was very hurt, frustrated, angry, and felt betrayed. Her sense of betrayal came not only from his having an affair with a much younger woman but also from the lies he told. In addition, Alex's children, who soon found out about it, felt betrayed and deeply disappointed in their father.

As it turns out, the relationship between Alex and Jennifer had been deteriorating for some time. The frequency and quality of their communication was ineffectual. They had been harboring resentments and grievances against each other for many years. None of the feeble attempts they had made to discuss the issues were successful. During the course of therapy, using the techniques presented in this book, Alex learned to forgive himself, to forgive his wife, to ask forgiveness from his children and wife, and to communicate more effectively. Jennifer, in turn, learned to forgive her husband for his affair and for denying it and to forgive herself for not confronting their marital problems a lot sooner. Alex broke off the affair. Gradually, over a number of months, Alex and Jennifer learned to forgive, to communicate more effectively, to start spending more quality time together, and to enjoy sex again. It took quite a while before Jennifer began to trust her husband and feel certain that Alex did not have any extracurricular contact with his secretary. A few months later, he transferred to another school district.

Alex also had to work on forgiving his father, whose perfectionism generated a lot of guilt in Alex, and that guilt impacted the way he communicated with his wife. As the forgiveness, communication, and trust grew, Alex and Jennifer's relationship became stronger and stronger. In addition, Alex's relationship with his children improved dramatically. Two years later, Alex and Jennifer report that they are happier than they have been since they married.

The following exercise is designed to facilitate inner and outer relationship healing through forgiveness.

Empty Chair Exercise[1]

This forgiveness process, graciously given to me by Martha Crampton, may be conducted alone, with a partner, friend, or with a therapist. It is best done with a facilitator. The intent is to bring healing to your relationship with a parent, sibling, extended family member, or significant other or, more precisely, to heal your relationship with the "inner significant other" that you carry in your own psyche. It would be a good idea to allow about thirty minutes to an hour for this process, though you may be able to do it in less time.

Create a peaceful space for your meeting with a significant person. Do this through your intention to bring healing and by calling upon the personal and spiritual resources that are available to you.

Place an empty chair facing you. "Invite" your significant person to join you. Imagine this person in the empty seat.

1 Tell this significant person about your unresolved feelings. This may include feelings such as pain, resentment, rage, anger, fear, disappointment, guilt, hurt, or unexpressed love. Tell this significant person what they did or didn't do that hurt you. Tell them how you felt about it. Try to avoid blaming statements, speaking instead in the first person about your own feelings and experience. If you express angry or hostile feelings, make sure that you also express the more vulnerable feelings underneath these.

Tell your significant person how your response to their behavior has emotionally and behaviorally affected your life. Acknowledge with the wisdom you now have today how your own patterns of behavior may have contributed to what happened in that relationship.

Tell them how you wanted them to be your ideal of the perfect significant person you wish they could have been. Tell them what your expectations were for how you wanted them to behave and how you wanted them to relate to you.

Make sure that you have expressed everything you wish to express at this time.

2 Change seats and, in your imagination, become the significant person. Don't be limited by the way you think they would respond in real life. Reach past their defensive part and try to connect with their inner essence, the part that would want to know the truth. As this significant person, receive what you have just been told. Let it in. Reflect back the facts and the feelings that you heard yourself express. Say how you feel about it.

Using your intuition, sense what it was like from their point of view. Feel how it was to be this significant person—how they felt about themselves and about their life. If you know or can sense it, move through the years of their life, beginning with their childhood on up to their adult years. As the significant person (sitting in their chair), tell yourself what your own life was like and what caused you to be the way you were when you were growing up. As the significant person, communicate anything further you wish to communicate to yourself.

3 Switch seats and take your own role again. Take a moment in silence to let in what the significant person communicated to you. Clarify for yourself what else you wish to communicate to them. Tell them how you feel now and what you wanted from them. See if you are ready to cancel your expectations/demands of this person. If so, tell them so, and tell them what you would have preferred from them. (In other words, see if you are ready to upgrade from expectations and demands to preferences. See if you are ready to release the "shoulds," such as, "you should have done X or you shouldn't have done Y.") Be honest with yourself and them. Once again, make sure that you have expressed everything you wish to express at this time.

4 Then switch chairs again and become this significant person. Speak to yourself, telling yourself how you now feel and how you wish you had been able to behave and relate at that earlier time. If, and only if, you feel like apologizing, do so. Express whatever positive feelings and intentions you now have to yourself. Be honest.

5 Switch seats again and be yourself. (You may need to go back and forth a few more times. It varies from person to person and relationship to relationship.) If you feel ready, release this significant person from your demands and expectations that they be what they could not be. Allow yourself to realize that you can prefer that they were a certain way without expecting it of them. See if you are ready to accept them as they are, as a fellow human being with their own life journey, their own struggles, their own pain and hurts, and their own strengths and limitations. Affirm your choice to take charge of your own life and to use your free will to create the life that you want from now on. If anything further needs to be communicated, let this happen now.

In your journal, write about your experiences.

APRIL'S RESPONSE

This really made me feel that, for the first time, I was able to say everything I've ever wanted to since my uncle hurt me. It helped me release a lot of feelings and thoughts that have been sitting inside of me.

Exercise: Violet Transmuting Flame Imagery

Imagery of the violet flame has been used for many years to transmute the negative energy of anger, resentment, blame, and attack thoughts. It is said to contain the energy of forgiveness, compassion, and kindness instead. Each of the seven rays has a defined quality of consciousness, in addition to a certain color and frequency of vibration. So when you call upon it and the violet flame in the name of the Higher or Divine Self, it comes down as a beam of healing and loving energy.

Saint Germaine is often referred to as the master of the seventh ray. It is said that each time you call upon St. Germaine, he brings you many healing opportunities. In any case, whether or not you call upon St. Germaine, using the imagery of the violet flame can have a powerful healing effect by greatly facilitating forgiveness, compassion, and kindness. Unlike some other approaches, the violet flame does not simply surround and remove emotional garbage, pain, and debris; it transforms it into pure light energy. In other words, the violet flame transmutes the dark, negative energy into light, positive energy, purifying it in the process.

1 Close your eyes and take some slow, deep breaths. Breathe slowly and deeply. Slowly and deeply. Now focus on your heart. You might even want to put one hand on your heart to help you focus.

2 Think of a relationship or situation that troubles you—where there is unforgiveness in your heart; think of the anger, hurt, resentment, guilt, disappointment, grudges, grievances, judgments you hold toward this person, situation, or yourself.

3 Think of an image of a violet flame getting stronger and stronger, entering your heart and surrounding and enveloping the dark, negative energy you are experiencing (the anger, hurt, resentment, guilt, disappointment, grudges, grievances, judgments).

4 Ask that the violet flame of forgiveness, compassion, and kindness dissolve and transmute the dark, negative energy you have been experiencing. (If you are so inclined, you can call upon angels, guides, archangels, spiritual masters, Infinite Intelligence, or St. Germaine to help you.) See the violet flame burning up the dark, negative energy and transmuting it into light, positive energy.

5 Ask that the violet flame be sent out to the hearts of everyone else involved in this difficulty, problem, challenge, or circumstance. Ask that the violet flame be sent to everyone you haven't forgiven and everyone you have blamed, judged, or done wrong in some way. Also ask that the violet flame be sent to everyone you believe has not forgiven you and everyone you think has blamed, judged, or done you wrong in some way. Then ask that the violet flame dissolve and transmute their dark, negative energy.

6 See the violet flame extending from your heart to the heart of all the other people involved in this difficulty, problem, challenge, or circumstance. As the violet flame enters their heart, imagine that there is an explosion of light, compassion, healing, and love in their heart. Imagine that the violet flame circulates throughout their body and mind and enters into every artery, vein, tissue, and cell of their body. Imagine that the violet flame that has circulated throughout their body reenters their heart and is then sent back to your heart, where an even greater explosion of light, love, compassion, and healing takes place. Imagine that as this process takes place, the negative energy in both of you or all of you is dissolved and transmuted into positive energy.

7 Ask that the violet flame imagery process is for the highest good and highest healing for yourself and for all parties involved and for the highest good of the universe.

8 Take three slow, deep breaths. Breathe slowly and deeply... deeply and slowly... slowly and deeply... deeply and slowly. Remind yourself to practice the violet flame imagery exercise frequently. (It can be done alone or along with other energy or transformational forgiveness exercises.) Take two more slow, deep breaths and then slowly, very slowly and gently, open your eyes.

In your journal, write about your experiences. Practice repeating the following two phrases frequently throughout the day. You can repeat it silently to yourself and/or out loud.

- I am the violet flame (repeat five times).
- I am the perfection of the violet flame manifesting in action (repeat five times).

APRIL'S RESPONSE

The violet flame exercise helps me slowly process all of the negative things I'm feeling and release them so I can create a more positive way of thinking. It brings a deep sense of peace to an unpleasant situation. It made me feel as though there was nothing wrong to begin with.

Ho'oponopono Forgiveness Exercise

Ho'oponopono is a Hawaiian healing process that stems from the meaning of the word. Ho'oponopono means "to set things right" or, in more simple terms, to fix what is. Although the process is simple, its use can be very powerful. However, the Ho'oponopono process requires that you accept certain basic beliefs and assumptions—challenging for many people. The core belief is that basically everything that you experience in your life comes from within you rather than outside you. In other words, there is no "out there" and "in here." This is considered a basic truth in Ho'oponopono, *and the clear implication is that you are one with all things at all times.* You are simply an extension of "source energy or Infinite Intelligence." So, if you are made out of this source energy, this Infinite Intelligence, you are also the creator of your own existence. Therefore, *everything* you experience you have created. You are 100 percent completely responsible. This includes all of your emotional responses and also what you see, hear, feel, smell, taste, and touch.

This means, of course, that you created everything you consider or judge as good, as well as everything you consider or judge as bad. Each of these things exists because on some level, according to Ho'oponopono, you want them to exist. *If everything that you perceive in the world exists because you perceive it and want it at some level to exist, you are, of course, a very powerful person.*

Everything then becomes a play of consciousness, for which you wrote the script whether you were consciously aware of it or not. This requires that you accept total responsibility for everything that happens to you or that you experience in your life. Once you fully grasp the idea of total responsibility, then you will realize that you have the power to change everything you experience in your life, because you are responsible for it being there in the first place. You are probably wondering how to do this. Well, the simplest answer is to express gratitude for everything in your life that pleases you and that you want to grow and expand and to forgive all the things in your life that you want to decrease, dissolve, or eliminate. *That is, be thankful for the light-filled, positive experiences and forgive the dark, negative experiences.* Because you are the creator of all these experiences, who are you actually being grateful toward or forgiving? According to Ho'oponopono, yourself. If you created something that is wonderful, you are thanking yourself for doing so, thus ensuring future occurrences of that same positive behavior. If you created something terrible, then you are forgiving yourself for doing it, thus making sure that it doesn't happen again in the future.

Because you are responsible, according to this point of view, for everything in your experience, it means that you are responsible for terrorism, illness, abuse, dysfunctional family relationships, school shootings, hostage situations, high gas prices, economic recessions, financial problems, taxes, affairs, housing and credit crises, and emotional, marital, family, and relationship problems. You are also responsible for the beauty of a rose, the love of a parent for a child or of a mate for their spouse, healing miracles, technological breakthroughs, childbirth and children, close, warm friendships, pets and animals, joyful experiences, magnificent churches, temples, and mosques, heroic deeds, outstanding athletic accomplishments, and deep peace of mind. You are, then, incredibly powerful, according to this Hawaiian Ho'oponopono point of view. You can, in fact, dramatically influence your mind and your life and the lives of others in a positive way, according to Ho'oponopono, by repeating the following simple phrase, *"I am sorry; please forgive me; thank you; I love you,"* over and over again. In Ho'oponopono, this is referred to as "cleaning." As you can see this phrase, *"I am sorry; please forgive me; thank you; I love you,"* offers an apology, asks for forgiveness, and expresses gratitude and love. This simple phrase must be repeated with feeling, frequently throughout the day, in response to any and all situations or experiences that are in even the slightest way upsetting or disturbing.

By assuming that you are responsible for everything that happens and repeating the phrase, *"I am sorry; please forgive me; thank you; I love you,"* with feeling, anything is possible and miracles can and do happen.

Practice this Ho'oponopono exercise often. Practice it every hour on the hour. Practice it in the morning, at lunchtime, in the afternoon, and before bed. Practice it during the week and on weekends. Practice it alone, and practice it with the other forgiveness exercises you have learned. Repeat *"I am sorry; please forgive me; thank you; I love you"* over and over again, with feeling. Then watch and see what changes take place in your life and experience. (For more information, see the sections on Ho'oponopono on *www. todayisthatday.com,* and Joe Vitale's excellent book, *Zero Limits.*[2]) After you have practiced it, write about what you experienced in your journal.

APRIL'S RESPONSE

This exercise really helps in giving me a more positive perspective on different things that come up in my everyday life. The more I say it, the better I seem to feel about everything. It really gives me a chance to change my way of thinking about things.

Many of my clients find that this simple yet apparently healing phrase, *"I am sorry; please forgive me; thank you; I love you,"* is very comforting and helps them see and experience things very differently. Collectively, all three exercises can substantially catalyze a further significant shift in forgiveness and healing on many levels: mental, emotional, energetic, relational, and spiritual.

CHAPTER 13

Reconnecting with Your Inner Treasure

"When you forgive others, it is really you yourself who is being forgiven.... Forgiveness is an attitude. Everything you learn becomes incorporated into that attitude until forgiveness happens automatically. For most people, especially during the first few years, forgiveness requires that you think about it. You become a master by having forgiving thought processes. *These right-minded thoughts eventually dominate your mind instead of the ego.... The world will* never *live in peace until they have inner peace, the inevitable result of true forgiveness.... True peace will come from true forgiveness.... And violence... will* never *come as a result of the... Holy Spirit, who teaches only love and forgiveness.... Your job is to teach forgiveness.... To teach is to demonstrate."*
—GARY RENARD, *The Disappearance of the Universe*

"By revealing our oneness with another, forgiveness frees us of the painful belief in separateness.... Forgiveness lifts us into holy encounters, in which two people set aside what separates them and experience salvation together.... Forgiveness is genuinely interactive. As others receive the gift of our forgiveness, they are healed, and as they return the gift to us through their gratitude, we

are healed. . . . The true perception that is exchanged in these [holy] encounters is a way of seeing the other person that overlooks all that would make us recoil from him or her. This true perception, then, is simply another way of talking about forgiveness. Forgiveness is the active ingredient in holy encounters. When we think of forgiveness, the picture in our mind should be that of a holy encounter."

—ROBERT PERRY, *Return to the Heart of God*

CAROLYN WAS TWENTY-TWO, WITH a child from a previous relationship. She worked as a nursing intern at a local hospital and was dating a twenty-five-year-old, single pharmaceutical salesman, Sam, who was very much in love with her. Carolyn and Sam had been dating for seven months when he discovered that she had been having an affair for over a year with her married, male nursing supervisor. Sam was astonished because the supervisor was not very attractive, while Sam was quite good looking and very attentive to her, or so he thought.

When she became pregnant a few weeks later, it was not clear whose child it was. This complicated an already strained relationship. Sam had been insecure before this, from a difficult childhood and because his girlfriend in a previous relationship had left him for another man. Carolyn, in turn, had low self-esteem. She had been criticized a lot as a child and then hurt deeply when the father of her previous child unexpectedly left her. Even though her supervisor was not that attractive physically and was married, she looked up to him and admired his work skills. He was attentive to her and very affectionate. She also had difficulty saying no, so when he made sexual advances to her, she went along with him despite her ambivalent feelings.

Sam found out about the affair and was crushed. He loved Carolyn very much, and though he was tempted to break off the relationship, he didn't. He wanted her to leave work, but she couldn't because of a one-year contract she had signed and the need for the money and the job experience. Sam greatly distrusted Carolyn and continually feared that she would get intimately re-involved with her boss. He was at least as angry at the boss as at Carolyn and distrusted his intentions. Carolyn kept assuring Sam that she was having minimal contact with her boss now, but Sam had difficulty believing her. Carolyn felt extremely guilty and self-critical, as she genuinely cared about Sam and wanted to marry him but was depressed as a result of what she had done and Sam's reactions to it.

It took a number of months in therapy, seeing Sam and Carolyn individually and as a couple, to help them begin to resolve all these issues. They both had to work hard on letting go of self-judgments and judgments of each other. The forgiveness process for Sam and Carolyn evolved over time, using many of the energy and forgiveness processes described in this book. As a result of therapy, Sam and Carolyn became much less emotionally reactive to each other. They learned to communicate better and to support each other. As they forgave, they engaged in more constructive relationship repair efforts and talked in calmer, quieter tones. They became better listeners and expressed their needs more clearly and gently and learned to compromise.

Eventually, they moved in together. Carolyn was very affectionate to Sam all along but especially so after they were living together. As they forgave themselves and each other, the trust gradually returned. They both started feeling more secure personally and in the relationship. Carolyn completed her nursing internship and found a job at another hospital. When the baby was born, it turned out to be Sam's, as Carolyn had said it would be. Soon after that,

Sam and Carolyn got married, and two months later they bought a house. Sam achieved outstanding success and won an award at work. Three years later, they report that they are very happy and getting along well.

The next three exercises will help you deepen your ability to forgive and connect with a profound inner source of healing and well-being. Ultimately, the goal of forgiveness is not only to feel better and heal your relationships but to help you reconnect with your highest, most loving, peaceful, wise, creative, and joyful Self—your inner treasure. In turn, your best and highest Self naturally wants to give and receive love and even miracles.

Letter-Writing Exercise: Forgiving an Important Relationship
This exercise is similar to the empty chair exercise on forgiving an important relationship, except it uses writing instead of empty chairs.

1 Pick a person (parent, spouse, ex-spouse, lover or ex-lover, friend, teacher, colleague, boss, co-worker, neighbor child, etc.) against whom you are holding grudges, grievances, hurts, anger, resentment, bitterness, disappointment, guilt, fears, frustrations, etc.

2 Write a letter to this person (don't send it, though), expressing all your grudges, grievances, hurts, anger, resentment, bitterness, disappointment, guilt, fears, and frustrations. Use the person's name. Don't hold back expressing whatever feelings, thoughts, beliefs, attitudes you have been holding on to for days, weeks, months, and even years. Make sure you "get it all out."

3 Wait a day or so and then rewrite the letter without all the blame, judgments, and attack thoughts that existed in the previous letter. Use the person's name. Take responsibility for your own feelings. If you have a friend, spouse, colleague, or therapist who can give you gentle, constructive feedback with the first letter, that may be beneficial for some people and may help eliminate the blame, judgments, and attack thoughts from this second letter. (For some people, the first letter will be sufficient if it is minimally attacking and blaming.)

4 Imagine you have sent the letter (don't actually send it, though). Now pretend that you are the person receiving the letter. Become that person who has received the letter from you. Write a letter back to yourself, using your name, expressing all the thoughts, feelings, beliefs, and attitudes that you think the receiver would say to you after getting your letter. Don't hold back. Here is an opportunity to role-play, as best you can in writing, the other person whom you believe triggered your deep emotional distress.

5 Write another letter from the other person to you (use your name). This time write an *ideal letter* to yourself from the other person. Assume that your original letter to this person was a call for help and for love. In this return letter, have them write to you expressing whatever it is that you would ideally like to hear from them. In other words, whatever desires, wants, feelings you would ideally like to hear and receive from the other person, write it to yourself. Whatever expression of caring, kindness, thoughtfulness, understanding, compassion, etc., you would like to hear and receive from them, write it to yourself, using your name.

6 Imagine you have received the letter from this person, the *ideal letter.* Write yet another letter from yourself to the other person, expressing your thoughts, feelings, reactions after receiving their letter. See if you are willing to let go of the expectations, judgments, demands, grievances, and blame that you have previously thought and felt for them. See if you are willing to upgrade from demands, expectations, and judgments to preferences; this means see if you are willing to have *preferred* that the other person behaved and communicated to you in a certain way but no longer *expect* it. See if you are willing to forgive them. See if you can focus on the struggles the other person had in their life: their challenges, difficulties, problems, and fears. See if you can sense the essence of the other person beneath their unskillful behavior toward you. See if you can see that they were crying out for love and help, though in a disguised way.

In your journal, write a summary of what you experienced and learned from this letter-writing exercise.

APRIL'S FIRST SERIES OF LETTERS

Dear Grandmom,

I'm not sure where to start as I sit here and write this letter to you. It has been eight months since we last spoke, through e-mail, and I guess my biggest question is why? At what point did you decide our relationship would end? We have been very close for as long as I could remember and then just like that, you're gone. Did I do something to offend you? Is our relationship strained as a result of Uncle Michael's feelings toward me? I am asking you this because I really feel like I stepped up and took a responsible role at one of the most difficult times in my life. Shortly after Dad died, I began to see a different side of you. I know you must be heartbroken over the loss of your son, but please remember I lost a father that day, too. You were the one that came to me and said I needed to stay in that house, that it was my home, and we would work everything out.

I guess we didn't quite work it out, which is why I am no longer living there now. I was paying you each month as much as I could for the taxes and insurance on top of paying all the regular bills. Even though I feel you were fair on the amount each month, I was kind of upset that as soon as Dad died, you wanted me to pay. That bothers me because you never made Dad pay a dime but couldn't get it quick enough from a twenty-year-old girl who at that point still didn't have a full-time job. I guess I would've felt better if I was putting money into a house that I could eventually own, but I now have no part of that house.

You always knew you had no intention of leaving that house to me and my sisters, and it pisses me off that you couldn't treat me like an adult and tell me. Every time it was brought up, you changed the subject. In time, I decided to make a change in my life and move on. I had to leave that house behind. When the time came to tell you that I was moving, I contacted you through our usual e-mailing and let you know exactly when I was moving and if you needed me to do anything specific before I moved. When you responded, you barely gave me a congratulations before going into a whole lecture as to why I didn't deserve the house. That's the last time we spoke. I just want to know why that was the last time I heard from you. You also told Cindy, a month after I moved out, that "everyone has their judgment day, so God bless the thief that stole my bedroom set."

How could you say something like that? It really does hurt me that you haven't said one word to me since that last e-mail. I am in a great relationship with an amazing guy, and we took the next step of our lives and moved in together. I finally found some happiness in my life, and yet in some way I feel like I'm being criticized for that. Bottom line is, it hurts that we don't have the relationship we used to, and it makes me angry that when you have a problem with me, you can never say it to me. I'm just not sure how it came to this.

April

Dear April,
I'm not really sure how things got this way, either. Losing your father broke my heart, and maybe in a way it has changed me. I didn't want things to be this way between us. I do appreciate you taking care of the house and paying the bills; I guess I just didn't know how to say it. I'm sorry that I didn't

explain to you and your sisters my intentions with the house from the beginning. Maybe I didn't stop and realize how much you were hurting, not only from your father but losing Donald as well. I am happy that you found Brian, and I wish nothing but good things for you. I hope we have a chance to someday continue with the relationship we once had.

Grandmom

Dear Grandmom,

I do accept your apology, and I understand that you were hurting as well. Maybe there could be some more effort on my part to speak with you again. I am still hurt, so it may take some time, but I do hope to reconcile at one point and put the past behind us.

April

APRIL'S SECOND SERIES OF LETTERS

Dear Donald,

I wish I was able to say this to you in person, but I can't. I feel like there is so much left unfinished between us. I wonder from time to time how you really felt about me at the end of it all. You were my first love, and you were amazing. When we got together, I only saw you and me forever. Some people say that's because I was young and naïve, but I always believed in us. We had a great relationship that, to this day, I'm still not sure why it ended. It took me a very long time to move on, and sometimes, when I think back, I'm still hurt by it. I can deal with it now because I have to, because I won't ever have the answers. I guess we were both at different places in our lives, and it just didn't work anymore, even if we still cared about each other. I never doubted your feelings for me ever. I just couldn't understand why the feelings suddenly changed. I am glad we found each other when we did, because you taught me how to love someone so completely and without judgment.

On the other hand, you also made me very insecure and unable to trust in my present relationship. In a way, I am grateful that things didn't work out, 'cause now I have Brian. He came into my life at one of my darkest points and gave me hope again. He gave me the chance to love again. I think, or at least I hope, you're looking down, and you're happy for me because I was lucky enough to have found another really amazing guy. You always told me you wanted me to be happy, and I finally am. I do still think about you and all the memories we made. That's the nice thing about memories... no one can take them away from you.

I'm so sad that you're not here anymore. It hurts me to think that you didn't get to live out the life you always wanted. It hurts me when I think about the pain your family is feeling every day without you. It hurts me most that I couldn't say good-bye. The last time I saw you was about twenty-four hours before you died, and I didn't say anything. Not one word. And just like that, you were gone. That feeling of guilt has weighed on me so heavily for so long. Right before you died, we were finally getting back to a normal place with each other, even if it was only as friends. I was happy that I was able to have a conversation with you like normal again. Although, I still got butterflies when I saw you. I just can't believe you're gone.

I went over this a hundred times in my head because I felt it was so unfair that God took you. However, when you died, I held tighter to my faith than I had when my dad passed. I felt like maybe God has a bigger plan for you. Bigger than I could ever understand, at least for now. I hope wherever you are, you're at peace and maybe even with my dad. You guys have to be my guardian angels now and watch over me. I know you two were always close. I want to apologize to you for taking out my grief over my dad on you. It wasn't fair to you, and I'm sorry. The hardest part of all of this is not having *any real closure to both the end of our relationship and the end of your life. Maybe one day I'll get that closure, but until then I will always hold you close to my heart, and I will never forget the most important thing you taught me... love. It's not good-bye, just a long "see you later."*

Love always,
April

Dear April,
I received your letter, and I just wanted to thank you. What you said meant a lot to me. I also feel there were many things left unfinished between us, but I think deep down in your heart you know how much I care about you and always will. You also gave me the special gift of love. You were the only person I ever shared that kind of love with, and I hold that close to me always. I can't explain why things ended the way they did. I guess I was just in a place where I wanted the freedom of being with my friends and taking some time for me. Maybe, in a way, I knew my time on Earth was ending. We taught each other a lot, and I'm sorry for hurting you. That was never my intention. I am happy to see that you have found someone to share your life with again. And you're right, I only want you to be happy. I don't want you to be sad about what happened to me. Everything happens for a reason, and in time we will all know what that reason is. For now, I want you to enjoy your life and keep those memories with you forever. I will always be around, just in a different way.

Love,
Donald

The next exercise, graciously shared by Robert Perry and adapted for this book, will help you connect to an inner treasure within you by opening a door to your most loving heart. When connected to your loving heart, you will be able to forgive yourself, and especially others, much more easily. The focus of this exercise, though, is that giving and receiving forgiveness and miracles are one. What you give is what you receive.

Exercise: Giving and Receiving Forgiveness and Miracles[1]

1 Close your eyes. Take three slow, deep breaths. Breathe in "peace" through your nose and breathe out "relax" through your mouth. Breathe slowly and deeply. Slowly and deeply. Breathing in and out. In and out. Slowly and deeply. Slowly and deeply. Now repeat the following phrase slowly in your mind: "I give the forgiveness and miracles I have received." Again: "I give the forgiveness and miracles I have received." Let yourself sink down deep into the quiet center of your mind. Breathe slowly and deeply. Calm and relax. Calm and relax.

2 As you approach the quiet center of your mind, you begin to see a treasure house, a beautiful, gleaming treasure house that radiates light and a sense of holiness. You immediately feel a sense of safety and warmth and welcome as you approach it. You notice a very large doorway at the entrance to the treasure house. As you approach the very large doorway, you wonder if you will be able to get in. Then you hear a gentle voice that says to you: "No one will be turned away from this new home, this treasure house, where your true Self, your inner light, waits for you; where your true happiness and love is."

3 The door of the treasure house swings silently open before you. As you enter, you behold the beautiful treasure that is stored in this place. Rather than gold and silver, you see a sacred garden with the most amazing lilies you have ever seen. The lilies literally shine with divine light and holiness. You begin to hear what sounds like the faint singing of angelic choirs in the air around the lilies. You realize that these are the lilies of forgiveness. These are miracles. You also begin to realize that the soil they are growing in is blessed soil, the blessed soil that nurtures forgiveness and miracles.

4   You are here to gather these miracles of forgiveness and take them back to the world. So you walk into the garden and begin to pick the lilies. As you pick each lily, you notice that two more lilies spring up in its place. You collect an armful of lilies.

5   You are now ready to go out into the world, into your day. You are now ready to give these miracles, these lilies of forgiveness, to everyone you encounter. As you go through your day, imagine yourself silently giving one of these lilies to each person you meet. Your lily is your acknowledgment that this person is a Being of divine light, just as you are, washed clean of their past. Imagine that as you give out these lilies of forgiveness, each person is reborn. So as you give the lily, say silently to each person: "You are forgiven, divine child of light."

6   Think of one person at a time that you have experienced some distress with, past or present. Then imagine gently giving this person a lily of forgiveness while you say: "You are forgiven, divine child of light." Then ask a Higher Power, the Holy Spirit, or Infinite Intelligence what lilies of forgiveness they would have you give in the coming hour and thank this force, power, or intelligence for the lilies they gave through you in the hour gone by.

7   Imagine now that many other people are giving you lilies of forgiveness, as you have given them. Imagine how beautiful they are and how sweet they smell. Feel the healing effect of these lilies of forgiveness. You cannot recognize, or become fully aware of, what you have received until you give it away. When you give forgiveness, you begin to recognize you have received forgiveness. What you give is what you receive, and what you receive is what you can give. You understand that you are healed when you give healing. You begin to accept that you have received the lilies of forgiveness for yourself when you forgive. Once again, imagine yourself distributing the lilies of forgiveness into the world, and as you do, know that you are forgiven. It is in giving away the miracles of forgiveness that you receive them.

8 Let yourself recognize that the storehouse of your mind is filled with miracles of forgiveness. Let yourself know that you can come to this storehouse, this treasure house, and receive the lilies of forgiveness. Know that a Higher Power or divine light or Infinite Intelligence has entrusted you with these lilies of forgiveness and wants you to give them away. Remember to pause often today to carry these treasures forth and offer them to the world. Know that this is one of the major purposes of your life, and so this is why you are here.

In your journal, write a summary of what you experienced from this exercise.

APRIL'S RESPONSE

The lilies of forgiveness [exercise] helps me understand that in order to get forgiveness from someone, I need to also give them forgiveness. If I'm not able to forgive someone, then it is unfair to say they should forgive me.

The next exercise will help you further release beliefs and emotions from the past that serve as a form of mental and emotional imprisonment. Like the previous exercise, it calls upon the spiritual resources within you. It will also help you to heal the emotional centers of your brain that store toxic feelings. You can use this exercise to help you reconnect with your inner or Higher Self. Many people benefit from all these exercises and find that the benefits are cumulative, but because you are unique, any given exercise may trigger more rapid healing in you than another process. In that case, you might want to single out for special attention this or any other exercise when it particularly appeals to you or seems to catalyze more rapid change.

Exercise: Fountain of Forgiveness and Love

1 Close your eyes. Take some slow, deep breaths. Breathing in through your nose and out through your mouth. Slowly and deeply.

Deeply and slowly. Now breathe in slowly and repeat the word "calm" on the in-breath and "relax" on the out-breath. Slowly and deeply. Deeply and slowly.

2 Now, with your eyes closed, imagine one, two, or three people about a foot or two in front of you, each one in their own prison cell. These are the people you have imprisoned in your mind and emotions with your negative thoughts, feelings, attitudes, and beliefs. One by one, tell each one of these people, each in their own prison cell, all your feelings, beliefs, attitudes, judgments, grievances, grudges, resentments, bitterness, hurts, pains, guilt, disappointments, sadness, and, in fact, everything you have blamed and punished them for in your mind. You are their jailor and they are your prisoners.

3 Be very honest with yourself. See if you are willing to let all this negativity go once and for all. If you are truly willing to let the past go, to let go of the hope of a different and better past, and to release them and yourself, then slowly pick up the key that you, their jailor, have next to you and walk over to each prison cell. One by one, put the key in the lock of the cell and let each person out of prison. As they walk away free, notice that by freeing them from imprisonment, you have freed yourself. Notice how much lighter you feel. Notice that the emotional and mental clutter in your mind has been released. Notice how much more at peace you are with yourself. Then take a few slow, deep breaths. Slow and deep.

4 Imagine yourself as a child, adolescent, and young adult standing in three different prison cells, a foot or two in front of you. One by one, review all the disappointments, hurts, pains, regrets, frustrations, resentments, anger, guilt, bitterness, shame you have toward yourself at each of these ages. Take your time and then express, one by one, all the thoughts, feelings, beliefs, and attitudes you have about yourself to the child, adolescent, and young adult imprisoned in each jail cell in front of you.

5 Once again, be clear and honest with yourself. See if you are willing to let the past go. As your own jailor, see if you are willing to free yourself from prison. See if you are willing to release the hope of a different and better past. See if you are willing to let go of the grievances, grudges, judgments, and attack thoughts you have against yourself. See if you are willing to forgive yourself. If the answer is yes, then pick up the key and, one by one, open the door to the prison cell of the child, the adolescent, and the young adult. Notice how much freer you feel.

6 As the child walks out of the prison cell, see yourself walking over and giving your child a very big, warm, loving hug. Feel yourself and your child becoming one as you share that loving embrace. Let yourself experience the love between you. Then as the adolescent walks out of the prison cell, see yourself walking over to the adolescent and giving your adolescent a very big, warm, loving hug. Feel yourself and your adolescent becoming one as you share that loving embrace. Let yourself experience the love between you. Finally, as the young adult walks out of the prison cell, see yourself walking over to the young adult and giving your young adult a very big, warm, loving hug. Feel yourself and your young adult becoming one as you share that loving embrace. Let yourself experience the love between you. Now imagine that your child, adolescent, and young adult blend into one another and become one person. Picture yourself holding, embracing, and loving that person and becoming one with that person.

7 Imagine that a radiant globe of light filled with infinite love and compassion is about two feet above your head. Imagine that the globe of light (your Higher Self or Soul) is showering an endless fountain of infinite, boundless, and radiant light on you. Imagine that this infinite light and love enters through the top of your head, into your head, and then into all the emotional centers of your brain, such as the amygdala, thalamus, hypothalamus, limbic system, etc. Imagine the light and love radiates into these emotional centers of the brain, healing everything it touches. Imagine that the infinite light and love then radiates into every particle and cell of your body, bringing healing, compassion, and joy to every cell of your body. Imagine that the love and light even enters the DNA in the cells, deepening the healing experience even more. Let yourself feel how loved you are by this infinitely wise, compassionate, and loving light. Know that this infinite, radiant, wise, and loving light goes with you wherever you go. Know that you are guided, protected, directed, blessed, and loved by this light.

8 Take five very slow, deep breaths. In through your nose and out through your mouth. In through your nose and out through your mouth. Breathe slowly and deeply. Deeply and slowly. Then gradually, very gradually, open your eyes and bring your consciousness back into the room.

In your journal, describe what you experienced during this exercise.

APRIL'S RESPONSE

This exercise really gave me a chance to think about the different aspects of my life and the feelings I've held on to for so long in many situations, particularly regarding my dad, Donald (my ex-boyfriend who died in a motorcycle accident), and my grandmom. It really releases a lot of the negative emotions I had been feeling. I was also able to release the feelings of guilt I had in being responsible for my father's actions when I was a child.

The exercises in this chapter have encouraged you to:

1. Use your writing skills and your ability to take the role of another person (i.e., your empathy skills) to facilitate healing through forgiveness.

2. Use your spiritual resources to connect with your deepest Self and learn that giving and receiving forgiveness and miracles are one.

3. Use your spiritual resources to help you release yourself from mental and emotional imprisonment developed from the past and release toxic feelings stored in the emotional centers of the brain.

We'll continue to work on these skills in the next chapters.

CHAPTER 14

Transformational Forgiveness and Cutting the Energetic Cord

"The most powerful way to heal is through forgiveness. When we forgive, we take something less personally, blame the person who hurt us less, and change our grievance story. Through learning the process of forgiveness, we can forgive anyone who has hurt us in any way.... Forgiveness is the feeling of peace that emerges as you...take responsibility for how you feel, and become a hero instead of a victim in the story you tell.... Forgiveness does not change the past, but it changes the present.... You can forgive and rejoin a relationship or forgive and never speak to the person again."
—FRED LUSKIN, *Forgive for Good*

"Historically, forgiveness has been addressed rather minimally and ineffectively in traditional therapies. We have always recognized that unforgiveness was a problem in human adjustment. But, we have tended largely to ignore it as a treatment issue. There are many reasons for such neglect I suppose, not the least of which is that we really were not sure how to eliminate it. Another is

*that many of us are uncomfortable and/or unfamiliar
with spiritual considerations. . . . I am convinced that
unforgiveness and related attitudes of resentment and
bitterness are among the deadliest dynamics in the
human psyche.*"
　　　—LARRY NIMS, BSFF Everyday Freedom eMagazine

"*To forgive we have to admit that we have been hurt
and that we have a right to feel hurt, angry, or resentful.
Forgiving does not require denying our feelings. In fact,
as we will see, unwillingness to admit that we have been
hurt is one of the major impediments to forgiving.*"
　　　—ROBERT D. ENRIGHT, *Forgiveness Is a Choice*

I N THEIR TERRIFIC BOOK *Finding Our Way Home,* Gerald Jampolsky and Diane Cirincione tell the following story:

*While in Belfast, we met a blind man who had started a
school that included both Protestant and Catholic children in
the same classrooms. He told us that he was showing these kids
that people of different faiths don't have horns sticking out of
their heads. He taught them how to live and work with each
other in harmony.*

*We asked him how long he'd been without sight, and
he told us that he was now forty and had been blind since
someone threw a bomb into his house when he was fourteen.
He added, "I believe that every negative circumstance can
be turned into a positive. I wouldn't be doing the work I'm*

doing if I hadn't had that experience. I discovered that there's another kind of vision—spiritual vision. I decided to see everyone through Christ's eyes and spend what time I had left making forgiveness and love my way of life."

Needless to say, our time in Belfast enriched our faith in miracles and in the power of forgiveness.

Within any circumstance, we can be open to hope and miracles in our lives.

One of the major and profound writings on forgiveness comes from *A Course in Miracles* (ACIM). In ACIM, the essence of forgiveness is defined as a shift in perception that helps you go from seeing a sinful and fearful world to seeing a loving and innocent one. Here, we will use a visualization technique, warmly given to me by Robert Perry and adapted from *A Course in Miracles*.[1] It will help you to rapidly see things differently and shift your perspective of yourself and another person whom you believe harmed or injured you in some way.

Exercise: Transformational Forgiveness

This exercise is labeled transformational forgiveness because it presents a point of view about forgiveness that contrasts with conventional approaches, which focus on perpetrators and victims, injury, harm, and sin. It also comes from an advanced spiritual perspective, which, if you are open to it, might further transform the quality of your life.

PART 1. TIME: ABOUT TEN MINUTES

1 Think of someone who arouses in you a negative reaction, such as anger, hurt, fear, guilt, resentment, bitterness, sadness, disappointment, shame, etc. As you read this list of negative reactions, one or more people or situations will spontaneously come to mind. Initially, pick one of these people.

2   Get in touch with your current perception of this person and all the negative things you think they did. Remember that forgiveness is a shift in perception, one in which you release your perception of another as harmful, hurtful, or sinful in some way and see them as loving, blessed, or even holy. Before you can release your current perceptions and feelings, you must first get in touch with them. This has two aspects:

a. Visualize their appearance. Just picture this person in your mind. This will bring up your negative perceptions (and feelings) of them.

b. Review the ways in which you think they have negatively affected you. In other words, mentally review their faults, neglect, mistakes, and perceived sins.

3   Consider the possibility of a new perception; that is, that they are actually your "savior." Consider that there is an alternative for your basic picture of who they are and what their relationship is to you. This alternative will dismiss your entire current perception of this person and contains three elements:

a. State your intention to see them as your "savior." The idea that your brother or sister (*generically speaking*) is your "savior" is a very misunderstood concept. It does not mean that they save you by pushing your buttons and thereby make you aware of your ego. It means that if you see them for who they really are, you will see a divine Being of light standing before you. And it is the divine Being of light who is your "savior."

b. See them shining blessings onto you and revealing your holiness and beauty, your magnificence. Many of you are familiar with the idea that an enlightened or awakened Being can transmit illumination to you simply by looking at you. Your brother or sister (*generically speaking*) is an illumined being; they just don't know it yet. But if you see them as they truly are, you will see that they are looking upon you with love and divine light and seeing perfect holiness and magnificence in you. This will reveal the divinity in you.

c. Have a sense of uniting with them. If you see your brother or sister as a divine being who recognizes holiness and blessedness in you, then the two of you are exactly alike. The only logical thing to do now is to unite with them in your mind.

PART 2. TIME: ABOUT TWENTY MINUTES

Find a quiet place and a comfortable chair. Read a sentence, close your eyes, and attempt to do what it says. Try to let each sentence sink in before going on to the next. Some sentences are ones you are meant to say directly to your "brother or sister" or to your Higher Self, Soul, or God. Give the exercise as much focused attention and concentration as you can. Try to be fully awake and alert before you sit down to do it. If you find the exercise helpful, there is no limit to how often you can use it. You may even want to use it every day as it relates to a particular person until you feel that your resentment toward that person is healed.

Composite Forgiveness Imagery Exercise[1]

1 Select one person you have used as a target for your grievances, grudges, and resentments and lay the grievances, grudges, and resentments aside. With your eyes closed, look at the person. Pick someone you do not like, who seems to irritate you or to cause regret in you if you should meet them; someone you actively despise or merely try to overlook. Someone, perhaps, you fear and even hate; someone you think you love who angered you; someone you call a friend, but whom you see as difficult at times or hard to please, demanding, irritating, or untrue to the ideal he should accept as his, according to the role you set for him. You know the one to choose; their name has crossed your mind already. They will do.

2 You will attempt to hold them in your mind first as you now consider them. See them as clearly as you can, in that same form to which you are accustomed. Notice their body with its flaws and better points as well. See their face, their hands and feet, their clothing. Watch them smile and see familiar gestures that they make so frequently.

3 Then review their faults, the difficulties you have had with them, the pain they caused you, their neglect, and all the little and the larger hurts they gave. Think of their mistakes and even of their so-called "sins." Catalog these perceived "sins" as, one by one, they cross your mind. Briefly consider all the negative and evil things you thought of about them.

4 Then think of this: what you are seeing now conceals from you the sight of one who can forgive you all your negativity and perceived sins; whose sacred hands can take away the nails which pierce your own and lift the crown of thorns which you have placed upon your bleeding head.

5 Let us ask a Higher Power, the Higher Self, Soul, Infinite Intelligence, or the Holy Spirit (pick one or two) for help. Let me perceive forgiveness as it is. Let this help me learn what forgiveness means. Today, you will go beyond the grievances, grudges, resentments, and hurts. You will not wait before the shield of hate and hurt but lay it down and gently lift your eyes in silence to behold radiant Beings of love and light. The radiant Beings of light and love wait for you behind your grievances, grudges, resentments, and hurts, and as you lay them down the radiant Beings will appear in shining light where each one stood before.

6 Then let us ask the Higher Power, the Higher Self, Soul, Infinite Intelligence, or Holy Spirit who knows this divine Being in their reality and truth that you may look on them in a different way and see your "savior" shining in the light of true forgiveness, given unto you. You will ask the Higher Power, the Higher Self, Soul, Infinite Intelligence, or Holy Spirit: "Let me behold my 'savior' in this one you have appointed as the one for me to ask to lead me to the holy and loving light in which they stand, that I may join with them." As you think of this person who grieved you, let your mind be shown the light in them beyond your grievances, grudges, resentments, and hurts. What is in them will shine so brightly in your grateful vision that you will merely love them and be glad. You will not think for a moment to judge them. Overlook their mind and body and see only the face of a radiant Being of light and love shining in front of you.

7   Now behold the radiant Being of light and love and look upon their purity. Be peaceful and still. In quiet, look upon their holiness, greatness, and magnificence and offer thanks that no guilt has ever touched them. There is no way to think of them but this, if you would know the truth about yourself. I thank You, Higher Power, Higher Self, Soul, Infinite Intelligence, or the Holy Spirit (pick one or two) and know that in their glory and radiance I will I see my own.

8   Say to your brother or sister: "Because I will to know myself, I see you as a radiant, holy, loving Being of light and my brother or sister." Look on your brother or sister and behold in them the whole reversal of the laws that seem to rule this world. In them is a child of light. See negativity or sin in them instead, and light and love and peace is lost to you. But see them as they truly are, and what is yours shines from them to you. Be willing, then, to see your brother or sister as sinless and without negativity, that a holy Being of light and love may rise before your vision and give you joy and peace. Your brother or sister's light, love, and holiness is sacred and a blessing unto you. Their light and love and holiness gives life to you.

9   Your brother or sister may not know who they are, but there is a light in their mind that does know. This light can shine deeply into yours. Say, then, to your brother or sister: "The light in you is all that I would see [use their name]." Light and joy and peace abide in you. Your sinlessness and holiness is guaranteed by a Higher Power,

Higher Self, Soul, Infinite Intelligence, or the Holy Spirit. Your brother or sister's sinlessness and holiness is given you in shining light to look on with the Higher Power, Higher Self, Soul, Infinite Intelligence, or the Holy Spirit's vision and rejoice.

10 Perceive them now as more than friend to you, for in that light their magnificence and holiness shows you your "savior," saved and saving, healed and whole. Before this light, their body disappears, as heavy shadows must give way to light. In glory will you see your brother and sister then. Behold them now, whom you have seen as merely flesh and bone, and recognize that blessings and light and holiness have come to you. Behold your friend, the Being of light and love who stands beside you. How holy and how beautiful they are! You thought they were negative and had sinned because you cast the veil of negativity and sin upon them to hide their loveliness. Yet still they hold forgiveness out to you, to share their holiness. Look on your risen friend and celebrate his magnificence and holiness.

11 Brother and sister, come and let me look on you. Your loveliness reflects my own. Your sinlessness and light and love are mine. You stand forgiven, and I stand with you. The light has come. I have forgiven you. Be very quiet now and look upon your shining "savior." No dark grievances obscure the sight of them. Within the darkness, see the "savior" from the dark and understand your brother or sister as their Higher Power, Higher Self, Soul, Infinite Intelligence, or the Holy Spirit's mind shows them to you. They will step forth from darkness as you look on them and you will see the dark no more.

12 Let them come forth to shine on you and give you back the gift of freedom and of love. See how eagerly they come, and step aside from heavy shadows that have hidden them, and let them shine on you in gratitude and love. The "savior" from illusions has come to greet you and lead you home with them. Ask this of them, that they may set you free: "Give me your blessing, holy child of light. I would behold you with the eyes of magnificence and greatness and see my perfect sinlessness and holiness in you." Take their blessing and feel how your heart is lifted and your fear released. And now the light in you must be as bright as shines in them.

13 How could they fail to welcome you into their heart with loving invitation, eager to unite with one like them in light and blessing and holiness? Come, let us join them in the holy, loving place of peace. Join them there. Now they have led you to the loving and holy light in which they stand.

14 And you have joined with them. "You stand with me in light [use their name]. You stand with me in light [use their name]. You stand with me in light."

Take a few slow, deep breaths. Breathe slowly and deeply. Then gradually, very gradually, open your eyes and bring your consciousness back into the room.

In your journal, describe what you experienced during this exercise.

APRIL'S RESPONSE

I thought of my grandmom during this exercise. I was able to see her as I once did, before all the negative feelings came up. Without my forgiveness, I cannot be forgiven, and by releasing all of that negativity I then see nothing but positives.

Exercise: Cutting the Energetic Cord and Forgiving Imagery Process

The energetic cord imagery exercise emphasizes that we are all tied together by invisible (at least to most people) energy cords or connections, like energy ropes. One effective way to release yourself from unhealthy energetic connections, especially where unforgiveness is operating, is to imagine yourself cutting the energetic and emotional cord that binds you to another person. This technique is even more effective if you transform the underlying beliefs that tied you emotionally together in the first place. This is where the previous transformational forgiveness imagery exercise or other imagery exercises in other chapters complement this exercise, just as this one complements the others. The processes and exercises in all the chapters are designed to give you many opportunities to practice forgiveness in many different ways. It is as if you were working on many threads of a mosaic. Each exercise or process is a forgiveness thread in the entire healing mosaic.

When you do this energetic cord-cutting process, you can picture yourself cutting the cords with just one person or with a number of people. If you do it with a number of people, do it slowly on one person at a time, using the name of that person. Some people doing this exercise are very emotionally sensitive and thus may become very tired for a while doing the exercise because a lot of emotional energy is being released. Others may feel energized or deeply relaxed. Generally, it is wisest to focus first on one or two people or situations where there is a lot of emotional charge. This could be someone currently in your life (child, spouse, in-law, boss, colleague, friend, employee, boyfriend or girlfriend, teacher, mentors, or any exes) or someone from your past (parents, grandparents, brothers and sisters, aunts, uncles, cousins, nephews, nieces, stepparents, stepchildren, and anyone who was considered "family" or ex-friends or an ex-mentor). It can also be a recent or long-ago deceased ancestor or even a child that is no longer alive as a result of illness, accident, an abortion, or miscarriage. Sometimes it may be someone you don't even know, such as someone who you felt abused by or who stole money from you or who injured you during war or during another violent situation. In these cases, you don't know who engaged in the behavior that felt like an "attack." You know the "attack" is a call for help and love, though in a disguised way. You also know you need to cut the emotional cord, the emotional attachments with this person or situation, release them or it, and move on.

1 Ask your Higher Power, Higher Self, Infinite Intelligence, the Holy Spirit, your Soul, or Divine Light to be with you. Some people may want to invite Archangel Michael to be with them, as he has been associated with the process of cord cutting. Visualize one or more persons toward whom you are experiencing negativity, such as anger, hurt, resentment, pain, fear, grievances, grudges, bitterness, guilt, shame, etc.

2 Imagine that there are cords that connect you and these people, for example, from your solar plexus to their solar plexus or from your heart or navel to their heart or navel. These cords represent your emotional attachment to these people. Ask Archangel Michael or your Higher Power, Higher Self, Infinite Intelligence, the Holy Spirit, your Soul, or Divine Light if you can borrow a sword or knife from them. Say out loud, "I now cut and release the cords with (say each person's name)." Picture yourself slowly cutting, one by one, the cords with each of these people.

3 Make it your intent to cut all the cords of all the people you have selected. Sense the freedom and emotional release that you experience as you do this. Also make it your intent to simultaneously release any limiting beliefs and attitudes that keep you attached emotionally to these people. Notice how your energy shifts as you cut the cords and release these people from your energy field.

4 As the cord-cutting process completes itself, say to these people, "I forgive you for anything you did or I thought you did that caused me hurt, distress, or pain." Then say to yourself, "I forgive myself for anything I did or thought I did that caused me to become and stay emotionally attached to you." Release all judgments, grievances, and grudges toward yourself, toward these people, and toward the circumstances in which you encountered them, as well as the energetic connection. Then hear back from them, "I forgive you and I release you." Know, however, that ultimately the only person you are forgiving is yourself.

5 Make it your intent that this cord-cutting process is for your highest good, the highest good of the other people (i.e., your relationships), and the highest good of the universe. See the energy connections dissolving and then disappearing as this healing process takes place. Know that as you dissolve these dysfunctional energy patterns, you are creating the space to allow new, more growth-producing energy patterns to develop. It is as if you are plucking out the weeds and beginning to plant new seeds in the energetic soil of your life.

6 When you have completed the cord-cutting exercise, take some slow, deep breaths. Breathe slowly and deeply. Slowly and deeply. Call in, once again, your Higher Power, Higher Self, Holy Spirit, Infinite Intelligence, or the Divine Light. Let this force, energy, intelligence, or power surround you with love and light. Let this light and love enter your heart and circulate around your heart. Feel the love in your heart as the light circulates there. Feel the connection with your deepest, undivided Self, the light of your true Self. Know that you are always guided, guarded, protected, and loved by this light and by your true Self. Hear the Voice of your Higher Self, the divine light say to you, "I am with you always."

7 Allow yourself to feel grateful for all the experiences and people in your life that contributed to your healing and growth. Allow yourself to feel grateful to yourself for creating or co-creating these people and experiences in your life. Allow yourself to feel grateful to your Higher Power, Higher Self, Holy Spirit, Infinite Intelligence, Soul, or the Divine Light for being there for you. If anyone has helped you with this process, allow yourself to feel grateful for them as well.

8 Continue to relax more and more. Breathe deeply and slowly ...slowly and deeply...calm and relax...relax and calm. Breathing slowly and deeply...deeply and slowly. Then slowly, very slowly, count from one to ten. When you get to ten, your eyes will be open and your consciousness will be back in the room. One... two...three...four...five...six...seven...eight...nine...ten.

In your journal, write about what you experienced during this exercise.

APRIL'S RESPONSE

I chose my dad and grandma for this exercise. By cutting the cord, I was able to release all the grievances and sadness over my dad's death, and I am able to be more at peace about it. With my grandma, it allowed me to release the anger and hurt over our relationship.

The transformational and energetic cord exercises have provided you with two additional powerful forgiveness processes that focus on both the spiritual and energetic components of forgiveness. Of course, any one or two exercises in this chapter or book could trigger a significant positive shift in you. Each one addresses the problem of unforgiveness from a slightly different angle. Because spiritual, energetic, emotional, mental, and relational aspects of forgiveness are all interrelated, doing all the exercises is more effective in promoting healing than just using any one alone. The more spiritual exercises, however, are also designed to help you realign with your deepest and highest Self, the core of your Being.

CHAPTER 15

Reconnecting with Your Divine Self

"The process of forgiveness essentially consists of three steps that lead us from our egos back to God.

1. The first entails the recognition that what we have attacked and judged against in another is indeed what we have condemned in ourselves.... The guilt is our own. We recognize it is not the other who needs to be changed, but ourselves....

2. The second step entails our understanding that the guilt, too, represents a decision, and one that can now be changed. The shift is not something we can do by ourselves, but it must be something we want. This can be our choice.... 'This time I choose with the Holy Spirit, and let Him make the decision of guiltlessness for me.'

3. This opens the way for the third step, which is the work of the Holy Spirit... [who] enters our world of fear and guilt.... The Holy Spirit asks only for our little willingness, that He may join it with the unlimited power of God's Will."

— KENNETH WAPNICK, *Forgiveness and Jesus: The Meeting Place of A Course in Miracles and Christianity*

A FEW YEARS AGO, I was invited to chair a symposium at an international conference. I asked quite a number of very talented, nationally and internationally known authors if they would be willing to present a paper at the conference. All were well known in their field. They all accepted the invitation—except one. This person was internationally known for his work on forgiveness but was very skeptical about presenting and wanted a rather high fee for presenting plus travel expenses, which no one else asked for. When I mentioned to him that all the other invited speakers had graciously accepted without these demands, he was dismissive and worried about giving this presentation. I was quite surprised, even bewildered, and a little annoyed. Despite my assurances and persistence, to my chagrin, he kept saying no. Frankly, I was hurt, frustrated, and angry. I had invited him because I thought he had something substantial to present in the area of forgiveness. I found it hard to believe, at first, that someone of his stature could be fearful about presenting his work at this conference. I did realize, of course, that fear is always a call for help and for love, though often in a disguised fashion.

I asked for guidance that night, and the response I received was "accept what is." So, reluctantly, I decided I would do that. Nevertheless, the following morning I was still feeling some irritation and disappointment, though trying to "accept what is." I went to my meditation room, as I do every morning, and decided to listen to some forgiveness CDs. One of them was by this same potential presenter. After listening to these forgiveness CDs for forty-five minutes, I felt calm, forgiving, peaceful, and truly ready emotionally and mentally to "accept what is." I looked at the clock and noticed that it said 8:45 A.M. I went to shower and dress and then I checked my e-mail. There was a message from this potential presenter sent at 9:10 A.M. He said that he had changed his mind, felt reassured, appreciated my persistence, and would gladly present at the conference for free and was no longer asking for travel expenses. Now he was very gracious and supportive. He thanked me for inviting him and for the opportunity to participate along with the other distinguished presenters. It then became obvious to me that we were both initially "thorny angels" to each other and then became "healing angels" through the power of forgiveness, peace, compassion, and love.

Ultimately, all the forgiveness exercises and processes are designed not only to facilitate personal and relationship healing but also to help you reconnect to your core Self, the place within you of deep peace, love, joy, harmony, balance, and wisdom. The core Self is usually visualized in this book in the form of white light.

The three exercises in this chapter are designed to further catalyze your ability to connect with your higher Self, spiritual intelligence, divine light, and inner wisdom. As previously mentioned, I encourage you to practice all these exercises in the order given in the book. Eventually, however, because you are unique you will want to select the ones you personally find most valuable in your life and work and use them more frequently and in the sequence you find most helpful.

These exercises also emphasize how interconnected we all are, and because all minds are joined at a deep level, as you learn to forgive more and more you contribute not only to your own healing but also substantially to the healing of the planet Earth. If you are finding it challenging or difficult to practice these exercises by yourself, I would encourage you to contact a forgiveness-oriented therapist, coach, facilitator, or group, preferably one trained in the approaches described in this book.

The first exercise focuses on forgiveness as a gift, a gift to yourself, to one another, and, ultimately, to the world. Forgiveness can then be seen as a holy encounter with yourself, others, and the world. Moreover, the most effective forms of forgiveness are conducted under the guidance of a higher force, power, spirit, teacher, or guide. Asking for help from that higher force, power, spirit, teacher, or guide should be one of the first things you do when beginning any forgiveness process, such as the ones in this chapter.

Exercise: Gift of Forgiveness Imagery Process[1]

This forgiveness imagery process was inspired by an excellent forgiveness audiotape by Robert and Mary Stoelting.

1 Close your eyes. Take some slow, deep breaths. Breathing in through your nose and out through your mouth. Slowly and deeply. Deeply and slowly. Now breathe in slowly and repeat the word "calm" on the in-breath and "relax" on the out-breath. Calm on the in-breath, relax on the out-breath. Slowly and deeply. Deeply and slowly.

2 Imagine a radiant white light coming down from over your head, from your Soul, Infinite Intelligence, or Higher Self. This white light is infinitely wise, compassionate, and loving. Let this light enter through the top of your head and radiate throughout your brain, entering all the emotional centers of your brain, such as the amygdala, thalamus, hypothalamus, and limbic system, and gently and softly bring peace and healing to each place in the brain it touches. Let the gentle white light then enter your neck and shoulders, and, as it does you relax more and more deeply...calmer and deeper...deeper and calmer. Then the light enters your back, arms, shoulders, and hands, and, as it does you find that you become calmer and calmer, relaxing even more deeply as you become slowly and gradually more and more at peace. Then this infinitely wise, loving, and compassionate light enters your heart. When it enters your heart, it circles around and deepens your love even more profoundly. It then enters your stomach, solar plexus, liver, and gall bladder, and you relax more and more...more and more. Then this compassionate and radiant light enters your legs, knees, feet, and toes, and you find yourself becoming even more deeply relaxed, calmer and more deeply relaxed. Finally, it enters all the cells of your body, right down into the DNA, where it brings even more love, compassion, wisdom, and healing.

3 Think of someone toward whom you have negative, unloving feelings, critical thoughts, beliefs. You know who it is. Reflect for a little while on the reactions you have toward this person (e.g., the hurt, anger, resentment, grievances, grudges, disappointment, guilt, bitterness, sadness, shame, etc.). Look closely at this person, in your mind's eye: their facial expressions, body posture, clothes, mannerisms. Thoroughly review all the things you dislike about them and the unloving thoughts and feelings you have toward them.

4 Imagine you are in a hallway. Imagine that a Higher Power, the Higher Self, Soul, Infinite Intelligence, Inner Counselor, or the Holy Spirit (pick one) is with you, guiding you down this hallway. At the end of the hallway is a room with a sign on it that says FORGIVENESS ROOM, but the door appears to be locked. The Higher Power, Higher Self, Soul, Infinite Intelligence, Inner Counselor, or the Holy Spirit has the key to this room and puts the key into the lock. The FORGIVENESS ROOM door gently opens, and you walk inside. Immediately, you notice that this room is filled with light, a bright but very loving light. Inside the room, you sense that there are angels of light who are there to help you, along with the Higher Power, the Higher Self, Soul, Infinite Intelligence, Inner Counselor, or the Holy Spirit. These angels of light love you unconditionally. You can feel their love surround you and radiate through you. You know immediately that they resonate with your essence as a being of light, love, and truth.

5 You ask these angels of light and the Higher Power, Higher Self, Soul, Infinite Intelligence, Inner Counselor, or the Holy Spirit (pick one) to help you to see this person differently, both with your eyes and with your mind. You ask them to show you this person's essence, the truth of who they are beyond their personality, behavior, temperament, and conditioning; beyond their emotions, attitudes, beliefs, and lifestyle. You ask them to show you how this person communicates love and how, even in disguised ways, the person asks for love. These great Beings of light and the Higher Power, Higher Self, Soul, Infinite Intelligence, Inner Counselor, or the Holy Spirit show you the infinite love that is the essence of this person beyond all appearances. They tell you that they love this person unconditionally, just as they love you. You are shown that the essence of this person is also love, light, blessings, and truth. You are then shown that all the negativity and upsets that you have experienced toward this person come from your own projections and illusions and that the essence of this person is no different from your own essence; the truth of this person is no different from the truth of your own Self. Then you are shown that at the core, you and this person are one, beyond surface features, behaviors, attitudes, beliefs, styles, and personality patterns. Both of your essences are light and love, truth and beauty, magnificence and greatness.

6 You are now able to "shift your perception" toward this other person. The love from your heart center flows easily now through you into the heart of the other person; that is, heart to heart. At a deep level, you also know that all minds are joined and that they are joined in love. Share with the other person your loving and forgiving thoughts. Take some time to do this now.

Realize that expressing love to the other person and forgiving them is a gift to yourself. Experience this gift of love within yourself. Thank this person, in your own mind, for being a mirror for you of your communication of love and your calls for love; thank them for being a mirror of the light within you that you couldn't fully see when you were projecting darkness upon them. Thank the angels of light who were and are always there for you—guiding, guarding, protecting, and loving you; thank the Higher Power, Higher Self, Soul, Infinite Intelligence, Inner Counselor, or the Holy Spirit, whoever you selected, for being with you wherever you go. Remember the phrase "I am with you always" and know that you are eternally grateful for the presence of these loving forces and energies of light.

APRIL'S RESPONSE

Step 6. Grandmom, I forgive you for anything you may have done that caused me hurt or anger. I accept you with open, loving arms for the person you are deep down in your soul.

7 Say a little prayer of gratitude on behalf of yourself and this other person who you now see was only calling out for help and love, as were you. Reflect for a moment and then say, "Thank you for all the blessings you have brought into my life; thank you for being you just the way you are; thank you for facilitating my healing; thank you, brother or sister (use the person's name), for reminding me who you and I really are, the essence, truth of my and our Being; thank you for helping me to remember the light of the Self within us. Amen."

Take a few slow, deep breaths. Breathe slowly and deeply. Then gradually, very gradually, open your eyes and bring your consciousness back into the room.

In your journal, describe what you experienced during these exercises.

APRIL'S RESPONSE

Step 7. This exercise gave me a chance to reflect on all the different feelings I've felt toward my grandmom from the time I was a little girl until now. It allows me to see that we're all human, and we all make mistakes, but everyone deserves and seeks love.

This exercise emphasized the significance of seeing that forgiveness is always a gift to yourself as well as to another. It also showed how true forgiveness is guided by a force beyond our ego-mind, an inner light that guides, directs, protects, and loves you if only you will listen to it.

Radical Forgiveness[2]

The term "radical forgiveness" was introduced by Colin Tipping. He was contrasting his approach to conventional forgiveness. Radical forgiveness, like transformational forgiveness, sees the larger spiritual picture. In conventional forgiveness, we see ourselves as victims of events and circumstances that happen to us and over which we have little or no control. In conventional forgiveness, bad, wrong, sinful, or evil things take place. This is not the case from the radical (or transformational) forgiveness perspective. Radical forgiveness occurs simply as a consequence of being open to the possibility that everything happens for a reason, and there are no mistakes.

If we could see the spiritual big picture (which we cannot), we would understand, according to radical forgiveness, that the situation was divinely guided and happened not *to* us but *for* us. It was meant to happen that way for the highest good of all concerned. Also, our Higher Selves actually called forth the experience for our healing and our spiritual growth.

Radical forgiveness is experienced as a shift in consciousness or a movement of energy, both within ourselves and throughout the situation itself, such that elements within the situation itself shift and change.

When we understand that our life is unfolding exactly as it should and that everything is divinely guided, we find peace—even in the most "unpleasant" situations or memories. When we understand that our enemies really love us (at the soul level), our hearts open, and we are released from the victim archetype.

Radical self-forgiveness happens in the same way—as a shift in energy. When we get it that there are no victims, we realize that there are no victimizers either—only players in the spiritual game that we call life, providing myriad situations for learning, growing, and healing.

The radical forgiveness experience helps you to achieve inner peace by helping you release all those old victim stories and self-destructive patterns and beliefs that have kept you out of joy, stolen your life, and blocked your abundance. Radical forgiveness occurs after you have had a chance to tell your story of what happened (or is happening), so you can have it witnessed and validated, and, even then, only after you have had an opportunity to recognize, accept, and fully vent your feelings in the safety of a loving and unconditionally accepting group or individual.

You will come to see how, even though it doesn't always feel like it, the Universe is truly supporting you in healing your victim stories so you can become who you were meant to be, and the Universe is constantly moving you in the direction of healing and spiritual growth. You may even become open to seeing that the people who seem to be the biggest problems in your life are the very ones who are your greatest teachers and who are offering you healing opportunities.

Some people may be skeptical of these ideas at first, though I have found that like many of the other exercises in this book, if you work them, they will work on you. They are very practical, helpful, and healing.

I recommend that you copy the following four written steps to radical forgiveness and the radical forgiveness written release letter so that you can use them again in the future. There will be many opportunities to practice forgiveness in the days, weeks, and months to come, and you may find that these written forgiveness exercises are particularly helpful to you.

Exercise: Four Written Steps to Radical Forgiveness[3]

When you find yourself making judgments, feeling self-righteous, or wanting to change something about a situation, use this process to bring your consciousness into the present, let go of the illusion, and align with spiritual truth.

1 "Look what I created." This first step reminds us that we are the creators of our lives and that we have, in fact, set up all the circumstances of the situation we find ourselves upset about, to help us learn and grow spiritually or heal a wound or core belief that keeps us out of our joy and bliss. Are you (circle one of the below alternatives):

IN AGREEMENT   WILLING   OPEN   SKEPTICAL   UNWILLING

2 "I notice my judgments and love myself anyway." This step acknowledges that, as humans, we automatically attach judgments, interpretations, questions, and beliefs to situations. We quickly create a victim story and try to lay blame on others. It's part of being human. So we must recognize and lovingly accept our feelings. They give us good feedback about our consciousness and they clue us in to our subconscious wounds and core negative beliefs. Are you (circle one of the below alternatives):

IN AGREEMENT   WILLING   OPEN   SKEPTICAL   UNWILLING

I AM FEELING: Angry, sad, frustrated, vengeful, _____ (add your own)

MY WOUNDS: Betrayal, abandonment, abuse, hurt, rejection, stolen from, let down, _____ (add your own)

3   "I am willing to see the hand of God in this situation."

a. This is where we attempt to reframe the story by becoming willing to be open to the idea that, in the sense that our Higher Selves have created this situation (as we said in step 1), then our life is unfolding exactly as it needs to unfold, and everything is in divine order. It is what we want and need for our soul's journey. Nothing wrong is happening and there is nothing to forgive. *(The key word here is "willingness." Only a very small amount of willingness to be open to this possibility is required.)*

b. This step also asks that we entertain the possibility that we have attracted the people with whom we are upset specifically to provide us with this experience. They are doing these things to us because our soul and theirs have contracted to do this for each other. They are not, therefore, our enemies but are our "healing angels," because without them we would not have the opportunity to grow or to heal those core negative beliefs. Are you (circle one of the below alternatives):

IN AGREEMENT   WILLING   OPEN   SKEPTICAL   UNWILLING

CORE BELIEFS: (Which of these can you identify with?)

Not good enough. Not worthy to receive.
Have to be perfect to be loved. Ugly.

Unlovable. Always will be abandoned.

Don't deserve love. Always will be betrayed.

This step also offers you the opportunity to see that what you see and hate in other people is precisely what you cannot stand in yourself and have denied, repressed, and projected onto them.

The things I dislike about _____ are:

Sorry about this, but IF YOU SPOT IT, YOU GOT IT!

"I am willing to recognize that _____ is mirroring something about me that I have denied and repressed, and I am now willing to love and accept that part of me, whatever it is, right now in this moment and to thank _____ for giving me the opportunity to heal." Are you (circle one of the below alternatives):

IN AGREEMENT   WILLING   OPEN   SKEPTICAL   UNWILLING

4 "I choose the power of peace." By accepting that divine purpose is served in this situation and that what appears to be occurring may be illusionary, we choose to surrender to spirit and to feel peace, knowing that we can use the power of peace in whatever actions are required of us. "I release all the feelings, judgments, and resentments I had in step 1 and choose peace." Are you (circle one of the below alternatives):

IN AGREEMENT   WILLING   OPEN   SKEPTICAL   UNWILLING

Note to _____: Having done this worksheet, I now feel _____.

Note to myself: Having done this worksheet, I _____.

In your journal, describe what you experienced during this exercise.

APRILS' RESPONSES TO THE FOUR WRITTEN STEPS OF THE RADICAL FORGIVENESS EXERCISE

Step 1: Look what I created.
Willing

Step 2: I notice my judgments and love myself anyway.
In Agreement

*Step 3: I am willing to see the hand of God in this
    situation.
Willing and Open
Step 4: I choose the power of peace.
Willing*

*This exercise allowed me to view things in a different
perspective. If I allow myself to believe that all things, good
and bad, that happen in my life are all part of a bigger plan,
it is easier to accept it and understand how to be more at
peace with it.*

Note any miracles or forgiveness experiences that occur over the next
few days as a result of doing this radical forgiveness worksheet.

The next exercise is a radical forgiveness written release letter. Use
it anytime you feel that a written exercise would be most useful
to you during the forgiveness process. It complements the other
forgiveness exercises and can be done quickly and easily. It also
activates, in written form, your spiritual intelligence or superconscious mind. Although I recommend practicing all the exercises in
this book at least one to three times, ultimately you will need to
use your intuition and experience in deciding which ones are most
helpful and beneficial to you, personally, and in what sequence.

Exercise: Radical Forgiveness Written Release Letter[4]

*Date: _____
Name: _____
To my spiritually intelligent self:
I, _____, hereby grant you, the part
of me that is spiritually intelligent, which I might call my
superconscious mind, and all other parts of myself that might
want to hold on to judgments, total permission to release all of
the misunderstandings, unfounded beliefs, misinterpretations,
and misguided emotions, wherever they may reside, whether*

in my body, my unconscious mind, my DNA, my conscious mind, my subconscious mind, my chakras, and even my soul, and I ask all those who want the best for me to assist in this releasing process.

I, _____, thank you, my spiritually intelligent self, for creating the experiences that created the situations causing my judgments and realize that on some level that the situation and the people involved have been my teachers and have offered opportunities for me to learn and to grow. I accept the experiences, without judgment, and do hereby release them forever.

I, _____, do hereby forgive _____.

I release him/her to his/her good and set him/her free. I bless him/her for having been willing to be my teacher. I sever all unhealthy attachments to this person and send him/her unconditional love and support. I am FREE!

I, _____, do hereby forgive myself and accept myself just the way I am and love myself unconditionally just the way I am, in all my power and magnificence. I, _____, do hereby release myself to my highest good and claim for myself freedom; fulfillment of my dreams, wishes, and goals; clarity; love; full expression; creativity; health; and prosperity.

Signed: _____ Date: _____

Witnessed by: _____ Date: _____

APRIL'S RESPONSE TO THE RADICAL FORGIVENESS WRITTEN RELEASE LETTER

To my spiritually intelligent self:
I, April, hereby grant you the part of me that is spiritually intelligent . . .

I, April, thank you, my spiritually intelligent self, for creating . . .

I, April, do hereby forgive my grandma and uncle. I release them . . .

I, April, do hereby forgive myself and accept myself just the way . . .

I, April, do hereby release myself to my highest good and claim for myself freedom . . .

Exercise: The Circle of Love Forgiveness Process[5]

The circle of love forgiveness process, which is adapted from a powerful forgiveness process developed by Steven Thayer, is the last exercise in the book. In a certain sense, it completes the circle you started many chapters ago by including everyone in the world in your forgiveness healing circle and extending love to all those people and yourself as well. Ultimately, it reemphasizes that we are all interconnected on planet Earth and all share the same divine and loving Self, though it is expressed in many different and unique ways. It also reiterates that you can experience forgiveness and healing most effectively when you are aware of the spiritual center within you that guides you, directs you, protects you, and loves you.

Use it anytime you want to see and experience the big picture that forgiveness ultimately offers you.

Close your eyes and relax. Take three slow, deep breaths. Breathe in through your nose and out through your mouth. Breathe slowly and deeply...deeply and slowly. Calm and relaxed...relaxed and calm. Now repeat silently to yourself the word "calm" on the in-breath and "relax" on the out-breath. Calm and relax...calm and relax. Slowly and deeply...deeply and slowly...calm and relax...calm and relax.

1 Now identify three people who you would like to forgive:
a. one person from your past
b. one person currently in your life
c. yourself

2 Put one hand on your heart. Focus on your heart. Think of some- one you love and the love you feel toward that person. Feel that love as strongly as you can. Now think of a few things, situations, or people you are grateful for. Feel that gratitude in your heart. Feel the love in your heart.

3 Imagine a ray of light going from the love in your heart to a place well above your head. See that loving ray of light connect above your head with the divine light and love of your Soul. Some people may want to connect with Infinite Intelligence, guides, masters, angels, or your Higher Self. Imagine that the divine light of your Soul and/or the Infinite Intelligence, guides, masters, angels, or your Higher Self loves you unconditionally. Ask that they now guide you, direct you, love you, and protect you as you go through this forgiveness process. Ask that this forgiveness process be for your highest good and highest healing and for the highest good and healing of everyone else involved in the process and for the universe at large.

The next few steps are forgiveness energy exchanges. Imagine the three people you previously selected. Imagine the person from your past, the person from your present, and yourself standing in a row about ten feet in front of you.

4 **The Past:** The first person who you would like to forgive is the person from your past. Think of their name. Have that person move closer to you until they are standing about three feet away. Imagine that you can roll the love in your heart into the shape and size of a bas- ketball or globe. Take the love from your heart and caress that globe filled with love. Now add more and more love to the globe by using your hands to pack the love into it. Hold the supercharged globe filled with love in your hands in front of your heart. Look this person in the eyes and then slowly push the love in the globe toward this person from your past whom you would like to forgive. Now experience this person taking the love into their heart. Let them fully take in the love. Wait until the energy stabilizes. Next (this is often a little harder) see the person you are forgiving do the same. See them take some love from their heart. See them pack more and more love into a globe. Look them in the eyes and let them place the love from that globe into your heart. Just let it in. Let it fully enter and absorb into your heart. Thank this person and have them move back with the others.

5   **The Present:**   The second person who you would like to forgive is the person currently in your life. Think of that person's name. Have that person move closer to you until they are standing about three feet away. Imagine that you can take a globe filled with love from your heart (about the size of a basketball). Now add more and more love to the globe by using your hands to pack the love into it. Now hold the supercharged globe filled with love in your hands in front of your heart. Look this person in the eyes and then slowly push the love in the globe toward the person from your current life whom you would like to forgive. Experience this person taking the love into their heart. Let them fully take in the love. Wait until the energy stabilizes. Next see the person you are forgiving do the same. See them take some love from their heart. See them pack more and more love into the globe of love. Look them in the eyes and let them place the love into your heart. Just let it in. Let it fully enter and absorb into your heart. Thank this person and have them move back with the others.

6   **Yourself:**   The third person is you. See yourself move closer to you until this image of you is standing about three feet away. Imagine that you can fill a globe about the size of a basketball with love from your heart. Now add more and more love to the globe by using your hands to pack the love into it. Now hold the supercharged globe filled with love in your hands in front of your heart. Look into your own eyes and then slowly push the love within the globe toward yourself and experience that other you taking the love into their heart. Let this image of yourself fully take in the love. Wait until the energy stabilizes. Next see the image of yourself do the same. See this image of you take some love from their heart. See them pack more and more love into a globe filled with love. Look them in the eyes and let them place the love into your heart. Just let it in. Let it fully enter and absorb into your heart. Let all that love sink in deeply, very deeply. Feel that love as it sinks into your heart, slowly and deeply...deeply and slowly. Thank yourself and have yourself move back with the others.

7 **The World:** Hold your arms out to either side, palms facing each other. Do it now. You can imagine doing this if there isn't room to physically do it for some reason. Let the love from your heart flow out through your right arm to the three people standing in front of you. Let the energy pass through these three people and let that energy of love flow back to you as you take it in through your left hand and up your left arm, all the way to your heart, thus completing the circle of love. Now add more people to the circle of love. Imagine more people that you would like to forgive standing in front of you in the circle of love. Add all of your family and friends, your neighbors, and your enemies into this circle of love. Let the love flow out your right arm and into your left arm passing through all these people, passing through the circle of love. Add more and more people until you see the entire population of the planet in front of you, as the love from your heart goes out through your right arm, through everyone in the world, and back into your left arm. The circle of love now includes everyone in the world. The circle of love is now complete. Finally, ask the divine light of your Soul, Infinite Intelligence, your guides, masters, angels, or Higher Self that the circle of love forgiveness process be for your highest good and for the highest good of all people in the circle of love.

8 Take five slow, deep breaths. Breathe slowly and deeply... deeply and slowly...calm and relax...relax and calm. In a few moments, you will be opening your eyes and bringing your consciousness back into the room. Some people, however, may benefit by engaging first in a final balancing and grounding. In this case, you can either hold your hands on top of your feet or place your left hand on your right knee and your right hand on your left knee. Take a few slow, deep breaths. Then slowly, very, very slowly, open your eyes and bring your consciousness back into the room.

Write in your journal what you experienced during this exercise.

APRIL'S RESPONSE

This exercise first allowed me to see that at times I have been very hard on myself throughout my life for many different reasons. As I learn to love myself unconditionally, I can have more positive experiences, and I can also love and accept others more. It then gave me a chance to reflect on all the people in my life that I am grateful for and love very much. When I allow the people I forgive into this circle, then I feel even more love and peace.

Ultimately, every person, situation, and circumstance in your life is designed to help you heal, forgive, and love and to catalyze or support you in your journey of awakening. Many times, this won't be fully apparent to you when you are going through the experience. The forgiveness exercises and processes in this chapter were further developed to help you experience and see that everything that happens is for your own personal and spiritual growth and enlightenment. Every experience, if perceived correctly, is designed to bring you and the people you interact with closer to oneness, love, peace, joy, happiness, resourcefulness, holiness, innocence, strength, and light. Forgiveness thus becomes a very powerful process for facilitating that journey.

CHAPTER 16

Self-Assessment Revisited

"Forgiving, then, is a new vision and a new feeling that is given to the person who forgives.... You will know that forgiveness has begun when you recall those who hurt you and feel the power to wish them well. Forgiveness is love's antidote for hate, beginning with passive hate, the loss of energy to wish people well. So, when we feel the slightest urge to wish that life would go well for them, we have begun to forgive; we have started to release those who hurt us from the blight of the harm they did to us."

—LEWIS B. SMEDES, *Forgive and Forget*

"Forgiveness is a letting go of the past suffering and betrayal,... [it] honors the heart's greatest dignity... it brings back the ground of love.... It is hard to imagine a world without forgiveness.... Without forgiveness our lives are chained, forced to carry the sufferings of the past and repeat them with no release. Consider the dialogue between two former prisoners of war: 'Have you forgiven your captors yet?' 'No never!' 'Well, then, they still have you in prison, don't they?' We begin the work of forgiveness primarily for ourselves."

—JACK KORNFIELD, *The Art of Forgiveness, Lovingkindness, and Peace*

THIS WOULD BE A good time to go back to the questionnaires you filled out in chapter 1 and fill them out again. This will give you an excellent idea of how much progress you have made. Some of you will have made tremendous progress, others perhaps less so. I encourage you, as previously mentioned, to reread the book three times and do all the exercises again, keeping a record in your journal. You may also want to seek out a forgiveness-oriented course, support group, coach, friend, or therapist, depending on how much progress you have made on your own.

In the section below, I have listed April's scores at five-week and ten-week intervals as we reassessed her progress. Remember, your progress might be faster or slower than hers. Whatever your scores are is okay. Be kind to yourself and be persistent.

April took her self-assessments for twenty weeks, reading and doing the rest of the exercises in the book in between, and noticed dramatic improvements in her happiness, life satisfaction, forgiveness, gratitude, affect (emotions), and beliefs after weeks five and ten. Her summary scores are presented below for the fifth and tenth weeks, and some of the bar graphs show her scores for fifteen or even twenty weeks. In addition, some of the bar graphs show changes that April made on other assessment measures not presented in this book.

Summary of April's Scores

SECOND ASSESSMENT SCORING: WEEK 5

Subjective Happiness Scale (SHS) Score	16
Satisfaction with Life (SWLS) Total Score	23
Heartland Self-Forgiveness Subscale Score	27
Heartland Forgiveness of Others Subscale Score	30
Heartland Forgiveness of Circumstances Subscale Score	25
Heartland Forgiveness Scale Total Score	82
Gratitude (GQ6) Total Score	36

THIRD ASSESSMENT SCORING: WEEK 10

Subjective Happiness Scale (SHS) Score   18
Satisfaction with Life (SWLS) Total Score   30
Heartland Self-Forgiveness Subscale Score   32
Heartland Forgiveness of Others Subscale Score   36
Heartland Forgiveness of Circumstances Subscale Score   35
Heartland Forgiveness Scale Total Score   103
Gratitude (GQ6) Total Score   36

The following graphs show the changes in April's scores on measures of anger, depression, life satisfaction, well-being, anxiety, total stress, gratitude, and forgiveness over fifteen and twenty sessions.

April's Bar Graphs

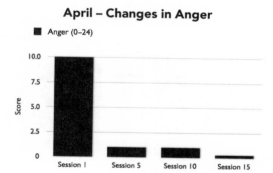

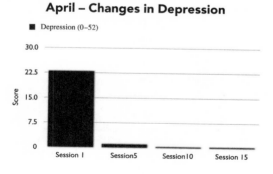

April – Changes in Satisfaction with Life

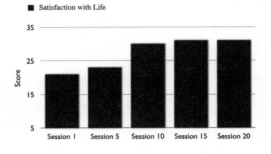

April – Changes in Well-Being

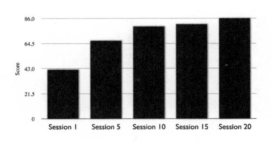

April – Changes in Anxiety

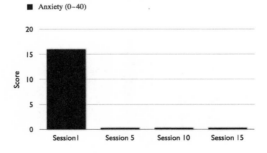

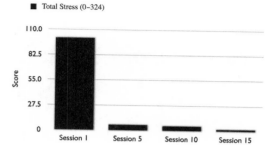

April – Changes in Total Stress

■ Total Stress (0–324)

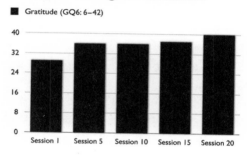

April – Changes in Gratitude

■ Gratitude (GQ6: 6–42)

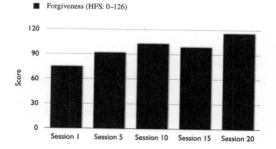

April – Changes in Forgiveness

■ Forgiveness (HFS: 0–126)

Try graphing your own progress as time passes.

CHAPTER 17

Twelve Frequently Asked Questions and Their Answers

O VER THE YEARS, I have been asked many questions about forgiveness—what it really is, how it plays out, why it's so important to do it, etc. Anticipating that you will have some questions, too, I have included the dozen most frequently asked questions and my responses. As you read the questions and answers below, write down your thoughts, feelings, and reactions in your journal.

Question 1. What is the difference between false and true forgiveness?

False forgiveness takes place:

a. when one person considers themselves better than the other person and forgives them with an obvious or subtle attitude of superiority; for example, I am better than you and therefore I will forgive you.

b. when one person considers themselves worse than or inferior to the other person. In this case, the person feels like a martyr and forgives from an attitude of inadequacy and often groveling. In both a and b, there is an inequality perceived between the forgiver and the recipient of the forgiveness, both before and after the forgiveness process.

c. the person forgiving does it conditionally. That is, they say to themselves (or the other person), I will forgive you, but you have to either promise never to do X again or you have to pay or repay me if I forgive you.

d. the potential forgiver will only forgive if the recipient of the forgiveness first apologizes or pays some debt to the person forgiving.

e. the forgiver perceives themselves as forgiving a "sin" or "evil" deed or action by the person being forgiven and basically considers the person to be forgiven blameworthy and guilty. The recipient of the forgiveness is not seen as innocent, let alone a blessed or holy brother or sister whose behavior was an error or mistake, based on fear and calling for help and love.

f. the forgiver focuses on the external behavior of the person being forgiven rather than on their essence or core, which is beyond their behavior. In other words, the forgiver tends to equate the other person with their behavior, which they see as defining them rather than see beyond that to something deeper and more central to who they really are. In all these cases (i.e., a through f), the forgiver sees themself as separate from the one being forgiven, both before and after the forgiveness process.

True forgiveness is done from a place of equality. The person being forgiven is seen as an innocent brother or sister *(generically speaking)*, whose behavior is fear driven, often heavily fear driven.

Moreover, the essence of both people is seen to be the same. The forgiver forgives in order to dissolve the separateness between themselves and their brother or sister. The recipient of the forgiveness is seen as blessed and even holy at their core, their essence, no different from the forgiver, just a person coming from fear and calling for help and love. When one person forgives, then they know that true forgiveness is for giving love and for helping them to reunite with their own undivided center of truth and love. This, in turn, generates peace and generates an energetic shift between the forgiver and the recipient of the forgiveness. The forgiver then experiences a sense of gratitude to the other person for being a "thorny angel," triggering the whole forgiveness process.

Question 2. Aren't there some things that are just basically wrong, bad, and evil and not subject to forgiveness?

There certainly are many religions, philosophies, theories, and perspectives that currently exist and have existed throughout time with that perspective. However, from the point of view taken in this book, everything and everyone is capable of being forgiven. Furthermore, it is the ego's way of thinking that generates right/ wrong, good/bad, innocent/evil, and black/white perspectives. Most of us grew up in families, cultures, religions, and nations that subscribe to one form or another of this thinking. This egoic thinking pattern is based on the illusion that we are somehow separate and, although very common and even natural at times, is quite limited and based on fear. The alternative thought system, based on the Higher Self, divine light, compassion, and love joins and unites rather than divides and separates. It is devoid of blame, judgment, guilt, and attack, which are the basis of polarized, black/white, ego-based thinking.

Of course, realistically, many people will move back and forth between these two thought systems until they are fully awakened and aligned with their true Self. It is not useful to deny that this "egoic thought system" exists within almost everybody. This just leads to more repression and projection and will then show up in distorted and dysfunctional ways. However, knowing that the "egoic thought system" exists allows for diminishing its unconscious projection onto others and for shifting, by choice, to a higher perspective based on Higher Intuition, Wisdom, Love, and Compassion.

Question 3. As a follow-up to the last question, isn't it true that "cheating" on your spouse, boyfriend, or girlfriend is bad and wrong? Isn't it bad to cheat on your taxes, steal money, lie, gamble to excess, be an alcoholic or drug addict, be a dealer of drugs, terrorize, murder, sabotage, steal, kidnap, prostitute, molest, or be an all-around nasty, negative, sarcastic, or mean person? Can you really expect people to forgive these kinds of people?

First of all, research shows that under certain conditions, we all have the capacity to engage in any of these behaviors to a certain degree. Second, there are many variations of the ego's voice that drives people. Many people have experienced various traumas of certain kinds in their life, often in early childhood. These life experiences, themselves driven by fear, trigger people to engage in unskillful and unresourceful behaviors that are often perceived as hurtful and harmful by others.

Because the world is as you see and experience it, every behavior by another person is, in turn, perceived through the personal (usually) egoistic lens of the recipient. The recipient then reacts or responds according to their own conditioning. If the recipient stays calm and peaceful, they can respond in a more resourceful, skillful way that sees that every communication and behavior is either an expression of love or a call for love. Even if the recipient does react emotionally rather than from a higher perspective, they can still practice forgiveness later and return to a more peaceful, loving state.

Of course, it may take some time before they are ready and willing to do this and yet it can be and has been done, even by people who have had children or spouses murdered, had spouses engage in affairs of many years, been raped, tortured, or terrorized. Basically, the "egoic" mind is based on fear, and this fear drives many kinds of behavior that are perceived as hurtful or harmful by others. Fear is a call for love, and by shifting our perception we can learn to see that.

Question 4. Why should I be the one to forgive? After all, my parents neglected, abused, criticized, and ignored me and still do. They favored my sister or brother over me and even sent me to live with my aunt or uncle or grandparents or a boarding school when I was young. I was molested or violated when young and humiliated by my peers. I had ADHD, was dyslexic, or had childhood cancer. I wish others would forgive me and all these people would apologize and make amends.

It is certainly understandable that you feel a lot of distress from these experiences. It is more useful, however, to imagine, as if you were playing a game, that you existed prior to birth as a soul. Imagine that you looked down upon the Earth right before you were going to incarnate in a human body and wondered what set of parents you wanted to select in this lifetime that would maximize your personal, relationship, and spiritual growth. Imagine that you also selected the time period, the culture, the religious group, and even the major people you would meet in this lifetime. Furthermore, imagine that you even could program in many of your major life experiences in order to maximize the possibilities of your personal, relationship, and spiritual growth.

Once you chose your parents and these situations, you were then born in this pretend game and promptly forgot the decisions you had made and why. From this perspective, your life with all these challenges unfolds in order to provide for the maximum opportunities for your personal, relationship, and spiritual growth. However, in order to grow as a person and strengthen yourself, you need to practice forgiveness. All of these people and circumstances then provide you with major growth opportunities that you have set up yourself, from this point of view.

Each time you forgive, you grow emotionally, relationally, and spiritually. Each situation becomes an opportunity to see things differently. It provides you with an opportunity to learn that your feelings do not have to be dependent on external forces and the behavior of other people. Moreover, if you completely forgive everyone and everything in your life, the possibility of true awakening, and even enlightenment, occurs.

Question 5. I don't really believe in the concept of forgiveness. I can believe in acceptance, perhaps, or tolerance but not forgiveness. Why should I forgive?

No one can or will force you to believe in forgiveness. As discussed in this book and other books, forgiveness is a powerful idea, perception, attitude, choice, energy, intention, and decision, with many positive benefits for you, the people you interact with, and potentially the whole planet. However, only you can make the decision to forgive and when you want to start the forgiveness process.

Forgiveness, as previously mentioned, requires a little willingness and a choice and a shift in perception, attitude, and energy. Acceptance is close to forgiveness and yet not quite there. Tolerance is quite a bit further away from forgiveness. It is best to allow yourself, however, to be where you are for now. If you are experiencing all the peace, love, joy, happiness, blessings, and relationship harmony that you want, that is fine. If you are not and want these qualities, then you might want to consider practicing forgiveness at some point in the future. Forgiveness is not something that you *should* do. You may, however, prefer to do it because it works for others and may, in fact, work for you in your life.

Question 6. Are you really trying to tell me I should forgive Hitler or Bin Laden or Saddam Hussein or any other dictator in the world?

No. No one is trying to tell you that you "should" do anything. Shoulds don't work and only create negative energy. However, it is not primarily the external Hitlers or Bin Ladens or Saddam Husseins that we need to forgive but the inner Hitlers or Bin Ladens or Saddam Husseins; that is, the inner dictators that we tend to project out onto other people. In other words, our attack thoughts in the form of the inner dictator, inner controller, inner mugger, etc., will get projected out onto other people unconsciously if we are not aware of them and don't forgive both ourselves and others. This is often referred to as our inner shadow, the inner darkness, or, as previously mentioned, the dark side of our egos.

By owning our projections and forgiving, we actually contribute not only to our own healing but also to the healing of the world. Having said that, it is essential that we own our projections, especially the inner dictator, the inner shadow. It is also very beneficial, and even necessary, to forgive the external "dictators" as well. This frees us from seeing ourselves as a victim of these people and releases us and them from negativity, guilt, resentment, fear, and pain. By forgiving them, we also forgive ourselves.

Question 7. You haven't used the terms "perpetrators" and "victims" like many other authors and clinicians do when discussing the concept of forgiveness. Why is that?

The terms "perpetrators" and "victims" not only have a judgmental bias to them, but they also emphasize the duality and separateness between the people involved. Moreover, these are terms that the egoic mind is more comfortable with, as is society in general. Furthermore, in many cases it is difficult to know, especially in a close relationship, who or what was the trigger that first created the emotional upset, because each party typically blames the other.

Using more neutral and positive terminology is more consistent with the frame of reference used in this book, and clinically it appears to be more useful. In addition, if all situations and people are in your life to facilitate your personal, relationship, and spiritual growth, then it is wiser and more constructive to be forgiving to these people and, at some level, to be grateful that they are in your life pressing your emotional buttons. The most growth usually comes when these "thorny" angels enter your life. Although it is not usually pleasant, these people and situations require the greatest amount of forgiveness, strength, and growth. As a teacher of mine once said, "They are spiritual growth machines. Be grateful they are there."

Question 8. The perspective you are taking toward forgiveness differs from the perspective taken in some other books, even books by very well-known authors, clinicians, and researchers in the field. Why?

Many people over the years have contributed enormously to the field of forgiveness from research, clinical, theoretical, and spiritual or religious points of view. This work stands on the shoulders of all these people. Every one of these people has contributed, usually quite substantially, to furthering forgiveness and healing on the planet. Many of these people have dedicated their lives to helping others forgive or clarifying through research various parameters regarding forgiveness, and they are all to be commended and respected for their hard work and efforts. Many of these authors, clinicians, and researchers have, in fact, contributed to my life, my knowledge, and my thinking. Nevertheless, I intend with this book to make a unique contribution to the literature and to people's lives. If I have succeeded, then the differences between the point of view presented here and those of other authors, clinicians, or researchers will be less important than the similar endeavor of all of us to help people forgive, heal, and perhaps to eventually wake up to their true Self.

Having said that, it is also true that I focus more on both energetic and spiritual approaches to forgiveness than some authors do and offer a wider range of integrative exercises and processes to forgiveness.

Question 9. What is the relationship between forgiveness, love, gratitude, and grace?

There is a close relationship between forgiveness, love, gratitude, and grace. First of all, they are qualities associated with the Higher Self or inner light rather than qualities of the ego-mind. Forgiveness is *for giving* love and gratitude, which in turn opens one up to the experience of grace. (Grace and gratitude come from the same root word—*gratus*, pleasing.)

From the highest perspective, the resentments, anger, hurt, bitterness, pain, grievances, grudges, and judgments made by the ego-mind—though often experienced as very unpleasant and often triggered by thorny as opposed to nurturing angels—provide the maximum opportunity for personal, relationship, and spiritual growth and healing. From this perspective, we can be grateful for the opportunity to practice forgiveness and for ultimately learning to experience truth, to give love, and to undo the illusions of the ego-mind. This, of course, is often quite challenging. Nevertheless, it allows you the opportunity to remember that, at the core, you and everyone else is a holy, innocent child of light and love.

It provides you the opportunity to see that inherent in every perceived difficulty is the seed of an equal or greater benefit. It provides you the opportunity to see that this "thorny" angel or "thorny" situation is actually your "savior," though initially disguised as such.

Question 10. How often should I forgive?

Keep practicing forgiveness until you are in a state of constant light rather than darkness, peace rather than conflict, clarity rather than confusion, love rather than fear, joy rather than sadness, and fully awakened. Whenever you feel any irritation, discomfort, or negative emotion, turn it over to a Higher Power, force, Self, or energy; the Holy Spirit or inner, divine light; or even to the Universe. Then listen within for guidance and practice one or more of the forgiveness exercises in this book. It is okay to practice forgiveness every day or even every hour. It is also common to have forgiven someone or yourself, to be at peace with yourself and/or with the other person or situation, only to discover later that some more or new feelings of anger, hurt, guilt, resentment, grudges, and grievances surface. If this happens to you, it is okay and totally appropriate to forgive yourself, this person, or situation again as new levels of need appear.

It is like peeling layers of an onion. You need to go deeper until everything has been cleared away or cleaned. Without overdoing it, the more you practice forgiveness, the more peace, love, joy, and harmony you will experience in your life.

In addition, the more you practice forgiving, the more you will develop a general disposition to forgiving and, ultimately, a different perception of reality.

Question 11. What is the relationship between forgiveness and assertiveness? Is it ever okay to express strong feelings and say "no"? Won't I be a doormat if I am always forgiving?

The quick answer is no, you will not be a doormat if you forgive all the time, and yes, it is okay to assert yourself. In fact, if you are true to yourself, you will assert yourself many times and say "no" many times because that is aligned with what you want and what you believe. This, in turn, prevents the buildup of negative emotions and feelings that you "should" have done or said something differently, or they "shouldn't" have done or said something, or they "should" have done or said something, and you didn't say what you felt or what your inner guidance was telling you to say or do. If you speak up when you are guided to do so, you will find that you judge yourself and others much less frequently and harshly, and you will need to forgive much less. In other words, you will not harbor grudges and grievances against yourself as often and will experience much less unforgiveness toward others.

Many people are overly nurturing and fear disapproval if they speak up and assert themselves. They then end up being disappointed, hurt, and let down, even though they are kind people. Sometimes it is beneficial for people to assert themselves in order to set a clear boundary with other people, a boundary that creates a safe place for themselves and then allows them to more easily practice forgiving from that safe place. In addition, sometimes your inner guidance will direct you to be assertive, not just on your own behalf but also on behalf of many other people as well. You might call this kind of assertiveness asserting on behalf of the bigger picture and the Higher Self rather than on behalf of the egoic mind. Forgiveness and assertiveness are best seen as complementary rather than as opposites.

Question 12. What is the relationship between forgiveness, awakening, oneness, salvation, and enlightenment?

The ultimate goal of forgiveness is awakening to your true Self, to the inner Beingness of yourself and others. In other words, when you have completely forgiven yourself, everyone else, and everything else completely, then the experience of separation between you and everyone else dissolves, and the experience of awakening, oneness, salvation, or enlightenment becomes a possibility. This goal may be more than most people are seeking. Still, it is the end goal of the practice of forgiveness and potentially available to everyone. As you extend forgiveness, so too do you receive forgiveness. As you extend love, so too do you receive love. As you extend gratitude, so too do you receive gratitude. As you extend blessings, so too do you receive blessings. As you offer light, so too do you receive light. Then the grace of awakening, oneness, salvation, and enlightenment becomes available to you.

Most people initially pursue the path of forgiveness for their own personal well-being and to reduce emotional distress. However, as you continue to pursue it diligently, you eventually discover that forgiveness can be a powerful catalyst for the transformation of consciousness, for planetary healing, and for spiritual awakening, oneness, salvation, and enlightenment.

Now write down any further questions you have in your journal!

CHAPTER 18

Review, Recommendations, and Returning Home

I F YOU HAVE COME with me through the past seventeen chapters, you have completed a powerful journey. Early in that journey, you planted some forgiveness seeds. If you have diligently and conscientiously followed most of the prescriptions recommended in these chapters, those forgiveness seeds have begun to sprout. You will be experiencing yourself as much closer to Home, to your authentic or true Self, to the divine light within you. You will have released a great deal of the emotional baggage you have been carrying around with you. You will have significantly improved one or more relationships. As you know from the introduction, I strongly recommend that you reread and do the exercises and processes in this book three times to develop a high degree of mastery of the forgiveness solution and realize the most benefits from it. But you should certainly feel very good about the work you've done so far.

Summary Pointers, Recommendations, and Practices to Help You Arrive Home to Your True, Authentic Self, Using the Forgiveness Solution

In the next two sections, I am going to summarize some of the key points we've covered in a worksheet format and make some recommendations for you to follow in the weeks, months, and years to come.

What follows is a brief summary of the forgiveness solution process in a worksheet format.

Forgiveness Solution Brief Worksheet

1   **Briefly, list up to four grudges, grievances, judgments, and attack thoughts you currently hold.**

Against yourself

  a. _____

  b. _____

Against someone else

  c. _____

  d. _____

2   **On a 10-point scale, how strong, currently, are your grudges, grievances, judgments, and attack thoughts against yourself or someone else?**

    (1 is very strong; 10 is very weak or not at all.)

  a. Against yourself _____

  b. Against someone else _____

3   **On a 10-point scale, how much peace, love, joy, happiness, and harmony are you currently experiencing?**

    (10 is a great deal; 1 is very little to none at all.) _____

Set the goal of forgiveness first: for example, peace, love, joy, happiness, and harmony in your relationships. This is actually the most important step in the forgiveness process.

4   **How willing are you to take 100 percent responsibility for all your experiences (feelings, thoughts, actions)?**

    (10 is completely willing; 1 is not at all.) _____

The more you are willing to take complete responsibility for your thoughts, feelings, and actions, the easier it will be for you to forgive. Say out loud: "I am willing to take complete responsibility for my thoughts, feelings, and actions."

5 **How strong is your current willingness to forgive yourself or this other person?**

(10 is very strong; 1 is very weak or not at all.) _____

Have a "little willingness"; choose consciously to be willing to forgive. Say out loud: "I am willing to forgive" or "I am willing to learn how to forgive."

6 **How strong is your current choice to forgive yourself or this other person?**

(10 is very strong; 1 is very weak or not at all.) _____

Choose consciously to forgive; that is, to begin to let go of and release judgments, grievances, attack thoughts, and shoulds. Say out loud: "I choose to forgive" or "I choose to learn how to forgive."

7 **How willing are you to choose to see things differently regarding this person or yourself?**

(10 is completely willing; 1 is not at all.) _____

Choose to see things differently; for example, choose to see that anger covers up fear, and fear is a call for love. (Again, choice empowers you. Learning to shift perception is essential in the forgiveness process.) Say out loud: "I am willing to see things differently."

8 **How aware are you that forgiveness is a process that unfolds over time?**

(10 is very aware; 1 is very unaware.) _____

Forgiveness of self and others is a process that unfolds over time. (Although forgiveness sometimes occurs dramatically, often it unfolds gradually over time.)

9 **How strongly are you holding on to the hope for a different and/or better past?**

(10 is not at all; 1 is very strongly.) _____

Choose to let go of the hope of a different and better past. (Most often, when you have not forgiven, you have been hoping and wishing that the past was different and better in some way.)

10   **How strong is your desire to be right?**
(10 is very weak; 1 is very strong.) _____
Choose consciously to be happy rather than right. (The ego-mind wants to be right. Our true Self wants to be happy.)

11   **How compassionate are you with yourself or someone else?**
(10 is very compassionate; 1 is not at all.) _____
Choose to be compassionate with yourself and others. (Being compassionate with yourself and others facilitates forgiveness.)

12   **How willing are you to see things from the other's point of view (shift perspective)?**
(10 is very willing; 1 is not at all.) _____
Choose consciously to see things from the other person's point of view and empathize with them. (The willingness and ability to shift perspective and to empathize is a great asset in the forgiveness process.)

13   **How willing are you to take one small step at a time in the forgiveness process?**
(10 is very willing; 1 is not at all.) _____
Remember that an inch is a cinch, a yard is hard; take one small step at a time. (Although forgiveness can sometimes occur rapidly, it is useful to think of taking small steps during the forgiveness process.)

14   **Have you turned the forgiveness process over to a Higher Power or force?**
(10 is all the time; 1 is never.) _____
Turn the forgiveness process over to the Higher Self within you, sometimes referred to as a Higher Power, the Holy Spirit, the Inner Center, wisdom, source, etc. (The "ego-mind" within us doesn't want to for-

give. Remember, forgiveness is a learned process, attitude, and shift in perception and beliefs. Most people need help from a higher part of their mind/Being.)

15 **Have you changed the grievance/attack story into one of preference or acceptance?**

(10 is all the time; 1 is not at all.) _____

Change the grievance/attack story (self or others) to one of acceptance or preference. (Everyone has a story around unforgiveness and holding on to grievances and judgments. Change the story to one of *preferring* that things had happened differently but *accepting* what actually happened so that you can move on. Also be willing to change your current story to one of *preferring* that things were currently happening differently.)

16 **Are you holding on to shoulds and unenforceable rules?**

(10 is not at all; 1 is all the time.) _____

Let go of "unenforceable rules" and shoulds, such as, "They should have done X; I should have done Y." (Similar to step 10. Stop "shoulding" on yourself or others, which is a judgment and attack on them or yourself.)

17 **Are you taking things very seriously or personally?**

(10 is not at all; 1 is all the time.) _____

Lighten up. Don't take things so seriously or so personally. (Whenever anyone is immersed in unforgiving thoughts and feelings, they usually take things too hard. Laughing, looking on the lighter side, and getting some distance on the experience/events helps a great deal.)

18 **Are you focusing on the positives, the goodness, the light in yourself and others?**

(10 is all the time; 1 is not at all.) _____

Remember that what you focus on expands. What you pay attention to grows. Focus on seeing/feeling the magnificence/greatness in each person, including yourself. You attract what you focus on. So learn to focus on the positives, the goodness, the light in yourself and others.

19 **Are you willing to see and learn that forgiveness is a key to happiness, peace, love, joy, and harmony in relationships?**
(10 is completely willing; 1 is not at all.) _____
Remember that forgiveness is a key to happiness, innocence, peace, joy, love, healing, compassion, kindness, empowerment, effective communication, emotional stability, and well-being, which are the essence of your core Self or Being. With practice, you *can* learn to recognize/remember that essence. (Ultimately, the forgiveness process allows you to rediscover who you really are at your core. It reconnects you with wholeness, resilience, resourcefulness, blessings, strength, giving, and unconditional love.)

20 **Are you practicing the exercises and processes you have learned, such as the Psychological Uplifter, Positive Pressure Point Techniques, forgiveness imagery, affirmations, and afformations?**
(10 is all the time; 1 is not at all.) _____
The Psychological Uplifter, Positive Pressure Point Techniques, and forgiveness imagery, affirmations, and afformations are some of the powerful techniques and processes in this book that will help you greatly accelerate the forgiveness process.

Add up the twenty numbers you wrote down next to the twenty pointers above. _____
Divide that score by two. _____
This score should be between 10 and 100; the higher, the better. (April's Score was 89 out of 100.)

Twelve Follow-Up Exercises and Practices
1 Once a month, retake the questionnaires on happiness, life satisfaction, gratitude, and forgiveness in chapter 1.

2 Once every month, write down a set of five to ten positive and forgiveness solution-related goals to focus on (see chapter 6).

3 Select three or more forgiveness affirmations (which are discussed in chapters 2, 4, and especially 7) and use them daily. Apply them to every distressing feeling, belief, relationship, and situation you encounter.

4 Select one or two afformations discussed in chapter 8 and practice them at least three times a week.

5 Practice using Psychological Uplifter 2, especially the Anything Is Possible step, daily (see chapter 9).

6 Select at least two of the Positive Pressure Point Techniques (energetic forgiveness) described in chapters 9 and 10 and practice them daily.

7 Select at least three of the forgiveness imagery exercises described in chapters 11 through 15 (transformational forgiveness) and practice one of them three to five times a week.

8 Practice repeating, "I am sorry; please forgive me; thank you; I love you" often throughout the day (see chapter 12).

9 Write a series of forgiveness letters and/or do the forgiveness worksheets at least once a month or more frequently (see chapters 13 and 15).

10 Reread *The Forgiveness Solution* and/or read a book listed in the "Recommended Reading" section (see p. 237).

11 Contact one of the "Resources Recommended" listed at the end of the book (see p. 245).

12 Check the forgiveness solution website at *www.forgiveness solution.com* for updates to the forgiveness solution processes, exercises, worksheets, research, questionnaires, quotes, and forgiveness stories and to share your experiences using the forgiveness solution. Also check the website for dates and times of workshops on the forgiveness solution.

Finally, may your life be blessed from the benefits of learning and using the forgiveness solution. May the forgiveness solution process lead you to a renewed and inspired purpose and vision in life. May you master the forgiveness solution process and teach others what you have learned. May the highest light guide you on your profound journey through life.

An old Cherokee Indian told his grandson: "We have two wolves in us who are fighting with each other. One wolf is fear, resentment, anger, guilt, greed, ego, and negative thoughts. The other wolf is love, peace, joy, forgiveness, compassion, kindness, and positive thoughts."

The grandson asked, "Which wolf will win?"

The Cherokee elder said, "The one we feed."

Notes

INTRODUCTION

1. Robert D. Enright, *Forgiveness Is a Choice: A Step-by-Step Process for Resolving Anger and Restoring Hope* (Washington, DC: American Psychological Association, 2001); Fred Luskin, *Forgive for Good: A Proven Prescription for Health and Happiness* (San Francisco: HarperSanFrancisco, 2002); Fred Luskin, *Forgive for Love: The Missing Ingredient for a Healthy and Lasting Relationship* (New York: HarperOne, 2007); Michael E. McCullough et al., "The Psychology of Forgiveness: History, Conceptual Issues, and Overview," in Michael E. McCullough, Kenneth I. Pargament, and Carl E. Thoresen, eds., *Forgiveness: Theory, Research, and Practice* (New York: Guilford Press, 2000); Everett Worthington, *Five Steps to Forgiveness: The Art and Science of Forgiving* (New York: Crown, 2001); Everett L. Worthington, Jr., ed., *Handbook of Forgiveness* (New York: Routledge, 2005); and Philip Friedman and Loren Toussaint, "The Relationship between Forgiveness, Gratitude, Distress, and Well-Being: An Integrative Review of the Literature," *International Journal of Healing and Caring* 6, no. 2 (2006): 1–10.

2. Everett L. Worthington, Jr., C. V. O. Witvliet, P. Pietrini, and A. J. Miller, "Forgiveness, Health, and Well-Being: A Review of Evidence for Emotional versus Decisional Forgiveness, Dispositional Forgivingness, and Reduced Unforgiveness," *Journal of Behavioral Medicine* 30 (2007): 291–302.

3. Jon R. Webb, K. Brewer, and D. Skaggs, "Gender Differences in the Relationship between Forgiveness and Health" (San Francisco: 115th Annual Convention of the APA, Division 38—Health Psychology, August 2007).

4. Frank D. Fincham, J. Hall, and S. R. H. Beach, "Forgiveness in Marriage: Current Status and Future Directions," *Family Relations* 55 (2006): 415–427.

5. Mark S. Rye, K. I. Pargament, W. Pan, et al., "Can Group Interventions Facilitate Forgiveness of an Ex-spouse? A Randomized Clinical Trial," *Journal of Consulting and Clinical Psychology* 73, no. 5 (October 2005): 880–892.

6. Philip Friedman, and L. Toussaint (2006), "Changes in Forgiveness, Gratitude, Stress, and Well-Being during Psychotherapy: An Integrative, Evidence-Based Approach," *International Journal of Healing and Caring* 6, no. 2 (2006): 11–28; and Loren Toussaint and Philip Friedman, "Forgiveness, Gratitude, and Well-Being: The Mediating Role of Affect and Beliefs," *Journal of Happiness Studies,* Springer Online (2008): DOI 10.1007/s10902-008-9111-8.

CHAPTER 3
1. *A Course in Miracles* (Mill Valley, CA: Foundation for Inner Peace, 1975).
2. Ibid.

CHAPTER 4
1. *A Course in Miracles* (Mill Valley, CA: Foundation for Inner Peace, 1975).
2. Dawson Church, *The Genie in Your Genes: Epigenetic Medicine and the New Biology of Intention* (Santa Rosa, CA: Elite Books, 2007).
3. David R. Hawkins, *Power vs. Force: The Hidden Determinants of Human Behavior* (Sedona, AZ: Veritas Publishing, 1995).
4. Esther Hicks and Jerry Hicks, *The Amazing Power of Deliberate Intent: Living the Art of Allowing* (Carlsbad, CA: Hay House, 2006).
5. Gerald G. Jampolsky, *Love Is Letting Go of Fear* (Millbrae, CA: Celestial Arts, 1979).
6. *A Course in Miracles.*
7. Gerald G. Jampolsky, *Forgiveness: The Greatest Healer of All* (Hillsboro, OR: Beyond Words Publishing, 1999).
8. *A Course in Miracles.*
9. Jampolsky, *Love Is Letting Go of Fear;* and Jampolsky, *Forgiveness.*
10. Marilee Adams, *Change Your Questions, Change Your Life: 7 Powerful Tools for Life and Work* (San Francisco: Berrett-Koehler, 2004).
11. Jampolsky, *Love Is Letting Go of Fear;* and Jampolsky, *Forgiveness.*
12. *A Course in Miracles.*

CHAPTER 6
1. Gary Craig, *The EFT Manual* (Santa Rosa, CA: Energy Psychology Press, 2008). EFT stands for Emotional Freedom Techniques.
2. Philip Friedman, *Integrative Healing Manual* (Plymouth Meeting, PA: Foundation for Well-Being, 2001); and Phillip Mountrose and Jane Mountrose, *The Heart & Soul of EFT and Beyond* (Sacramento, CA: Holistic Communications, 2006).

CHAPTER 7
1. Werner Erhard, *Erhard Seminar Training (est)* (Philadelphia: 1977).

CHAPTER 8
1. Edmund Jacobson, *Progressive Relaxation: A Physiological and Clinical Investigation of Muscular States and Their Significance in Psychology and Medical Practice* (Chicago: University of Chicago Press, 1938).

2. Joseph Wolpe and Arnold A. Lazarus, *Behavior Therapy Techniques: A Guide to the Treatment of Neuroses* (Oxford, NY: Pergamon Press, 1966).

3. Philip Friedman, *Creating Well-Being: The Healing Path to Love, Peace, Self-Esteem, and Happiness* (Saratoga, CA: R&E Publishers, 1989).

4. Noah St. John and D. Berar, *The Great Little Book of Afformations* (Chicago: MetaPublishing, 2006).

CHAPTER 9

1. Craig, *The EFT Manual;* Mountrose and Mountrose, *The Heart & Soul of EFT and Beyond;* Fred Gallo, *Energy Tapping: How to Rapidly Eliminate Anxiety, Depression, Cravings, and More Using Energy Psychology* (Oakland, CA: New Harbinger Publications, 2008); Tapas Fleming, *TAT Professional Manual* (Redondo Beach, CA: TATLife, 2007); Sheila S. Bender and Mary Sise, *The Energy of Belief: Psychology's Power Tools to Focus Intention and Release Blocking Beliefs* (Santa Rosa, CA: Energy Psychology Press, 2008); John H. Diepold, Victoria Britt, and Sheila Bender, *Evolving Thought Field Therapy: The Clinician's Handbook of Diagnoses, Treatment, and Theory* (New York: Norton, 2004); Daniel J. Benor, *7 Minutes to Natural Pain Release: Tapping Your Pain Away with WHEE, the Revolutionary New Self-Healing Method* (Santa Rosa, CA: Energy Psychology Press, 2008); Asha Clinton, *Advanced Integrative Therapy* (West Stockbridge, MA: 2008); Larry Nims and Joan Sotkin, *Be Set Free Fast* (Goodyear, AZ, 2007); Steve Reed, *Quick Remap: Self-Help Book* (Richardson, TX: self-published, 2007); David Feinstein, Donna Eden, and Gary Craig, *The Promise of Energy Psychology: Revolutionary Tools for Dramatic Personal Change* (New York: Jeremy P. Tarcher/Penguin, 2005).

CHAPTER 10

1. Philip Friedman, "Miracle Acupressure Tapping Technique (MATT)," in *Integrative Healing Manual* (see chap. 6, n. 2).

2. Tapas Fleming, *TAT Professional Manual* (Redondo Beach, CA: TATLife, 2007).

3. Philip Friedman, "Active Choice Technique (ACT)," in *Integrative Healing Manual.*

CHAPTER 11

1. Friedman, *Creating Well-Being* (see chap. 8, n. 3).

2. Friedman, *Integrative Healing Manual* (see chap. 6, n. 2).

3. Martha Crampton, White Light Self-Forgiveness Exercise (New York: 1999). Adapted with permission.

4. Friedman, *Integrative Healing Manual.*

CHAPTER 12

1. Martha Crampton, Empty Chair Exercise (New York: 1990). Adapted with permission.
2. See *www.todayisthatday.com/blog/do-you-ho-oponopono;* and Joe Vitale and Ihaleakala Hew Len, *Zero Limits: The Secret Hawaiian System for Wealth, Health, Peace, and More* (Hoboken, NJ: Wiley, 2007).

CHAPTER 13

1. Allen Watson and Robert Perry, *A Workbook Companion: Commentaries on the Workbook for Students from A Course in Miracles,* vol. 2 (West Sedona, AZ: Circle Publishing, 2006): Lessons 181–365. Adapted with permission.

CHAPTER 14

1. Based on an adaptation of "A Course in Miracles Composite Forgiveness Exercise," developed by Robert Perry, of the Circle of Atonement, with his permission. See *www.circleofa.org/articles/CompositeForgivenessExercise.php* for specific references to the numbers, pages, and lessons in *A Course in Miracles.*

CHAPTER 15

1. Inspired by a forgiveness audiotape (1995) from Pathways of Light *(www .pathwaysoflight.org);* used with permission from the directors, Robert and Mary Stoelting.
2. Summary of the basic teachings of radical forgiveness by Colin Tipping from his website, *www.radicalforgiveness.com* and his book *Radical Forgiveness: Making Room for the Miracle* (Marietta, GA: Global 13 Publishers, 2002). The summary and the two exercises are used with his permission.
3. Ibid.
4. Ibid.
5. Adapted from the IET® (Integrated Energy Therapy®) forgiveness process audio CD program by Steven J. Thayer © 2002 The Center of Being, Inc.; used with permission from The Center of Being, Inc. See *www.LearnIET.com.*

Recommended Reading

FORGIVENESS-RELATED BOOKS

Burroughs, Tony. *The Code: 10 Intentions for a Better World.* San Francisco: Red Wheel/Weiser, 2008.

A Course in Miracles. Mill Valley, CA: Foundation for Inner Peace, 1975.

Dalai Lama. *The Wisdom of Forgiveness: Intimate Conversations and Journeys.* New York: Riverhead Books, 2004.

Doyle, DavidPaul, and Candace Doyle. *The Voice for Love.* Ashland, OR: The Voice for Love, 2006.

Enright, Robert D. *Forgiveness Is a Choice: A Step-by-Step Process for Resolving Anger and Restoring Hope.* Washington, DC: American Psychological Association, 2001.

Ford, Debbie. *Why Good People Do Bad Things: How to Stop Being Your Own Worst Enemy.* New York: HarperOne, 2008.

Friedman, Philip. *Creating Well-Being: The Healing Path to Love, Peace, Self-Esteem, and Happiness.* Saratoga, CA: R&E Publishers, 1989.

Jampolsky, Gerald. *Forgiveness: The Greatest Healer of All.* Hillsboro, OR: Beyond Words Publishing, 1999.

Luskin, Fred. *Forgive for Good: A Proven Prescription for Health and Happiness.* San Francisco: HarperSanFrancisco, 2002.

Perry, Robert. *The Path of Light: Stepping into Peace with A Course in Miracles.* West Sedona, AZ: Circle Publishing, 2004.

Ponticello, Tony. *After Enlightenment: 16 Articles about A Course in Miracles.* San Francisco: Community Miracles Center, 2009.

Renard, Gary. *The Disappearance of the Universe: Straight Talk about Illusions, Past Lives, Religion, Sex, Politics, and the Miracles of Forgiveness.* Carlsbad, CA: Hay House, 2004.

Rosenthal, S., and Reeve, S. R. *With Forgiveness.* Ashland, OR: Pass Along Concepts, 2006.

Sai Maa Lakshmi Devi. *Petals of Grace: Essential Teachings for Self-Mastery.* Crestone, CO: Humanity in Unity, 2005.

Swami Chidvilasananda. *Enthusiasm.* South Fallsburg, NY: SYDA Foundation, 1997.

Tipping, Colin. *Radical Forgiveness: Making Room for the Miracle.* Marietta, GA: Global 13 Publications, 2002.

Vitale, Joe, and Ihaleakala Hew Len. *Zero Limits: The Secret Hawaiian System for Wealth, Health, Peace, and More.* Hoboken, NJ: Wiley, 2007.

Wapnick, Kenneth. *The Message of A Course in Miracles.* Roscoe, NY: Foundation for "A Course in Miracles," 1997.

Williamson, Marianne. *The Age of Miracles: Embracing the New Midlife.* Carlsbad, CA: Hay House, 2008.

Worthington, Everett. *Five Steps to Forgiveness: The Art and Science of Forgiving.* New York: Crown, 2001.

ENERGY HEALING-RELATED BOOKS

Bender, Sheila, and Mary Sise. *The Energy of Belief: Psychology's Power Tools to Focus Intention and Release Blocking Beliefs.* Santa Rosa, CA: Energy Psychology Press, 2008.

Benor, Daniel J. *7 Minutes to Natural Pain Release: Tapping Your Pain Away with WHEE, the Revolutionary New Self-Healing Method.* Santa Rosa, CA: Energy Psychology Press, 2008.

Craig, Gary. *The EFT Manual.* Santa Rosa, CA: Energy Psychology Press, 2008.

Diepold, John H., V. Britt, and S. Bender. *Evolving Thought Field Therapy: The Clinician's Handbook of Diagnoses, Treatment, and Theory.* New York: Norton, 2004.

Feinstein, David, D. Eden, and G. Craig. *The Promise of Energy Psychology: Revolutionary Tools for Dramatic Personal Change.* New York: Jeremy P. Tarcher/ Penguin, 2005.

Fleming, Tapas. *TAT Professional Manual.* Redondo Beach, CA: TATLife, 2007.

Friedman, Philip. *Integrative Healing Manual.* Plymouth Meeting, PA: Foundation for Well-Being, 2001.

Gallo, Fred. *Energy Psychology: Explorations at the Interface of Energy, Cognition, Behavior, and Health.* Boca Raton, FL: CRC Press, 2005.

———. *Energy Tapping for Trauma.* Oakland, CA: New Harbinger Publications, 2007.

Mountrose, Phillip, and Jane Mountrose. *The Heart & Soul of EFT and Beyond.* Sacramento, CA: Holistic Communications, 2006.

Nims, Larry, and J. Sotkin. *Be Set Free Fast.* Goodyear, AZ: 2007.

PROFESSIONAL READING LIST

Adams, Marilee. *Change Your Questions, Change Your Life: 7 Powerful Tools for Life and Work.* San Francisco: Berrett-Koehler, 2004.

Bender, Sheila, and Mary Sise. *The Energy of Belief: Psychology's Power Tools to Focus Intention and Release Blocking Beliefs.* Santa Rosa, CA: Energy Psychology Press, 2008.

Benor, Daniel J. *7 Minutes to Natural Pain Release: Tapping Your Pain Away with WHEE, the Revolutionary New Self-Healing Method.* Santa Rosa, CA: Energy Psychology Press, 2008.

Burroughs, Tony. *The Code: 10 Intentions for a Better World.* San Francisco: Red Wheel/Weiser, 2008.

Callahan, Roger. *Tapping the Healer Within: Using Thought Field Therapy to Instantly Conquer Your Fears, Anxieties, and Emotional Distress.* Lincolnwood, IL: Contemporary Books, 2001.

Carson, James W., Francis J. Keefe, Veerainder Goli, et al. "Forgiveness and Chronic Low Back Pain: A Preliminary Study Examining the Relationship of Forgiveness to Pain, Anger, and Psychological Distress." *Journal of Pain* 6, no. 2 (2005): 84–91.

Choquette, Sonia. *Your Heart's Desire: Instructions for Creating the Life You Really Want.* New York: Three Rivers Press, 1997.

Church, Dawson. *The Genie in Your Genes: Epigenetic Medicine and the New Biology of Intention.* Santa Rosa, CA: Elite Books, 2007.

Clinton, Asha. *Advanced Integrative Therapy.* West Stockbridge, MA: 2008.

Cloke, Kenneth, and Joan Goldsmith. *Resolving Personal and Organizational Conflict.* San Francisco: Jossey-Bass, 2000.

A Course in Miracles. Mill Valley, CA: Foundation for Inner Peace, 1975.

Craig, Gary. *The EFT Manual.* Santa Rosa, CA: Energy Psychology Press, 2008.

Crampton, Martha. White Light Self-Forgiveness Exercise. New York: 1999.

Dalai Lama. *The Wisdom of Forgiveness: Intimate Conversations and Journeys.* New York: Riverhead Books, 2004.

Diener, Ed, Robert A. Emmons, Randy J. Larsen, and Sharon Griffin. "The Satisfaction with Life Scale." *Journal of Personality Assessment* 49, no. 1 (1985): 71–75.

Diepold, John H., V. Britt, and S. Bender. *Evolving Thought Field Therapy: The Clinician's Handbook of Diagnoses, Treatment, and Theory.* New York: Norton, 2004.

Doyle, DavidPaul, and Candace Doyle. *The Voice for Love.* Ashland, OR: The Voice for Love, 2006.

Emmons, Robert A., and Michael E. McCullough. "Counting Blessings versus Burdens: An Experimental Investigation of Gratitude and Subjective Well-Being in Daily Life." *Journal of Personality and Social Psychology* 84, no. 2 (2003): 377–389.

Enright, Robert D. *Forgiveness Is a Choice: A Step-by-Step Process for Resolving Anger and Restoring Hope.* Washington, DC: American Psychological Association, 2001.

Farrow, Tom F. D., Ying Zheng, Iain D. Wilkinson, et al. "Investigating the Functional Anatomy of Empathy and Forgiveness." *NeuroReport* 12, no. 11 (August 2001): 2433–2438.

Feinstein, David, D. Eden, and G. Craig. *The Promise of Energy Psychology: Revolutionary Tools for Dramatic Personal Change.* New York: Jeremy P. Tarcher/ Penguin, 2005.

Fincham, Frank D., J. Hall, and S. R. H. Beach. "Forgiveness in Marriage: Current Status and Future Directions." *Family Relations* 55 (2006): 415–427.

Fleming, Tapas. *TAT Professional Manual.* Redondo Beach, CA: TATLife, 2007.

Ford, Debbie. *Why Good People Do Bad Things: How to Stop Being Your Own Worst Enemy.* New York: HarperOne, 2008.

Fredrickson, Barbara. *Positivity.* New York: Crown Publishers, 2009.

Fredrickson, Barbara L., and Marcial F. Losada. "Positive Affect and the Complex Dynamics of Human Flourishing." *American Psychologist* 60, no. 7 (October 2005): 678–686.

Friedman, Philip. "Integrative Psychotherapy." In Richie Herink, ed. *The Psychotherapy Handbook.* New York: New American Library, 1980.

———. *Creating Well-Being: The Healing Path to Love, Peace, Self-Esteem, and Happiness.* Saratoga, CA: R&E Publishers, 1989.

———. *Friedman Well-Being Scale and Professional Manual.* Plymouth Meeting, PA: Foundation for Well-Being and Menlo Park, CA: Mind Garden, 1992.

———. *Friedman Belief Scale and Research Manual.* Plymouth Meeting, PA: Foundation for Well-Being, 1993.

———. *Friedman Affect Scale.* Plymouth Meeting, PA: Foundation for Well-Being, 1998.

———. *Integrative Healing Manual.* Plymouth Meeting, PA: Foundation for Well-Being, 2001.

———. "Integrative Energy and Spiritual Therapy." In Fred Gallo, ed. *Energy Psychology in Psychotherapy: A Comprehensive Sourcebook.* New York: Norton, 2002.

———. "Pressure Point Therapy." In Phillip Mountrose and Jane Mountrose. *The Heart & Soul of EFT and Beyond.* Sacramento, CA: Holistic Communications, 2006.

Friedman, Philip, and Loren Toussaint. "The Relationship between Forgiveness, Gratitude, Distress, and Well-Being: An Integrative Review of the Literature." *International Journal of Healing and Caring* 6, no. 2 (2006): 1–10.

———. "Changes in Forgiveness, Gratitude, Stress, and Well-Being during Psychotherapy: An Integrative, Evidence-Based Approach." *International Journal of Healing and Caring* 6, no. 2 (2006): 11–28.

Gallo, Fred. *Energy Psychology: Explorations at the Interface of Energy, Cognition, Behavior, and Health.* Boca Raton, FL: CRC Press, 2005.

———. *Energy Tapping for Trauma.* Oakland, CA: New Harbinger Publications, 2007.

Gallo, Fred, and Harry Vincenzi. *Energy Tapping: How to Rapidly Eliminate Anxiety, Depression, Cravings, and More Using Energy Psychology.* Oakland, CA: New Harbinger Publications, 2008.

Gottman, John M. *Why Marriages Succeed or Fail.* New York: Simon & Schuster, 2005.

Hawkins, David R. *Power vs. Force: The Hidden Determinants of Human Behavior.* Sedona, AZ: Veritas Publishing, 1995.

Hicks, Esther, and Jerry Hicks. *The Amazing Power of Deliberate Intent: Living the Art of Allowing.* Carlsbad, CA: Hay House, 2006.

Jacobson, Edmund. *Progressive Relaxation: A Physiological and Clinical Investigation of Muscular States and Their Significance in Psychology and Medical Practice.* Chicago: University of Chicago Press, 1938.

Jampolsky, Gerald. *Love Is Letting Go of Fear.* Millbrae, CA: Celestial Arts, 1979.

———. *Forgiveness: The Greatest Healer of All.* Hillsboro, OR: Beyond Words Publishing, 1999.

Jampolsky, Gerald, and Diane V. Cirincione. *Finding Our Way Home: Heartwarming Stories That Ignite Our Spiritual Core.* Carlsbad, CA: Hay House, 2008.

Kaplan, Berton H. "Social Health and the Forgiving Heart: The Type B Story." *Journal of Behavioral Medicine* 15, no. 1 (1992): 3–14.

Lawler, Kathleen, and Rachel Piferi. "The Forgiving Personality: Describing a Life Well Lived?" *Personality and Individual Differences* 41, no. 6 (2006): 1009–1020.

Lawler, Kathleen, Jarred Younger, Rachel Piferi, et al. "The Unique Effects of Forgiveness on Health: An Exploration of Pathways." *Journal of Behavioral Medicine* 28, no. 2 (April 2005): 157–167.

Leach, M. M. "Interpersonal Forgiveness: A Linguistic Analysis of the Process." Paper presented at the 5th Annual Loyola Mid-Year Conference on Religion and Spirituality. Baltimore, MD, 2007.

Luskin, Fred. *Forgive for Good: A Proven Prescription for Health and Happiness.* San Francisco: HarperSanFrancisco, 2002.

———. *Forgive for Love: The Missing Ingredient for a Healthy and Lasting Relationship.* New York: HarperOne, 2007.

Lyubomirsky, Sonja, and Heidi Lepper. "A Measure of Subjective Happiness: Preliminary Reliability and Construct Validation." *Social Indicators Research* 46, no. 2 (February 1999): 137–155.

Mackie, Greg. *How Can We Forgive Murderers? And Other Answers to Questions about A Course in Miracles.* West Sedona, AZ: Circle of Atonement, 2003.

McCullough, Michael E., et al., "The Psychology of Forgiveness: History, Conceptual Issues, and Overview." In Michael E. McCullough, Kenneth I. Pargament, and Carl E. Thoresen, eds., *Forgiveness: Theory, Research, and Practice.* New York: Guilford Press, 2000.

McCullough, Michael E., Robert A. Emmons, and Jo-Ann Tsang. "The Grateful Disposition: A Conceptual and Empirical Topography." *Journal of Personality and Social Psychology* 82, no. 1 (2002): 112–127.

McCullough, Michael E., Lindsey M. Root, and Adam D. Cohen. "Writing about the Personal Benefits of a Transgression Facilitates Forgiveness." *Journal of Consulting and Clinical Psychology* 74, no. 5 (October 2006): 887–897.

Mountrose, Phillip, and Jane Mountrose. *The Heart & Soul of EFT and Beyond.* Sacramento, CA: Holistic Communications, 2006.

Nims, Larry, and J. Sotkin. *Be Set Free Fast.* Goodyear, AZ: 2007.

Perry, Robert. *The Path of Light: Stepping into Peace with A Course in Miracles.* West Sedona, AZ: Circle Publishing, 2004.

———. *Return to the Heart of God: The Practical Philosophy of A Course in Miracles.* West Sedona, AZ: Circle Publishing, 2007.

Piedmont, Ralph, and Philip Friedman. "Spirituality, Religiosity, and Quality of Life." In *Handbook of Social Indicators and Quality of Life Research.* New York: Springer, in press.

Ponticello, Rev. Tony. *After Enlightenment: 16 Articles about A Course in Miracles.* San Francisco: Community Miracles Center, 2009.

Reed, Steve. *Quick Remap: Self-Help Manual.* Richardson, TX: self-published, 2007.

Renard, Gary. *The Disappearance of the Universe: Straight Talk about Illusions, Past Lives, Religion, Sex, Politics, and the Miracles of Forgiveness.* Carlsbad, CA: Hay House, 2004.

———. *Your Immortal Reality: How to Break the Cycle of Birth and Death.* Carlsbad, CA: Hay House, 2006.

Roman, Sanaya. *Divine Manifesting as Your Divine Self,* audiocassette course. Medford, OR: LuminEssence, 2007.

Rosenthal, S., and Reeve, S. R. *With Forgiveness.* Ashland, OR: Pass Along Concepts, 2006.

Rye, Mark S., K. I. Pargament, W. Pan, et al. "Can Group Interventions Facilitate Forgiveness of an Ex-spouse? A Randomized Clinical Trial." *Journal of Consulting and Clinical Psychology* 73, no. 5 (October 2005): 880–892.

Sai Maa Lakshmi Devi. *Petals of Grace: Essential Teachings for Self-Mastery.* Crestone, CO: Humanity in Unity, 2005.

Schwartz, Robert M., Charles F. Reynolds, Michael E. Thase, et al. "Optimal and Normal Affect Balance in Psychotherapy of Major Depression: Evaluation of the Balanced States of Mind Model." *Behavioural and Cognitive Psychotherapy* 30, no. 4 (2002): 439–450.

St. John, Noah, and D. Berar. *The Great Little Book of Affirmations.* Chicago: MetaPublishing, 2006.

Stoelting, Robert, and Mary Stoelting. "Forgiveness," audiotape. Kiel, WI: Pathways of Light, 1995.

Swami Chidvilasananda. *Enthusiasm.* South Fallsburg, NY: SYDA Foundation, 1997.

Thayer, Steven J. "IET Forgiveness Process," audio CD. Woodstock, NY: The Center of Being, Inc., 2002.

Thompson, Laura Y., C. R. Snyder, Lesa Hoffman, et al. "Dispositional Forgiveness of Self, Others, and Situations." *Journal of Personality* 73, no. 2 (January 2005): 313–360.

Tipping, Colin. *Radical Forgiveness: Making Room for the Miracle.* Marietta, GA: Global 13 Publications, 2002.

Toussaint, Loren, and Philip Friedman. "Forgiveness, Gratitude, and Well-Being: The Mediating Role of Affect and Beliefs." *Journal of Happiness Studies,* Springer Online (2008): DOI 10.1007/s10902-008-9111-8.

Toussaint, Loren, and Jon R. Webb. "Forgiveness, Mental Health, and Well-Being." In Everett L. Worthington, Jr., ed., *Handbook of Forgiveness.* New York: Routledge, 2005.

Toussaint, Loren L., David R. Williams, Marc A. Musick, and Susan A. Everson. "Forgiveness and Health: Age Differences in a U.S. Probability Sample." *Journal of Adult Development* 8, no. 4 (October 2001): 249–257.

Vitale, Joe, and Ihaleakala Hew Len. *Zero Limits: The Secret Hawaiian System for Wealth, Health, Peace, and More.* Hoboken, NJ: Wiley, 2007.

Waltman, M. A. "The Psychological and Physiological Effects of Forgiveness Education in Male Patients with Coronary Artery Disease." Dissertation Abstracts International: Section B: The Sciences & Engineering, 63(8-B), (2003): 3971.

Wapnick, Kenneth. *The Fifty Miracle Principles of A Course in Miracles.* Roscoe, NY: Foundation for "A Course in Miracles," 1992.

————. *Forgiveness and Jesus: The Meeting Place of A Course in Miracles and Christianity.* Roscoe, NY: Foundation for "A Course in Miracles," 1994.

————. *The Message of A Course in Miracles.* Roscoe, NY: Foundation for "A Course in Miracles," 1997.

Watson, Allen, and Robert Perry. *A Workbook Companion: Commentaries on the Workbook for Students from A Course in Miracles,* vol. 2, lessons 181–365. West Sedona, AZ: Circle Publishing, 2006.

Webb, Jon R., K. Brewer, and D. Skaggs "Gender Differences in the Relationship between Forgiveness and Health." San Francisco: 115th Annual Convention of the APA, Division 38—Health Psychology, August 2007.

Williamson, Marianne. *Everyday Grace.* New York: Riverhead Books, 2002.

————. *The Age of Miracles: Embracing the New Midlife.* Carlsbad, CA: Hay House, 2008.

Wolpe, Joseph, and Arnold A. Lazarus. *Behavior Therapy Techniques: A Guide to the Treatment of Neuroses.* Oxford, NY: Pergamon Press, 1966.

Worthington, Everett. *Five Steps to Forgiveness: The Art and Science of Forgiving.* New York: Crown, 2001.

Worthington, Everett L., Jr., ed. *Handbook of Forgiveness.* New York: Routledge, 2005.

————. *The Power of Forgiving.* Philadelphia: Templeton Foundation Press, 2005.

Worthington, Everett L., Jr., C. V. O. Witvliet, P. Pietrini, and A. J. Miller. "Forgiveness, Health, and Well-Being: A Review of Evidence for Emotional versus Decisional Forgiveness, Dispositional Forgivingness, and Reduced Unforgiveness." *Journal of Behavioral Medicine* 30 (2007): 291–302.

Recommended Resources

ACEP (Association of Comprehensive Energy Psychology)
349 West Lancaster Ave., Suite 101
Haverford, PA 19041
619-861-2237 (ACEP)
www.energypsych.org

BDB Group
John Diepold, Sheila Bender,
Victoria Britt
37 Franklin Pl.
Montclair, NJ 07042
856-778-9300
www.tftworldwide.com

Be Set Free Fast (BSFF)
Larry P. Nims
3674 North 159th Ave.
Goodyear, AZ 85395
623-466-4112
www.besetfreefast.com

Caroline Myss Education Institute (CMED)
Caroline Myss
333 Second St.
La Salle, IL 61301
800-910-MYSS (6977) or 815-220-8723
www.myss.com

Center for Attitudinal Healing
c/o Corstone
33 Buchanan Dr.
Sausalito, CA 94965
415-331-6161
www.attitudinalhealing.org
www.corstone.org

Center for Integrative Psychotherapy
Mary Sise
582 New Loudon Rd.
Latham, NY 12110
518-785-8576
www.integrativepsy.com

Circle of Atonement
Robert Perry
P.O. Box 4238
West Sedona, AZ 86340
928-282-0790
www.circleofa.org

Community Miracles Center
Rev. Tony Ponticello and
Rev. Larry Bedini
2269 Market St.
San Francisco, CA 94114
415-621-2556
www.miracles-course.org

Deb Chamberlin: Singer-Songwriter-Model-Vocal Coach-Voice Over
36 Windmill Dr.
Clementon, NJ 08021
856-435-6398
www.debchamberlin.com

Debbie Ford
3639 Midway Dr., Suite B295
San Diego, CA 92110
800-655-4016
www.debbieford.com

EFT (Emotional Freedom Techniques)
Gary Craig
P.O. Box 269
Coulterville, CA 95311
707-785-2848
www.emofree.com

Everett Worthington
Virginia Commonwealth University
Department of Psychology
White House
806 West Franklin St.
Richmond, VA 23284-2018
804-828-1150
www.has.vcu.edu/psy/people/
worthington.html

Foundation for "A Course in Miracles"
Ken Wapnick
41397 Buecking Dr., Dept. H
Temecula, CA 92590-5668
951-296-6261
www.facim.org

Foundation for Well-Being
Philip H. Friedman
P.O. Box 627
Plymouth Meeting, PA 19462
610-828-4674
www.integrativehelp.com
www.philipfriedman.com
www.forgivenesssolution.com

Holistic Communications
Phillip and Jane Mountrose
P.O. Box 279
Arroyo Grande, CA 93420
805-931-0129
www.gettingthru.org

Humanity in Unity
Sai Maa
Temple of Consciousness
4462 Ridgecrest Way
P.O. Box 190
Crestone, CO 81131
719-256-4176
www.HumanityInUnity.org

InnerSource
Donna Eden and David Feinstein
1055 Benson Way, Suite 55
Ashland, OR 97520
541-482-1800
www.innersource.net

Institute for Radical Forgiveness Therapy & Coaching, Inc.
Colin Tipping
26 Briar Gate Ln.
Marietta, GA 30066
972-202-9926
www.radicalforgiveness.com

Loren Toussaint
Department of Psychology
Luther College
700 College Dr.
Decorah, IA 52101
563-387-1647
http://loren.toussaint.googlepages.com/

LuminEssence Productions
Sanaya Roman
P.O. Box 1310
Medford, OR 97501
541-770-6700
www.orindaben.com

Michael McCullough
Department of Psychology
Department of Religious Studies
University of Miami
P.O. Box 248185
Coral Gables, FL 33124-0751
305-284-8057
www.psy.miami.edu/faculty/mmccullough/

Miracle Distribution Center
3947 East La Palma Ave.
Anaheim, CA 92807
714-632-9005
www.miraclecenter.org

Pathways of Light
Robert and Mary Stoelting
13111 Lax Chapel Rd.
Kiel, WI 53042
800-323-PATH (7284)
www.pathwaysoflight.org

Psychological Services—Energy Psychology
Fred Gallo
Hickory Professional Center
60 Snyder Rd.
Hermitage, PA 16148
724-346-3838
www.energypsych.com

Raymond W. Holman Jr. Photography
Raymond W. Holman, Jr.
1712 Girard Ave.
Philadelphia, PA 19130
215-205-7414
www.rholmanjrphoto.com

The Stillpoint Foundation and School of Integrative Life Healing
Dr. Meredith Young-Sowers
22 Stillpoint Ln.
Walpole, NH 03608
603-756-9281 or 800-847-4014
www.stillpoint.org

SYDA Foundation
P.O. Box 600
371 Brickman Rd.
South Fallsburg, NY 12779-0600
845-434-2000
www.siddhayoga.org

TATLife
Tapas Fleming
PMB 7000-379
Redondo Beach, CA 90277
310-378-7381 or (outside the U.S.)
877-674-4344
www.tatlife.com

The Voice for Love
DavidPaul and Candace Doyle
P.O. Box 3125
Ashland, OR 97520
541-488-0426
www.thevoiceforlove.com

Acknowledgments

I am extremely grateful to many people for contributing to the writing of *The Forgiveness Solution*. I want to thank the members of my family: my deceased parents Leonard and Miriam Friedman for all their support and love over the years, my sister Elaine and brother-in-law Eric, my sister-in-law Marguerite Friedman, and my mother-in-law and father-in-law, Oliver and Chloe Molinaro. I especially want to thank my wife Teresa and son Mathew Friedman, who were continually supportive and encouraging. My wife Teresa, in particular, did much of the early editing of the book, which I very much appreciated, and listened constantly to me during the inevitable ups and downs of the writing and publishing process.

I want to thank Loren Toussaint, my talented and bright colleague who analyzed, wrote, and published three studies on forgiveness and gratitude with me and gave me constructive feedback on an early draft of *The Forgiveness Solution;* and Tony Scioli, a colleague who was of enormous help while I was searching for and finding a publisher and writing this book. Also, I want to thank my co-author, Ralph Piedmont, who wrote a book chapter with me that included a summary of the forgiveness and gratitude literature, and chaired, for many years, a conference where I could present my research work on forgiveness while it was in progress. It was also at this conference on spirituality and psychology that I met Robert Emmons, Mike McCullough, Everett Worthington, Jon Webb, and Mark Rye, noted authors and researchers on forgiveness (and gratitude) who very graciously contributed stories, scales, or ideas for this book. Everett Worthington, in particular, contributed stories, quotes, and research and directed me to other forgiveness-oriented resources or people. I am very appreciative to all of them.

In what I refer to as phase one of the writing and publisher-seeking process, I want to thank Mitch Myerson and Michael Port, who taught the excellent 90-Day Product Factory telecourse; my Success Magnet leader, Cara Lumen; and my "buddies" in that course, Beth Borray and Sandie Hum, who were not only very encouraging and supportive but very helpful with useful ideas for writing a book proposal and the early chapters of the book. My longtime spiritually oriented and creative colleague and friend, Martha Crampton, was also of enormous support and assistance during both this phase and the second phase of the writing of *The Forgiveness Solution*. Martha also contributed two imagery processes with a psychosynthesis flavor to *The Forgiveness Solution* book that I improvised and adapted with her kind permission. I am saddened that she passed on just as the book was being completed. Fred Gallo, a friend and colleague, was also very supportive in the first stage of the process and also taught me all the basics of energy therapy I needed to know back in the early 1990s. Fred also published a key early chapter with my ideas in it in one of his wonderful edited books.

In phase two of the writing process, no one was more helpful and valuable than April, who inspired the writing of the last twelve chapters of *The Forgiveness Solution* and gave me excellent feedback on all the exercises and processes, most of which are included in the book. Without her, I am not sure this book would ever have been written. She was truly an angel in disguise.

I am particularly grateful to Jerry Jampolsky, whom I have known for twenty-five years. Jerry has been extremely influential in the writing of *The Forgiveness Solution,* not only by his direct contributions to the book through stories and quotes (along with his wife Diane Cirincione) but also because of his being a gracious and inspiring model for much of my work. Ken Wapnick has also been a model for the ideas in this book going back many years, and, more recently, Robert Perry has been extremely helpful in many ways, including donating forgiveness imagery processes and quotes and also for reading and giving me feedback on certain chapters of the book. For this I am most appreciative. In addition, Tony Ponticelli, Paul Tuttle, Greg Mackie, Gary Renard, DavidPaul and Candace Doyle, Robert and Mary Stoelting, Marianne Williamson, and Beverly Hutchinson McNeff, through their excellent books, workshops, audios, videos, newsletters, stories, feedback, and/or quotes, have been very helpful; to them, I am also very appreciative.

I also want to thank the following people for generously donating and/or inspiring exercises, processes, scales, quotes, and ideas used in this book: Ed Diener, Sonya Lyubomirsky, Laura Thompson, Tony Burroughs, Tina Stober, Colin Tipping, Steven Thayer, Larry Nims, Philip and Jane Mountrose, Tapas Fleming, Robert Fritz, Arjuna Ardagh, Doreen Virtue, Sonia Choquette, Caroline Myss, Debbie Ford, Fred Luskin, David Feinstein, Donna Eden, Dan Benor, Asha Clinton, Pat Carrington, Dawson Church, Jack Canfield, Gary Craig, Steve Reed, John Freedom, Kathy Milano, Joe Vitale, Esther and Jerry Hicks, Mary Sise, and Sheila Bender.

I also want to thank the following clients (pseudonyms used) who graciously contributed, directly or indirectly, stories to this book: Alex, April, Ben, Carolyn, Charlene, Ellen, Hiraldo, Jane, Jennifer, Sam, and Ted; and my friends who listened patiently for many hours as I talked about the sometimes challenging journey of writing a book or who contributed to the book in some small but significant way: Francie and Bill Pagell, Bruce and Cathy Fay, Bob Dreyfus, Barry Ginsberg, Jacqui McDonald, Joe Klemas, Deb Chamberlin, and all the wonderful members of the Windmill Intenders Circle who supported me during many months of this process. They were all supportive and encouraging as the publishing and editing journey evolved.

I want to thank Pat Cleveland from my Siddha yoga group, who especially encouraged, inspired, and supported me during phase two of the writing process of *The Forgiveness Solution,* as well as my entire yoga/meditation community for their love and support over the years. Deb Chamberlin, the warm and joyful leader of the Windmill Intenders Circle, also graciously posed as the superb model for all the pictures in this book (though by training she is a talented singer and singing coach), and Raymond Holman from my yoga group took the excellent pictures of Deb, which I greatly appreciate. Blaine Oelkers and the members of the Think and Grow Rich teleclass he facilitated were also very helpful and supportive, for which I am very grateful. The loving blessing givers, Kathy Stock and the Stock family, Norma Feldman, Kristina Matteo, Jeanne Susie, Poornima and Ganesh Guruajan, Scott and Nancy McBride, and Steve Stroph, were continually sources of nurturance, peace, and support during the writing process, and I am very grateful to them for being in my life.

My many spiritual teachers provided the general inspiration and many of the ideas for this book in one form or another. In particular, Gurumayi Chidvilasananda, Baba Muktananda, Sai Maa, Mother Meera, Adyashanti, Sanaya Roman, Meredith Young-Sowers, Bob Bauman, Ammachi, Amma and *A Course in Miracles* were sources of profound knowledge, love, light, and blessings. My gratitude to them all is infinite and eternal. The courses, workshops, audiotapes, videos, DVDs, and in-person blessings I received from them were invaluable and priceless. I cannot thank them all enough. The personal and spiritual growth writings, audios, videos, and DVDs of Ken Wilber, Andrew Cohen, Eckhart Tolle, Genpo Roshi, Bill Harris, Wayne Liquorman, and Steve and Barbara Rother were also very valuable, and I thank them deeply as well.

I want to thank my agent Jeff Herman, who helped me negotiate the book contract, for all his constructive feedback and help; and Randy Rolfe, a friend and colleague, who graciously directed me to Jeff a number of years ago. I am thankful to both of them for their encouragement, suggestions, and support.

I also want to thank some of my teachers and mentors, who were very helpful early in my career and who indirectly influenced the writing of *The Forgiveness Solution* for all their wonderful ideas, techniques, and inspiration: Fred Keller, Len Berkowitz, Vernon

Allen, Brenden Maher, Arnold Lazarus, Joe Wolpe, Aaron Beck, Ivan Boszormenyi-Nagy, Geraldine Sparks, Jim Framo, Carl Whitaker, Rick Crocco, David Moultrup, and Jay Haley.

Finally, last but certainly not least, I want to thank my publisher Conari Press and in particular Caroline Pincus, my editor, for all they contributed to edit, design, publicize, and publish *The Forgiveness Solution*. Without their superb skills, there would be no *Forgiveness Solution* published in this form. Caroline Pincus saw the value of *The Forgiveness Solution* early on and was constantly a source of support, encouragement, wisdom, advice, and constructive feedback. I am greatly appreciative of her help and guidance. In addition, Susie Pitzen, her assistant, was very helpful in the second half of the editorial and all of the book design process, and I am most appreciative to her as well. Bonni Hamilton, the head of publicity and her assistant, Allyson May, were very supportive and encouraging throughout the marketing and publicity process and I thank them very much, too.

About the Author

Photo by Raymond W. Holman, Jr.

Philip Friedman, Ph.D., is a licensed clinical psychologist and psychotherapist living and working in a suburb outside Philadelphia. Dr. Friedman is widely published in professional journals and books. He is also the director of the Foundation for Well-Being and the author of *Creating Well-Being: The Healing Path to Love, Peace, Self-Esteem and Happiness and the Integrative Healing Manual,* as well as a complete audio course on creating well-being.

Dr. Friedman currently serves as an adjunct professor at the Institute of Transpersonal Psychology faculty in Palo Alto, CA, and is co-founder of "Integrative Therapy" (IT) and "Integrative Healing" (IH) and is the founder of the "Positive Pressure Point Techniques" (PPPT), a form of energy therapy used in this book. He is also a diplomate in Comprehensive Energy Psychology.

Dr. Friedman conducts seminars on the forgiveness solution, gratitude, energy and transformational healing, and well-being. You can contact him through his websites:

www.philipfriedman.com and
www.forgivenesssolution.com

To Our Readers

Conari Press, an imprint of Red Wheel/Weiser, publishes books on topics ranging from spirituality, personal growth, and relationships to women's issues, parenting, and social issues. Our mission is to publish quality books that will make a difference in people's lives—how we feel about ourselves and how we relate to one another. We value integrity, compassion, and receptivity, both in the books we publish and in the way we do business.

Our readers are our most important resources, and we value your input, suggestions, and ideas about what you would like to see published. Please feel free to contact us, to request our latest book catalog, or to be added to our mailing list.

Conari Press
An imprint of Red Wheel/Weiser, LLC
500 Third Street, Suite 230
San Francisco, CA 94107
www.redwheelweiser.com

APR - - 2010

CLIFTON PARK-HALFMOON PUBLIC LIBRARY, NY

0 00 06 0355453 6